InstallAnywhere Tutorial and Reference Guide

InstallAnywhere Tutorial and Reference Guide

Zero G Team

♦Addison-Wesley

Boston • San Francisco • New York • Toronto • Montreal
London • Munich • Paris • Madrid
Capetown • Sydney • Tokyo • Singapore • Mexico City

Many of the designations used by manufacturers and sellers to distinguish their products are claimed as trademarks. Where those designations appear in this book, and Addison-Wesley was aware of a trademark claim, the designations have been printed with initial capital letters or in all capitals.

The authors and publisher have taken care in the preparation of this book, but make no expressed or implied warranty of any kind and assume no responsibility for errors or omissions. No liability is assumed for incidental or consequential damages in connection with or arising out of the use of the information or programs contained herein.

Zero G Software, Inc., Zero G, ZeroG.com, the Zero G logo, InstallAnywhere, the InstallAnywhere logo, InstallAnywhere.NET, the InstallAnywhere.NET logo, PowerUpdate, PowerUpdate.com, the PowerUpdate logo, LaunchAnywhere, and SpeedFolder are trademarks or registered trademarks of Zero G Software, Inc., in the United States, other countries, or both.

The publisher offers discounts on this book when ordered in quantity for bulk purchases and special sales. For more information, please contact:

U.S. Corporate and Government Sales
(800) 382-3419
corpsales@pearsontechgroup.com

For sales outside of the U.S., please contact:

International Sales
(317) 581-3793
international@pearsontechgroup.com

Visit Addison-Wesley on the Web: www.awprofessional.com

Library of Congress Cataloging-in-Publication Data

InstallAnywhere tutorial and reference guide / Zero G Team.
    p. cm.
   Includes index.
   ISBN 0-321-24610-1 (pbk. : alk. paper)
 1. Computer software—Development. I. Zero G Team.

   QA76.76.D47I544 2005
   005.3—dc22
                                    2004008887

Copyright © 2005 by Zero G Software, Inc.

All rights reserved. No part of this publication may be reproduced, stored in a retrieval system, or transmitted, in any form, or by any means, electronic, mechanical, photocopying, recording, or otherwise, without the prior consent of the publisher. Printed in the United States of America. Published simultaneously in Canada.

For information on obtaining permission for use of material from this work, please submit a written request to:

Pearson Education, Inc.
Rights and Contracts Department
75 Arlington Street, Suite 300
Boston, MA 02116
Fax: (617) 848-7047

ISBN 0-321-24610-1
Text printed on recycled paper
1 2 3 4 5 6 7 8 9 10—CRS—0807060504
First printing, July 2004

Contents

Preface   xi

Introduction   xvii

Chapter 1   Introduction to InstallAnywhere   1
     What Is InstallAnywhere?   2
     Requirements   2
     Editions   4

Chapter 2   The InstallAnywhere End-User Experience   5
     The End-User Experience   6
     The Client-Side Installer Experience   6
     The Server-Side Installer Experience   12

Chapter 3   The InstallAnywhere Developer Experience   19
     The InstallAnywhere Wizard   20
     Building Your First Installer   21

Chapter 4   Key Concepts in InstallAnywhere   25
     Authoring Environments   26
     Installer Types   26
     Installer Modes   27
     Install Sets, Features, and Components   27
     Installer Interface GUI   28
     Actions   30
     Rules   31
     Uninstaller   31
     LaunchAnywhere   31
     PowerUpdate   32
     InstallAnywhere Variables   32
     Magic Folders   33

SpeedFolders   35
Project File   36
Manifest Files   36

Chapter 5   Basic Installer Development Strategies   39

Installation Planning   40
Installation Goals   40
InstallAnywhere Installation Planning Worksheet   41

Chapter 6   An Introduction to the Advanced Designer   43

Exercise 6.1 Building an Installer with the Advanced Designer   45
Defining Installer Projects and the Product Registry   53
File Settings—Timestamps and Overwrite Behavior   54
Platforms   56
Locales   57
Rules before the Pre-Install Task   57
Creating Debug Output   57
Virtual Machines   57
Quick Quiz   58

Chapter 7   Build Options   61

Generic UNIX Build   62
VM Packs   62
Distribution   63

Chapter 8   Basic Installer Customization   65

Customizing Your InstallAnywhere Installer's Look and Feel   66
Exercise 8.1 Exploring Look and Feel   66
Introducing Conditional Logic   73
Exercise 8.2 Using Installer Rules   75
Exercise 8.3 Using Rules to Control Visual Elements   76
Exercise 8.4 Managing Installer Flow Based on End-User Input   78
Quick Quiz   81

Chapter 9   Installer Organization   83

Install Sets, Features, and Components   84
Organizing Features and Components   88
Exercise 9.1 Using InstallAnywhere's Basic Installer Organization   90
Adding Components   93
Assigning Files to Components   93

Removing Empty Components		93
Integrating Components Already Installed on Target Systems		93
Adding Features		94
Quick Quiz		94

Chapter 10   Introduction to Advanced Actions and Panel Actions   95

Actions	96
Exercise 10.1 Using Panels in Pre-Install	98
Exercise 10.2 Using Files Task Actions	99
Quick Quiz	100
List of Actions	101

Chapter 11   Managing Installation Locations with Magic Folders   115

Magic Folders and InstallAnywhere Variables	116
Exercise 11.1 Magic Folders	118
InstallAnywhere-Provided Magic Folders	119

Chapter 12   Applying Basic and Intermediate Development Concepts   123

Concept Review	124
Debugging InstallAnywhere Installers	125

Chapter 13   Advanced Installer Concepts   131

Console Installers	132
Exercise 13.1 Building a Console-Enabled Installer (Return of OfficeSuite)	133
Silent Installers	135
Exercise 13.2 Building a Silent-Mode Installer	136

Chapter 14   Uninstaller Issues   137

About Uninstaller	138
Feature Uninstall	138
Uninstaller for Multiple Products	139

Chapter 15   Source and Resource Management in InstallAnywhere   141

How Source Paths Work	142
Managing Source Files	144
The Resource Manager	144
Exercise 15.1 Creating Source Paths	147
Quick Quiz	148

Chapter 16 Advanced Interface Options — 149
Installer Panel Additions — 150
Exercise 16.1 Creating Installer Logic Using Jump Labels and Actions — 152
Quick Quiz — 152

Chapter 17 Advanced Organizational Concepts — 153
Integrating the Find Component in Registry Action — 154
Merge Modules and Templates — 154
Importing a Design-Time Merge Module — 161
Exercise 17.1 Creating Merge Modules — 162
Quick Quiz — 163

Chapter 18 Integrating InstallAnywhere with Automated Build Environments — 165
InstallAnywhere Command-Line Build Facility — 166
Build Tools — 167
Exit Codes — 168
ANT Build Integration — 170

Chapter 19 Custom Code — 175
Writing Custom Code — 177
Quick Quiz — 190

Chapter 20 Developing and Using Custom Code Actions — 193
Custom Code and InstallAnywhere Variables — 194
Accessing InstallAnywhere Variables via Custom Code — 194
Executing External Scripts and Executables via Custom Code Action — 196
How to Write Custom Errors in the Installation Log — 201
Exercise 20.1 Create a Custom Code Action — 202
Exercise 20.2 Create a Custom Code Panel — 202
Exercise 20.3 Create a Custom Code Console Action — 203
Exercise 20.4 Create a Custom Code Rule — 203
How to Package and Execute Custom Code with an Installer — 203
Plug-Ins — 204

Chapter 21 Localizing and Internationalizing InstallAnywhere Installers — 207
Dynamic and Static Text — 208
Localization and the Internationalized Designer — 209
Specific Localization Concerns — 209
Localizable Elements — 214

Appendix A	Standard InstallAnywhere Variables	217
Appendix B	Provided Magic Folders	223
Appendix C	Actions	227
Appendix D	Build Tools	239
Appendix E	Exit Codes	241
Appendix F	Parameters	243
Appendix G	Language Codes	247
Appendix H	Localizable Elements	249
Appendix I	LaunchAnywhere Executable Properties	253
Appendix J	Quick Quiz Answers	257
Index		259

Preface

About This Book

Our team of experts from Zero G, with more than 100 man-years of experience in software deployment, worked together in the writing of this book, a massive, collective undertaking that took many months of combing knowledge-base articles, working directly with the developers who created InstallAnywhere, and assimilating feedback from customers around the globe. You can see that in this collaboration, software engineers, product managers, and technical support experts had a big job on their hands. The book that they delivered is concise and intuitive, often hiding the real complexity and power of the software. The chapters ahead contain page after page of fundamental software deployment and installation knowledge that simply can't be found anyplace else.

Of course, you would expect someone who works with these people every day to say something like that. But the truth is that I'm very excited about this software manual, and not just because it is from Zero G. I am excited because it gives software developers access to undoubtedly the most experienced, knowledgeable team of multiplatform software deployment experts in the world.

Don't be surprised if by the time you put this book down, you're already thinking about new ways to tackle software installations, viewing some of your software projects differently, and beginning to use InstallAnywhere in ways you never expected.

How to Approach This Book

The right approach to any learning experience is essential. Any kid in kindergarten can tell you that an afternoon nap makes learning easier. Later, he's likely to discover, as I did, that staying up all night before a final exam in college is not a very good idea and that a class in advanced microbiology is best approached with his girlfriend as his lab partner. Software developers and engineers may not need naps in the afternoon, but learning still requires preparation, time, and the support of colleagues.

The authors have made this book easy to approach and have taken great care to leverage existing computing metaphors and familiar exercise-based lessons, written in plain English, that make sense. As you begin to use this book, you'll notice how it is organized. It is designed in linear coursework steps that are meant to teach new skills methodically in a successive progression from basic to advanced concepts. Each chapter builds upon knowledge imparted in previous ones, starting with an introduction of the InstallAnywhere software in Chapter 1 and ending with specialized custom code tutorials in the final chapters.

Although an experienced engineer may find it easy to follow advanced lessons without having read previous chapters in the book, the best way to learn any new software is to start at the beginning of the manual and work through each chapter from start to finish. As a software engineer, I know that finding time for the continuing education necessary to stay on top of the latest technology trends is often very difficult and reading an entire book can be challenging. The authors have designed this manual with that in mind.

Even if you're an expert engineer, we're confident that a textbook approach to this volume will yield powerful results from InstallAnywhere. A more methodical reading of these pages will arm less experienced users of InstallAnywhere with a solid foundation of knowledge upon which they can start adding intermediate and advanced skills. Whatever the level of skill developers may start with, the result for experts and novices alike is the same: effortless, adaptive learning at their own pace.

It is the adaptive nature of the authors' work that I find among the best qualities of the book. Not everyone learns the same way, and not everyone who buys this book intends to use it for the same purpose. The one thing that was clear to the authors from the outset, however, was that good software manuals are used often and are rarely too far out of reach at a software developer's desk. As this is a reference volume, you'll find that each lesson is complete in itself, which means that you can add this book to the ones you keep handy for troubleshooting and quick answers to your "how to" questions.

How to Use This Book

The authors break down the material in this manual into 21 numbered chapters, each of which should be regarded as a single lesson. Each lesson consists of exercises, concept reviews, or a combination of both, as well as various other learning tools that you'll become familiar with as you read, such as best practices, quick quizzes, hints, and notes.

- **Exercise:** A chronological explanation of each step involved in solving a problem, presented as a task-oriented activity that can be repeated to reinforce understanding and increase skills. Exercises should ideally be mastered before readers move on to the next chapter.
- **Concept review:** A study tool that often incorporates minitasks and activities with an examination of a computing principle or metaphor. Concept reviews must be reinforced through actual conceptualization.
- **Best practices:** The ideal and customary way of doing common tasks, best practices are determined only after having been proven, often through years of hands-on experience.
- **Quick quiz:** At the end of a chapter, the quick quiz tests your knowledge by posing questions and providing the answers in Appendix J. They reinforce skills learned in the chapter and help you evaluate your progress and identify areas that require further study.

Once you become comfortable with this format, you may decide that you learn most efficiently by first working through the exercises, or you may discover that you like to jump right to the quick quiz at the end of a chapter and then work backward to find the answers. The authors have made this book easy to use, no matter what your personal preference is.

Knowing What to Expect

This manual is used in formal Zero G product training courses that take place on both coasts several times each year. By following the flow of lessons in this book from start to finish, you can duplicate the flow of training that would take place over a period of three days were you to attend an InstallAnywhere training course, also called Zero G University. Don't be disappointed if you take more than three days to get through the manual, however. Zero G University is led by highly knowledgeable InstallAnywhere instructor engineers, who have conducted training courses for years. It's unrealistic to expect the same result without the trainer in the room with you. If you have more time, take advantage of it, and your own training is likely to be a more rewarding experience as a result. If you'd like to find out more about Zero G University, you can go to the Zero G Web site at www.ZeroG.com.

One interesting concept from the three-day training course that you may find useful is that this book can be divided into three distinct parts, one for each of the days of the course itself. The authors chose not to write this distinction into the book, but you may decide to apply three parts to your learning plan as you budget time and determine training priorities. You may even decide that you'd like to concentrate on one or two of the parts in the book that you feel are most relevant to the work you do. There are a lot of circumstances in which a strategy for grouping the chapters in this book will be required. Here's how Zero G does it.

- **Part 1 (Day 1) covers Chapters 1 through 9:** InstallAnywhere basics and breadth.
- **Part 2 (Day 2) covers Chapters 10 through 17:** Advanced actions and panels.
- **Part 3 (Day 3) covers Chapters 18 through 21:** Extending functionality with custom code.

Those who complete the InstallAnywhere Training Course most often note that they are able to produce better-looking, more complex installers in a lot less time. There's no reason why you shouldn't have a similar experience after using this manual. The authors understood with the writing of this book that it had to produce a similar experience, no matter the learning environment. To accomplish this, they identified four goals that the manual aims to achieve for users (and consequently, attendees of the training course).

1. **Add value:** Users who successfully complete the coursework presented in the manual should better understand the value they bring to their organization with their newly acquired knowledge and should feel personally rewarded with a more refined and marketable skill set.
2. **Time and cost savings:** Users who master the use of InstallAnywhere should feel assured that they will experience shorter time to market and a reduced volume in documentation associated with their own software. They should also be more aware of possible savings associated with better quality assurance and reduced support costs.
3. **Seamless customization:** Users should walk away from their learning experience with the skills they need to create customized installers that match their own product's unique look and feel, thereby extending the value of their own brand.
4. **Improved implementation:** Users should acquire a knowledge of best practices and smarter software strategies using InstallAnywhere and feel confident in sharing their knowledge to promote better collaboration across workgroups and more powerful, improved implementations overall.

Acknowledgments

The authors of this book spent many months planning, strategizing, writing, and rewriting to produce this volume. Their dedication and effort must be recognized in the context of the complex materials they assimilated and the fast-paced, frenetic environment of a company like Zero G, where they often had to juggle many large projects in addition to the book writing. They are Robert Brown, Tim Miller, Carrie Smith, Drew Tappan, and Wayne Tombo, and I extend a very special thank you to them on behalf of Zero G for their outstanding work. In addition, many others who are too numerous to name individually contributed ideas, comments, and reviews for this book. We thank them, too, for their contributions, without which this book would not be possible.

Trent Wheeler
San Francisco, California
March 2004

Editor's Note: Trent Wheeler leads the development of InstallAnywhere, Zero G's flagship multiplatform deployment product line. He has also served Zero G in developer technical support as director of technical operations and product management.

Introduction

An Introduction to Installation Issues

A well-planned installation and deployment strategy should be part of any serious software development project. When the installer is an afterthought, end-users usually get a poor first impression. In practice, however, this critical requirement is sometimes ignored until the software is complete. Why wait until the product is ready to be released before thinking about deployment? Regardless of whether the end-user is a member of the general public, a consulting client, or another group within your own organization, it's unlikely that the product will simply be checked out of a source control solution and the resources laid immediately into their final operational location.

Once you have made your Gold Master, how does the software make its way to your customers? Will it be enough simply to deliver an archive such as a ZIP or Java archive (JAR) file or a UNIX tarball? This method allows you to deliver a number of different types of files as a single unit. That's certainly one way to do it, and it is easier than having your end-user log in to a source control solution or copy individual files. However, this method has inherent weaknesses. Rarely can a collection of files simply be laid into a file system and ready for one-click execution without some measure of configuration. What if the application requires installation into several locations? What if portions of the installation require configuration prior to use?

Today's sophisticated software applications require complex configurations, and complex configurations require installation utilities. You can choose from a variety of methods and types of installation utilities. Windows and Macintosh users are familiar with the executable installer (e.g., InstallAnywhere), while users of UNIX systems are accustomed to deployment schemes that utilize complex scripts or native package managers.

Installation utilities allow you to provide your end-users with a familiar interface, assuring a positive product installation experience with a minimum of inconvenience.

Many ready-made solutions are available for specific target platforms. For example, RPM is a packaging system that generally functions only on Linux (although it has been introduced to other mainstream UNIX and UNIX-like systems). Such targeted solutions are not useful for multiplatform deployment. Multiplatform deployment, although once unusual, is no longer a fringe issue. More platform-agnostic software development is being done in languages such as Java, Perl, Python, PHP, and those outlined by the .NET standards. In order to keep pace with this new development landscape, you need a tool that deploys and configures your applications on many different platforms.

Multiplatform Installation

If your product is intended for multiplatform deployment, you need InstallAnywhere. InstallAnywhere deploys your applications to many different systems, while you build and create only a single project. Using Java, InstallAnywhere installers run on nearly any platform for which a Java Virtual Machine is available, from the ubiquitous Windows desktop, to the high-end, headless UNIX servers used in e-Business and Web services applications.

Complex application delivery requires an installer that allows complete configuration and precise control over uncounted variables. A multiplatform installer is preferable over a simple archive because you can dynamically configure your applications and deliver associated (or other necessary) applications along with your own packages. For example, if your application is a database-based tool, you may need to include the database engine necessary for your application to run. A single installer can be used as a "master" installer and manage the entire installation process for your end-users. This method is often referred to as a "suite" installer or a "software stack" installation.

You never get a second chance to give a first impression, and if an end-user's first experience with your product is difficult, disorienting, or time-consuming, you're already "in the hole" in terms of credibility. End-user confidence is enhanced when you use a multiplatform installer. By providing your end-users with a comfortable, easily accomplished installation of your product, your end-users' product experience is immediately positive.

Many of today's end-users grew up on Microsoft Windows or Macintosh operating systems. Even those whose primary platform is a commercial UNIX (like Solaris or IRIX) are familiar with the modern graphical user interfaces implemented by these operating environments. The custom graphics features in InstallAnywhere provide instant familiarity without sacrificing the power behind the pretty front end. Additionally, InstallAnywhere provides powerful "silent" features, allowing you to integrate your installation with any number of automation processes.

CHAPTER 1
Introduction to InstallAnywhere

- **What Is InstallAnywhere?**
- **Requirements**
- **Editions**

What Is InstallAnywhere?

InstallAnywhere is the most powerful multiplatform software installation solution available. InstallAnywhere deploys software onto any platform and configures applications for optimal performance. InstallAnywhere supports the platforms that run the enterprise, including the latest editions of Windows, Mac OS X, Solaris, Linux, NetWare, HP-UX, AIX, and many more.

InstallAnywhere creates installers that meet the demands of diverse computing environments and that dynamically adapt to the systems on which they are deployed, making even the most complex software configuration easy. Its intuitive architecture brings intelligence to the process of installing any kind of software, including desktop software, enterprise software, or multitiered Web services, onto any client or server platform and configuring those applications for optimal performance. InstallAnywhere handles all installation details automatically, minimizing time to deployment and increasing developer productivity.

By delivering an ideal mix of power, ease of use, and functionality, the award-winning InstallAnywhere family has become the preferred choice of multiplatform developers worldwide. Software innovators like Adobe, Borland, HP, i2, IBM, Intel, Iona, Lucent, Nortel, and Sun are just some of the software industry's leaders who depend upon InstallAnywhere for fast, powerful, and intuitive installers.

Requirements

When developing an installer, just as when developing software, you must think in terms of the authoring environment, where you create the installer, the target environments, and the various operating systems and configurations where the installer will be deployed.

Authoring Environment

Requirements
- 128MB free RAM
- Minimum of 8-bit color depth (256 colors)
- Minimum 1024 × 768 resolution

Operating Systems Supported
- Windows Server 2003, XP, 2000, NT, Me, 98
- Mac OS X, Mac OS X Server
- Solaris/SPARC
- Linux/Intel: Red Hat, SuSE, UnitedLinux, Debian, and others
- HP-UX
- AIX

Language-localized versions of InstallAnywhere Enterprise Edition (for French, German, and Japanese developers) are available on the Windows platform only. Full platform support and full support for 29 languages are also included.

Installer Environment
- 32MB of free RAM
- Minimum of 8-bit color depth (256 colors)
- Minimum 640 × 480 screen resolution

Operating Systems Supported
- Windows Server 2003, XP, 2000, NT, Me, 98
- Linux/Intel: Red Hat, Red Hat Enterprise Server, UnitedLinux, TurboLinux, SuSE, and others
- Linux/PPC
- Mac OS X
- Solaris SPARC, Intel
- HP-UX (PA-RISC and Itanium2), Tru64, FreeBSD
- AIX
- z/OS, OS/390
- Other UNIX platforms
- NetWare

Java VMs Supported
- Sun: 1.1.8, 1.2.2, 1.3.X, 1.4.X
- IBM: 1.1.8, 1.3.X, 1.4.X

- Apple: 1.3.X, 1.4.X
- HP: 1.3.X, 1.4.X

Editions

There are three editions of InstallAnywhere. Each edition is designed to meet product deployment needs for different types of customers. This manual describes the features available in the Enterprise Edition. Although some specific differences are called out throughout the manual, for a detailed chart of which features are available in each edition, see www.ZeroG.com/goto/editions.

Enterprise Edition

Enterprise Edition provides the ultimate in configuration options, user interaction, and client/server features. It simplifies complex installations and provides maximum developer customization. The Enterprise Edition is available in English, French, German, or Japanese. Each Enterprise Edition has full international support to create installers in 29 different languages.

InstallAnywhere Mac OS X Edition

Designed specifically for Cocoa, Carbon, Classic, or Java applications, InstallAnywhere is the only installer you'll ever need to create installers for Mac OS X that are flexible, intuitive, and royalty free.

Standard Edition

The Standard Edition offers more features and customizability than any other product in its class. It is ideal for desktop application deployment and has international support for nine languages.

CHAPTER 2

The InstallAnywhere End-User Experience

- **The End-User Experience**
- **The Client-Side Installer Experience**
- **The Server-Side Installer Experience**

The End-User Experience

There is no difference in InstallAnywhere's usability whether you are creating client-side or server-side application installers. The needs of installations are different; server-side installations generally require more choices, more configuration options, and more experience of the person performing the installation. The following examples show some of the options InstallAnywhere offers for these different types of installers.

The Client-Side Installer Experience

The InstallAnywhere application is itself installed using an installer built with InstallAnywhere. (We'll call this installer the "InstallAnywhere installer," just like you might call your installer "My_Product installer.") Going through the process of installing InstallAnywhere is a useful exercise in observing the end-user experience of installing a client-side application, and that's what we are going to do next. The InstallAnywhere installer is built completely with InstallAnywhere and makes use of many of the InstallAnywhere features we'll cover in our exercises.

The first objective is simplicity. When your end-user visits your download page, you want to present a "single-click install." This is accomplished by the InstallAnywhere Web Installer Applet (Figures 2.1 to 2.20). Because InstallAnywhere automatically creates HTML pages configured with the InstallAnywhere Web Installer Applet, not only is the end-user's experience simple, but your work is done for you (we'll talk more about that later).

Conveniently, at the completion of this demonstration, you'll have installed the InstallAnywhere product that we'll be using for the remainder of the book.

The Client-Side Installer Experience 7

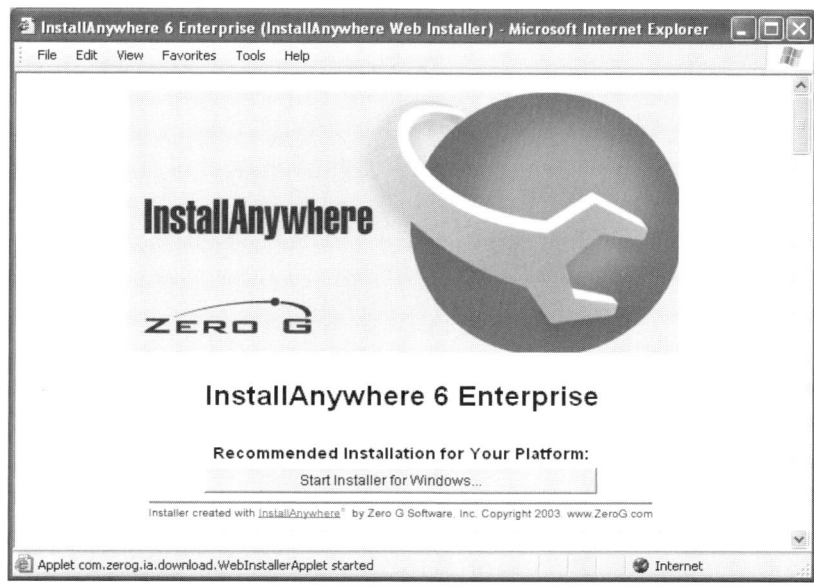

Figure 2.1 *The InstallAnywhere Web Install Applet.* When the user selects the **Start Installer** button, the applet will check for disk space, download the installer, and execute that installer.

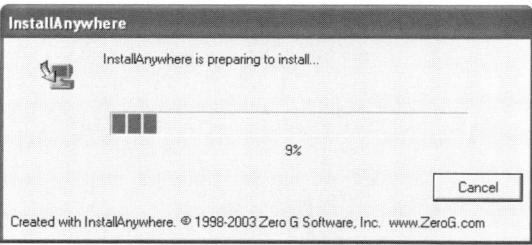

Figure 2.2 *Applet Downloading InstallAnywhere.* InstallAnywhere's installer utilizes some of InstallAnywhere's advanced user interface (UI) customization options. For example, note the background images and the dynamic list of installation steps used in the installer. These features are available when you use InstallAnywhere's advanced Swing-mode UI.

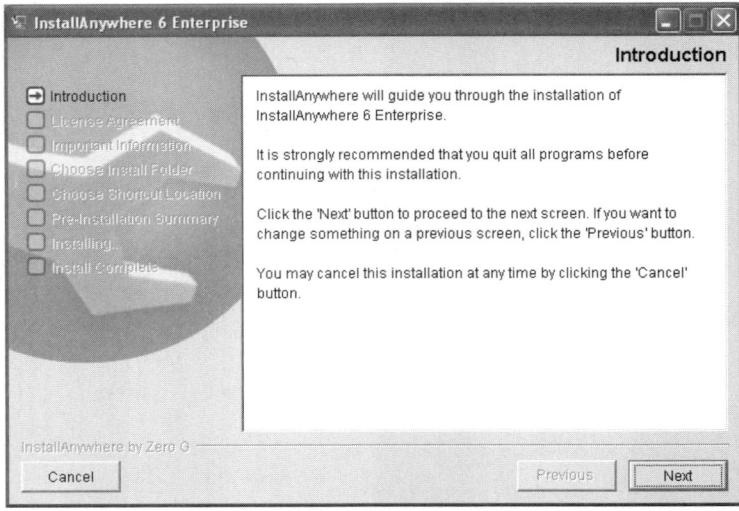

Figure 2.3 *Informational Pages.* The left pane of the Installer can present a list of steps that the installer will perform. These steps will be updated as the installation progresses. In the right pane the Installer can present information and accept information from the end-user.

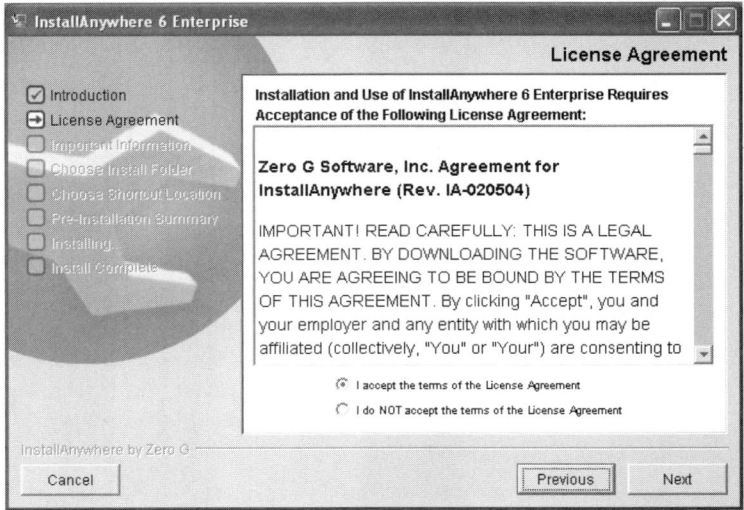

Figure 2.4 *Present Options to the End-User.* The InstallAnywhere installer presents a license agreement that the user must accept.

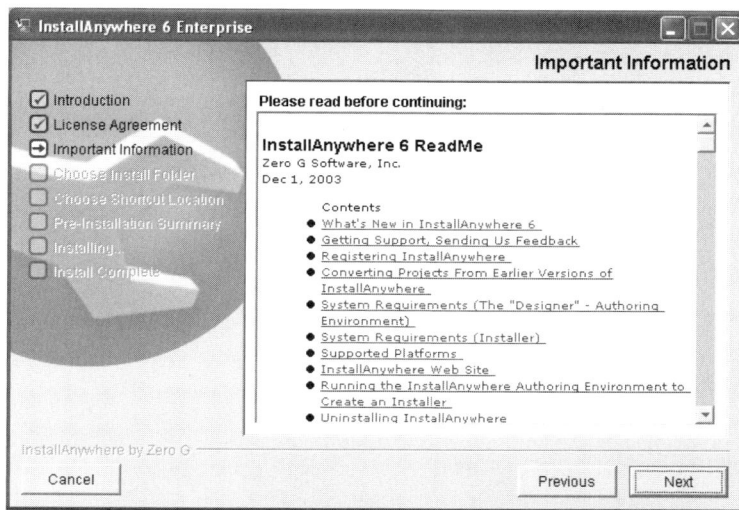

Figure 2.5 *Present HTML from within the Installer.* A great deal of information can be packaged in the installer, even HTML, including links.

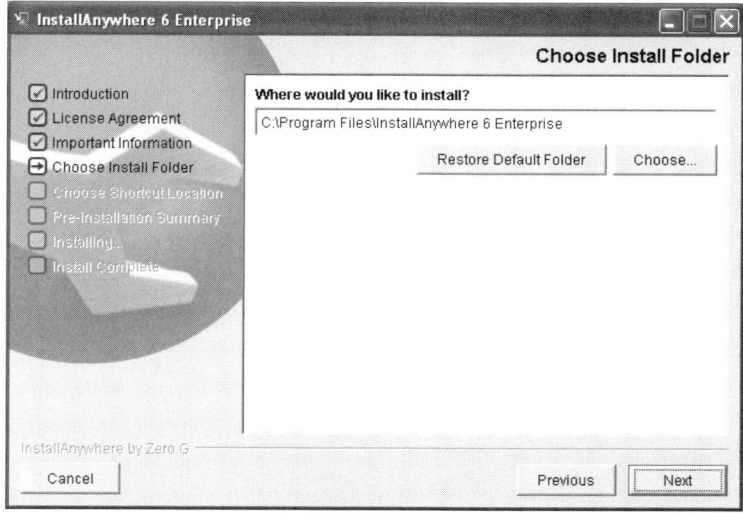

Figure 2.6 *Request Installation Configuration Information.* The installer can request installation configuration information from the end-user; in this case, the installation location, itself, is requested.

Chapter 2 ■ The InstallAnywhere End-User Experience

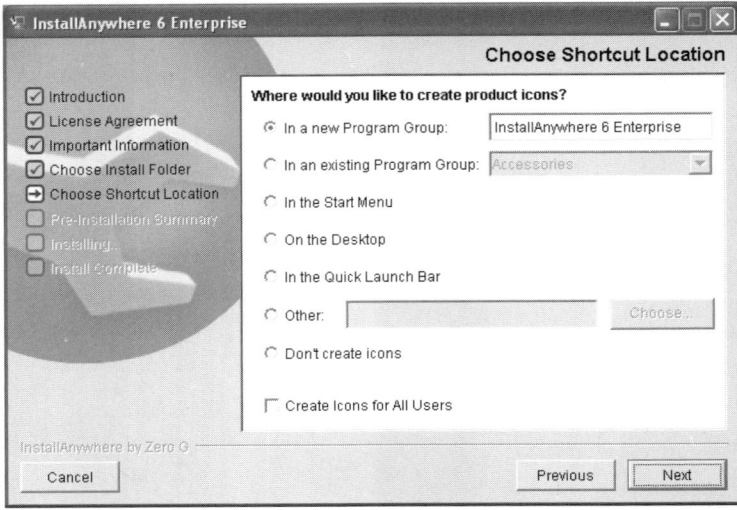

Figure 2.7 *End-User Shortcut Definition.* The InstallAnywhere installer requests that the user choose a location for shortcuts to be installed. When the installation is done on a UNIX system, the same panel would reflect links, rather than shortcuts, and on a Macintosh system the user would choose where to install aliases.

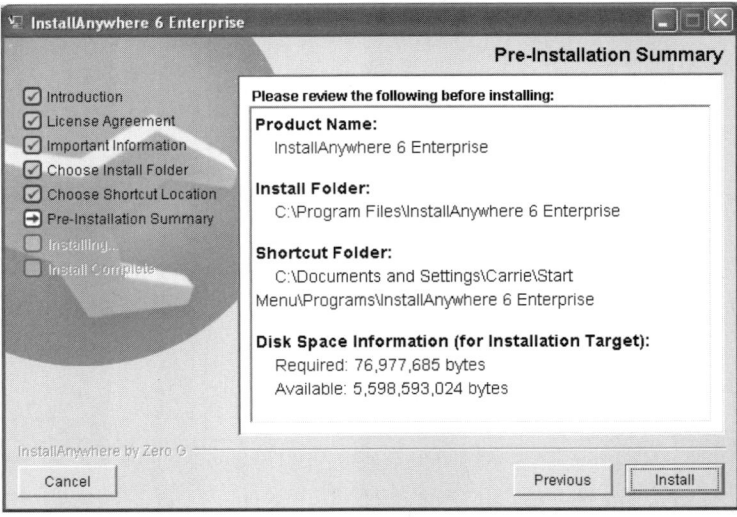

Figure 2.8 *Summary.* The InstallAnywhere installer displays a summary of information gathered in the installation so far. This summary includes disk space calculations and user choices.

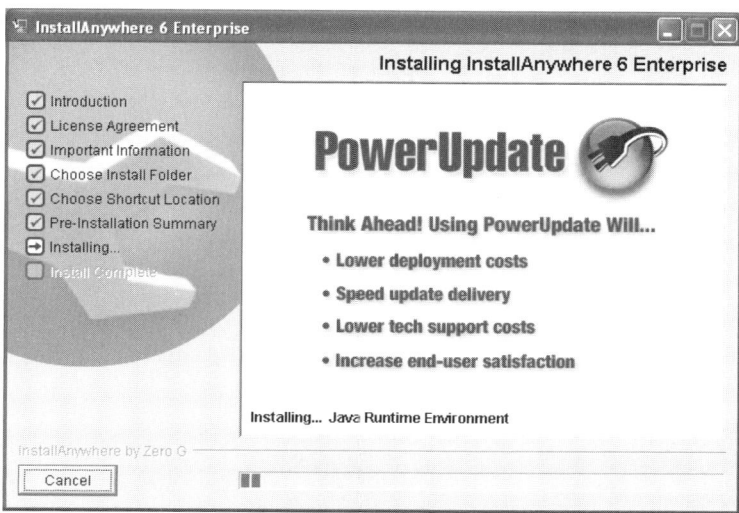

Figure 2.9 *Present Billboards, Animated Graphics, and Progress Bar.* Finally, the installer proceeds to lay down files. During the actual file install, the user is presented with a progress bar and textual feedback. The installer can display animated graphics about the product or about other available products offered (in this case by Zero G).

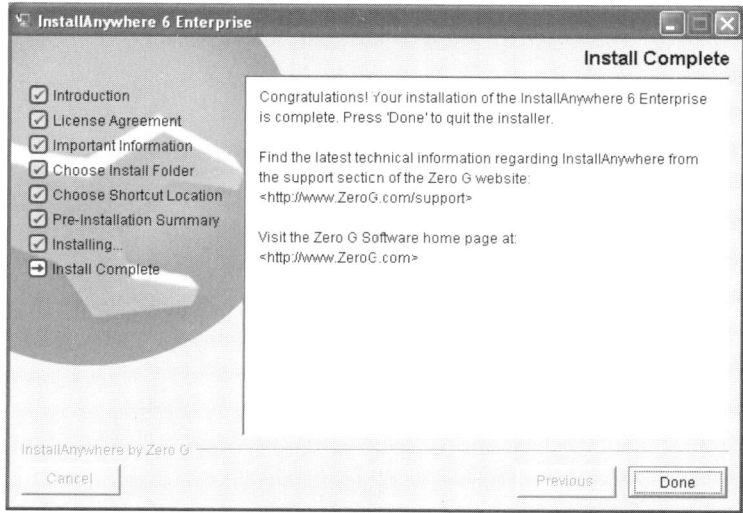

Figure 2.10 *Install Complete.* When the file installation is complete, the installer presents a panel indicating that the install has been a success (or should there be any errors, that errors have occurred).

The Server-Side Installer Experience

InstallAnywhere also includes features that can be used in the installation of server-side products. The needs of a server product installation are often different from those of a client application. Server-side installations normally require more information from the user, and the installation may or may not run in a graphical environment.

Using the same intuitive development interface as client-side installations and, in graphical environments, the same graphic installer, the user can be presented configuration choices to assist with the configuration of the installation.

Figure 2.11 *Installer Branding.* As in a client-side installer, InstallAnywhere provides you the opportunity to brand your product. For server-side installations, InstallAnywhere also provides the option to use Console-mode installers (which require no graphical environment) and/or Silent-mode installers that either accept all defaults or retrieve configuration information from a response file.

The Server-Side Installer Experience 13

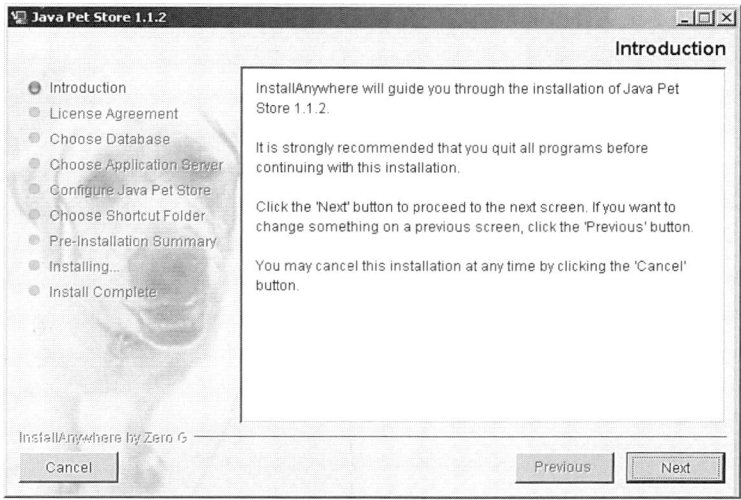

Figure 2.12 *Presenting Information.* The **Introduction** panel allows you to present your end-user with information about the installer, the installed product, or any configuration steps that may be necessary.

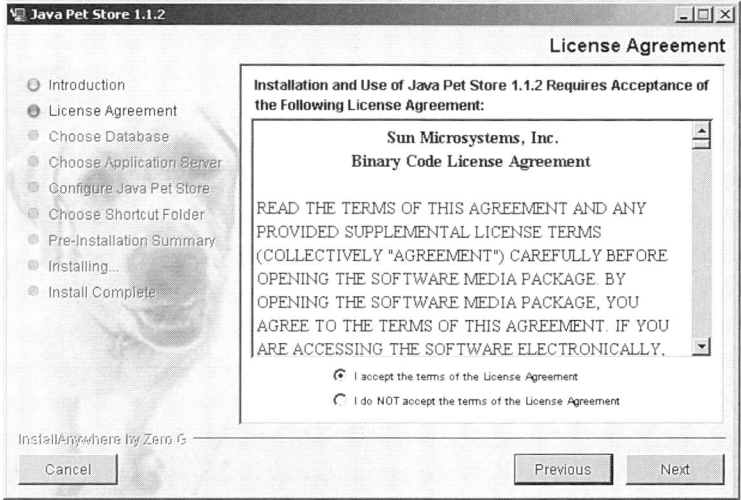

Figure 2.13 *License Agreement Panel.* The **License Agreement** panel presents your users with a license agreement and requires them to accept the agreement before continuing. There is an analogous console available for Console-mode installs.

14 Chapter 2 ■ The InstallAnywhere End-User Experience

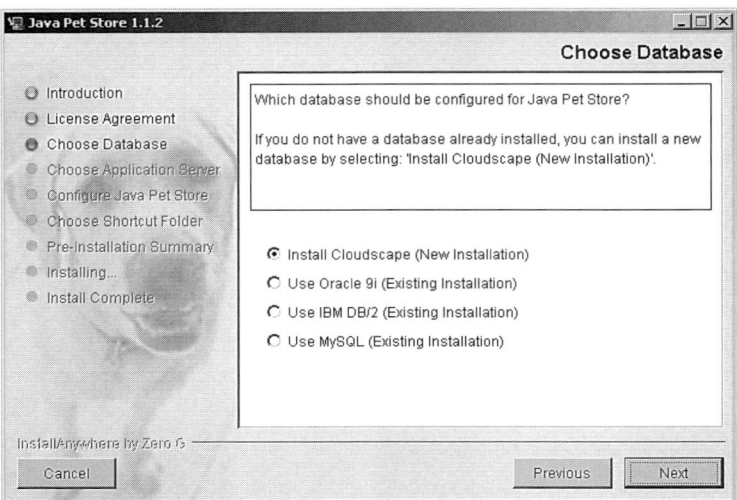

Figure 2.14 *Get User Input Panel.* Using InstallAnywhere's **Get User Input** panel, the user is able to choose configuration options, in this case, which database to use for the installed product's data storage operations.

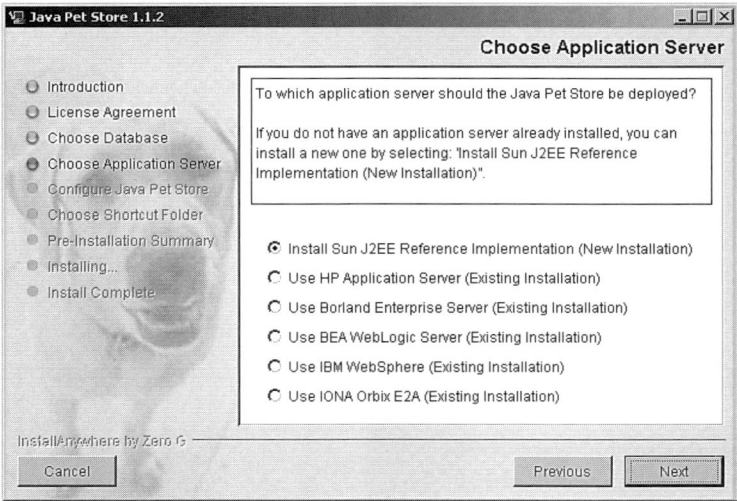

Figure 2.15 *Configure Get User Input Panel.* Again, using InstallAnywhere's **Get User Input** panel, the developer requests input from the user. This panel requires the user to choose an application server. The **Get User Input** panel does not require you, as a developer, to write any code and can be configured in a matter of seconds.

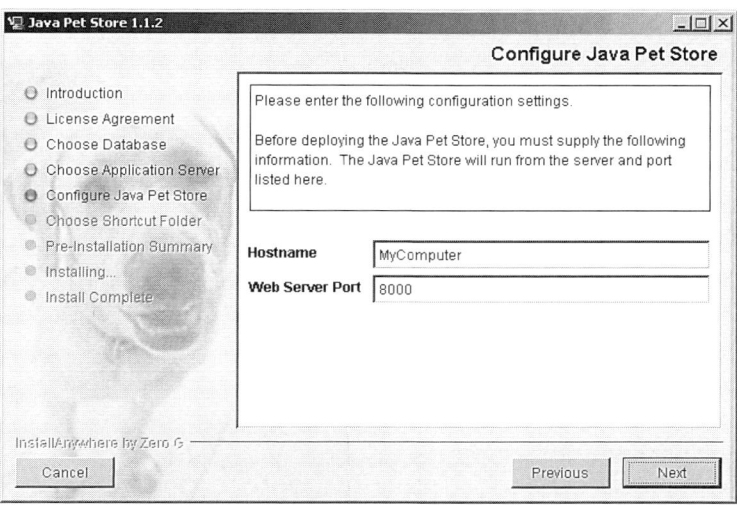

Figure 2.16 *More Get User Input Options.* In another instance of the **Get User Input** panel, the user is asked to choose a hostname and server port for the installation. Note that the **Get User Input** panels we have seen in this demonstration allow radio buttons and text fields. You can also choose to include check boxes, lists, or pop-up items.

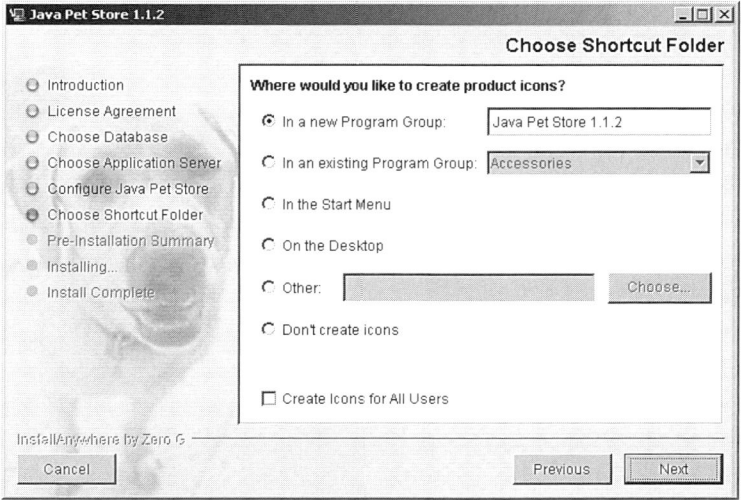

Figure 2.17 *Provide User with Configuration Options.* The installer asks the user where to install the shortcuts, or links, allowing the user to manage the installed product.

16 Chapter 2 ■ The InstallAnywhere End-User Experience

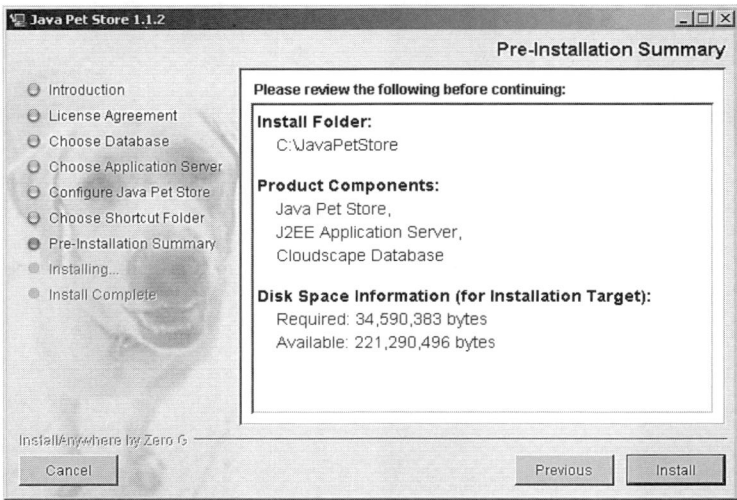

Figure 2.18 *Server-Side Summary.* Like the previous client-side installer, InstallAnywhere allows you to present the end-user with a summary of the choices made in the installer. This panel can be customized to reflect whatever information you would like. This panel is replicated in Console mode as well.

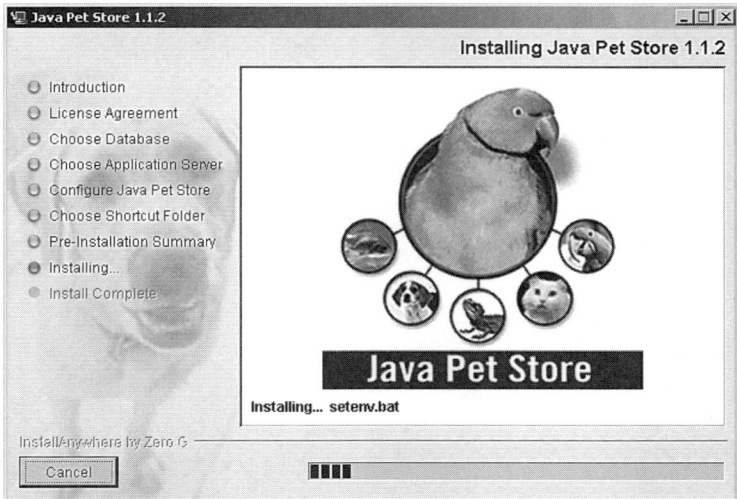

Figure 2.19 *Billboards.* During installation, the installer displays "billboards" to the user through the installation process. These images can be customized to present product or marketing information, or even entertainment.

The Server-Side Installer Experience 17

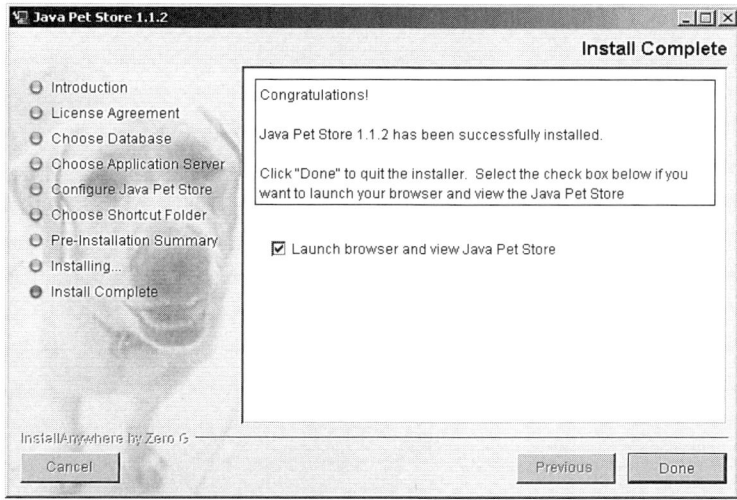

Figure 2.20 *Java Pet Store Installation's Final Panel.* The final panel in the Java Pet Store installation allows the user to select an option to launch the browser and view the Java Pet Store. In the background, transparently to the user, the installer has installed and configured the database, the Web server, and in this case, the J2EE reference implementation. The user can now access the Java Pet Store.

CHAPTER 3

The InstallAnywhere Developer Experience

- **The InstallAnywhere Wizard**
- **Building Your First Installer**

INSTALLANYWHERE HAS TWO authoring modes: The Project Wizard makes the process easier, but also makes choices for developers, while the advanced designer gives developers greater control of an installer project.

InstallAnywhere launches to the first frame of the Project Wizard unless the default preference has been changed in **Edit | Preferences**. To access an existing InstallAnywhere project, open the file, then select **Advanced Designer**, rather than selecting **Next** to continue on through the wizard.

The general process for developing an InstallAnywhere project is

1. Creating new projects
2. Setting Info
3. Pre-install actions
4. Files tasks
5. Post-install actions
6. Setting installer UI options
7. Configuring the project uninstaller
8. Building
9. Testing

The introductory tutorial builds an installer using the Project Wizard, which does not allow configuring pre-install or post-install actions.

The InstallAnywhere Wizard

InstallAnywhere provides two distinct interfaces for creating projects and building InstallAnywhere installers. In this section, we'll cover the InstallAnywhere Project Wizard. This innovative, intuitive wizard guides you through the creation of a basic InstallAnywhere project customized for your product.

Developers can build their first installer in less than five minutes with the six-step Project Wizard. This intuitive design tool also sets the classpath and finds the main class for a Java application automatically.

Building Your First Installer

It is possible to build a basic installer with the Project Wizard in six steps and about five minutes. The following tutorial teaches how to build an installer for a sample Java application, called OfficeSuite for Java, which is included in the InstallAnywhere folder.

1. Creating new projects
   a. Launch InstallAnywhere.

      On the first screen, the **Create New Project** option should already be selected.

   b. Click **Save As** to save and name the project.

      The **Save New Project As** dialog appears. By default the project is named `My_Product`, but any name could be used.

   c. Click **Save** to confirm the name and close this dialog.
   d. Click **Next** to move to the next step of the Project Wizard.

2. Setting info

   Set Info defines basic information about the installer, such as the product name (as displayed on the installer), the name of the installer to be produced, the name of the destination folder, and the application name.

   a. Type the information in the appropriate textboxes. For this tutorial, use the following:

      Product Name: OfficeSuite
      Install Folder Name: OfficeSuite
      Application Shortcut Name: OfficeSuite

   b. Click **Next** to move to the next step in the Project Wizard.

3. Files tasks
   a. Add files.

      i. Click **Add Files**. The **Add Files to Project** dialog appears. Browse through the list to find the OfficeSuite Source Files folder. The OfficeSuite Source Files folder is within the InstallAnywhere installation folder.

ii. Click **Add All** to add the Images and Docs and OfficeSuite 2000 folders, which are inside the OfficeSuite Source Files folder.

These files should appear in the **Files to Add** list.

iii. Click **Done**.

The selected files should appear in the **File/Folder Hierarchy**.

iv. Click **Next** to move to the next step in the Project Wizard.

b. Choose the main class.

Choose Main Class selects the starting class for the application. This frame also allows developers to specify custom icons (in GIF format) for the LaunchAnywhere executable file.

i. Click **Automatically Find Main Classes** at the bottom of the screen.

ii. Select the main class.

iii. Specify a custom icon for the LaunchAnywhere executable by clicking **Change** and choosing a 32 × 32 or a 16 × 16 pixel GIF for the application icon. (Note: ICO files are not supported.) Navigate to the Images and Docs folder and select **OfficeIcon.gif**.

iv. Click **OK** to confirm and close the dialog.

The icon will appear on the main screen.

v. Click **Next** to move to the next step in the Project Wizard.

NOTE Unless you are installing a Java application, skip ahead by clicking **Next** without specifying a main class. The **Choose a Main Class** dialog appears. Click **No** to move to the next step.

c. Set the classpath.

Set Classpath automatically configures a Java application's classpath.

i. Click **Automatically Set Classpath**. InstallAnywhere will calculate which files need to be added to the classpath. A small "CP" icon will appear at the bottom of those folders.

ii. Click **Next** to move to the next step in the Project Wizard.

Building Your First Installer 23

4. Building the installer

    The first several items on the **Build Installer** screen, from Mac OS X through UNIX (All), represent installers that are double-click-able on their respective platforms. The final option, **Other Java-Enabled Platforms**, is a "pure" Java installer that can be invoked from the command line on any Java-enabled platform. Developers may also choose to build installers with an embedded virtual machine. Installers that are built without VMs are smaller and download faster than installers bundled with one. The **InstallAnywhere Web Install** process will allow end-users to choose the appropriate installer for their system.

    a. Pick the appropriate destination platforms and click **Build**.

        The installer folder will be placed in a subdirectory in the same location as the project file. This location cannot be changed.

5. Testing

    a. Now that an installer has been built, it can be tested by clicking **Try It**.

    b. After deploying the sample installer

        - On Windows, go to the OfficeSuite program group and select **OfficeSuite**.
        - On UNIX, "cd" to the directory where the program was installed and type "OfficeSuite."
        - On Mac OS X, double-click the **OfficeSuite** icon on the desktop.

    c. After launching OfficeSuite for Java, quit by selecting **Exit** from its **File** menu.

        It is possible to post the installer folder to a Web server and install the software onto another platform as well.

TIP Hold down the Control (ctrl) key while the installer launches to see the debug output (Windows only).

---

    d. Run the completed installer.

        When building for a platform other than that on which the installer is being developed, transfer that installer and run it manually. By default, installers will be located in the `Build_Output` directories found in the same folder as the `.iap_xml` project file. Within the `Build_Output` folder, will be `Web_Installers` and/or `CDROM_installers`. From within each of these directories, choose the platform to test. For the CD-ROM installer, transfer the entire contents of the `CDROM_Installers` folder.

CHAPTER 4

Key Concepts in InstallAnywhere

- **Authoring Environments**
- **Installer Types**
- **Installer Modes**
- **Install Sets, Features, and Components**
- **Installer Interface GUI**
- **Actions**
- **Rules**
- **Uninstaller**
- **LaunchAnywhere**
- **PowerUpdate**
- **InstallAnywhere Variables**
- **Magic Folders**
- **SpeedFolders**
- **Project File**
- **Manifest Files**

THE KEY CONCEPTS CHAPTER gives a conceptual framework for InstallAnywhere installer development. InstallAnywhere provides many complex options for creating installer functionality.

Authoring Environments

InstallAnywhere offers two authoring environments. One environment is the Project Wizard, which guides developers through creating a new installer quickly. The other environment is the advanced designer, which provides much finer control over installer functionality. The advanced designer allows you to define multiple install sets, add customized splash screen graphics, execute commands from within the installation process, or use many other advanced features. It is possible to build an installer in the Project Wizard and then switch to the advanced designer to add functionality.

Installer Types

InstallAnywhere offers two types of installers: Web installers and CD-ROM installers. Merge modules and templates, which are essentially InstallAnywhere subprojects, are also installer types.

Web

Web Installers are packaged into a single executable file by platform, and are appropriate for distribution over the Web or via e-mail. They use a self-extractor to prepare the source files at the start of the installation and, therefore, require more available temporary disk space.

CD-ROM

In a CD-ROM installer all of the resources are located in an external archive. There is still a self-extractor, but it only extracts the installer engine. Therefore, CD-ROM installers take up less temporary space and start up faster, but they are not appropriate for Web or electronic distribution. CD-ROM installers are also good for distribution on DVD and can span multiple CDs or DVDs.

Merge Modules

Merge modules are essentially installer subprojects that can be created independently of one another and later merged together. A merge module is a reusable collection of installation functionality. It is just like an installer, complete with features, components, panels, actions, and files; however, a merge module cannot be installed without being part of an InstallAnywhere project. Instead, use merge modules to include the functionality of one installer within another installer.

Templates

A template is the starting point for every new installer project. A template can be a simple empty project, or it can contain everything a regular project would contain, such as license agreements, custom graphics and billboards, and even files. Templates provide a convenient way to maintain the look and feel of different versions of installers.

Installer Modes

InstallAnywhere installers can run in three different interactive modes.

- **GUI:** This is the graphical user interface with wizard panels and dialogs.
- **Console:** Also known as the command-line interface, this is for remote installations over TELNET or on systems without a graphical windowing environment.
- **Silent:** This type of installer does not interact with the user at all and is suitable for distribution when all of the settings are already known or provided in a response file.

Install Sets, Features, and Components

Install sets, features, and components are one of the most important concepts to understand when using the InstallAnywhere installer development environment.

InstallAnywhere provides levels of granularity for end-user installation options. Install sets and features may be selected by the end-user. Install sets are groupings of features such as Typical Install or Minimal Install. Features are meant to identify the specific units of functionality of your product. While both install sets and features are made up of files, there is not necessarily a direct correlation between these larger organizational groupings and the files.

Components are groupings of the specific files and actions of your product and are invisible to the end-user. A component may also include a group of registry changes or other elements needed to make a feature work properly. Components are used for the organized sharing of resources and for versioning; they are uniquely identified and are the organization tool of the installer developer, not the installer user. A developer could create a component for each feature in the application, a component for shared libraries used by all the features, and a component for the help system.

Although developers may assign files, folders, and actions directly to product features, it is best to think of features as groupings of components. Install sets such as typical or minimal install are groupings of features. The interaction between the three levels should be addressed when planning which options to present to the end-user.

Installer Interface GUI

Most aspects of an InstallAnywhere installer's user interface can be modified. As a developer of an InstallAnywhere installer, you can alter text strings as well as graphics, such as the splash screen, installer screens, panel additions, background images, and billboards. Developers may even add their own animated GIF files to provide a multimedia experience.

Localization

Nearly every text string in an InstallAnywhere project can be localized. Translations of the text of built-in InstallAnywhere screens and dialogs are already provided. The Enterprise Edition supports 29 different locales, and the Standard Edition supports 9.

If developers want to modify text strings further by locale, the string files are output each time an installer is built in a folder called Project Locales, which will be next to the build output folder. The files are named by locale code. For example, the default English (locale code, en) locale file has the name custom_en.

Each locale file contains the text string grouped by the name of the action to which it belongs. Developers may alter the text string, and upon the next build of the installer, the new localized text will be displayed with the action.

Look and Feel

InstallAnywhere provides many options for altering the look and feel of the installer.

Splash Screens

InstallAnywhere installers present a splash screen at the initial launch of the installer. This screen is displayed for a few seconds while the installer prepares the wizard. The splash screen is an ideal introduction to your product and is an opportunity to set its mood and image. The splash screen will also appear on the HTML page generated for the Install-Anywhere Web Install Applet. It can be a GIF, a PNG, or a JPEG file of any size, although the preferred size is 470 × 265 pixels.

GUI Panel Additions

The **Additions to GUI Installer Panels** option allows developers to display a list of steps or an image along the left side of the installer's panel.

Background Images

This Background Image feature allows you to create a truly unique installer. The background image is the graphical background for every panel in your installer. Background images are only supported in Swing GUI installers.

Billboards

Billboards are graphics that the installer will display during the installation of files. Billboards generally convey a marketing message, a description of the product, or simply something fun for the end-user to see as the file installation is occurring. Each billboard added will be displayed for an even amount of time, based on actions within the installation. If an installation has very few files, and many billboards, each billboard will only be displayed for a short time.

Billboards can be GIF, PNG, or JPEG files, and should be 587 × 312 pixels in size. Billboards can even use animated GIF files, providing the end-user with a richer media experience during installation.

Actions

InstallAnywhere supports an extensible action architecture that gives developers the ability to perform operations during installation. Some of these actions are as simple as installing files and folders and as complex as creating or modifying text files, executing custom code during the installation process, or extracting contents from a compressed file.

Actions may occur in the background, not requiring any user input, or may require user input. General/install actions do not require any user input. Panel actions and console actions request user input. Panel actions display a graphic element that requests user input. Console actions display a command-line request.

General Actions

Most general actions occur transparently to the end-user. They do not require any user input.

Panel Actions

Panel actions are requests for user input that appear inside the graphical installer wizard.

Console Actions

Console actions are command-line requests for user input and are used during command-line installation.

Plug-in Actions

Custom code can be integrated with the InstallAnywhere designer and will appear as a plug-in.

Rules

InstallAnywhere rules can be applied to any action within the Install-Anywhere installer, as well as to organizational units such as install sets, features, and components.

InstallAnywhere uses variable-based Boolean rules to control most aspects of installer behavior. The rules logic allows developers to create simple and complex logic systems that determine which actions will occur. The rules can be structured based on end-user input or on conditions determined by the installer.

Uninstaller

InstallAnywhere automatically creates an uninstaller for each project. The uninstaller can be removed manually. The InstallAnywhere uninstaller typically removes all files and actions that were installed during the installation, although you can control this behavior as desired.

The uninstaller is much like the installer. It is a collection of panels, consoles, and actions. It keeps track of what the installer has done and contains a record of every action run during install time. All pre-uninstall panels, actions, and consoles run first. Then, the uninstaller removes files and performs the uninstall operation of any action found in the files tree. Lastly, post-uninstall actions are run.

LaunchAnywhere

A native executable used to launch a Java application, LaunchAnywhere is Zero G's Java application launcher technology. LaunchAnywhere technology creates double-click-able icons on Windows and Mac OS X. On UNIX platforms, a command-line application is created.

A LaunchAnywhere Java application launcher automatically locates an appropriate Java Virtual Machine (JVM), either bundled with the application or already installed on the system, and sets the Java options and settings (such as heap size), depending on the developer's specifications. LaunchAnywhere sets the classpath; redirects standard out and standard error; passes in system properties, Environment variables, and command-line parameters; and launches the Java application. LaunchAnywhere hides the console window by default for GUI applications, or it can be set to display the console for text-based applications. All LaunchAnywhere settings are configured within InstallAnywhere and are automatically set when the installer installs the application.

PowerUpdate

PowerUpdate—Zero G's multiplatform software updating and delivery solution—updates any kind of software on any client or server platform. PowerUpdate ensures that end-users will always have the latest version of the deployed application, eliminating the need to contact customers whenever there is an update, patch, or new release, thereby reducing the volume of customer support calls and minimizing the need to contact end-users every time an application is modified.

PowerUpdate can easily be added to an application using the built-in Install PowerUpdate Client action.

InstallAnywhere automatically keeps itself updated using PowerUpdate. If an update is available, a message will appear giving developers the option to get the update.

For more information on PowerUpdate, see www.zerog.com/goto/powerupdate.

InstallAnywhere Variables

During installation, InstallAnywhere keeps track of dynamic values through the use of variables. Almost every dynamic value in InstallAnywhere, such as the path that a Magic Folder (see below for definition of Magic Folder) refers to, is represented by an InstallAnywhere variable. Variables may be modified or accessed in order to affect the functionality or behavior of an installer.

InstallAnywhere variables are the key to any InstallAnywhere-based installation. They allow developers to control the flow of information and the flow of the installation. They let developers store information from the system and information input by end-users, then create rules to determine operations based on that information. Developers can even output that information to configuration files or other resources to be used by the application.

Magic Folders

InstallAnywhere uses Magic Folders to define installation locations. These Magic Folders are a way of keeping track of installation locations. InstallAnywhere can install to any Magic Folder or subfolder of a Magic Folder. Magic Folders represent a specific location, such as the user-selected installation folder, the desktop, or the location for library files. At install time, the installer determines which operating system it is running on and sets the Magic Folders to the correct absolute paths. Many Magic Folders are platform-specific, and many are predefined by InstallAnywhere. You can install to nearly any standard location on any supported platform. InstallAnywhere also provides user-controlled Magic Folders, which can be set as the developer needs them.

NOTE Not all Magic Folders are available in every edition.

Magic Folder Examples

InstallAnywhere uses Magic Folders to define most installation locations. They can represent either a fixed or variable path and can be used to place a single file in the appropriate location on different target platforms. Many Magic Folders are predefined by InstallAnywhere and in Enterprise Edition allow you to install to nearly all standard locations across our supported platforms (see Table 4.1).

Table 4.1 Magic Folder Examples

Folder Name	InstallAnywhere Variable	Destination
User Installation Directory	$USER_INSTALL_DIR$	This is the installation folder, as specified by the end-user. You can specify a default value for this variable in the **Project Info** screen in the advanced designer by choosing a location in the Default Install Folder area of the screen.
Programs Folder (platform default)	$PROGRAMS_DIR$	This is the default application directory on the destination system (the Program Files folder on Windows, the Applications folder on Mac OS, and the logged-in end-user's home account on UNIX).

"End-User Installation Directory" ($USER_INSTALL_DIR$) resolves to the folder the end-user selects as the desired installation directory when the installer is running.

"Programs Folder" ($PROGRAMS_DIR$) resolves to the default application folder for the target platform's operating system. If a particular Magic Folder does not make sense on a target platform, actions that create files (Install File or Create Alias, Link, Shortcut) will not install them. Actions that do not install files, such as Execute Command, are not affected and will run normally.

In the Properties section of each Install File and Create Folder action is a list from which to select that item's destination, such as its Magic Folder. Some user-environment Magic Folders now resolve on Linux. They will detect which GUI environment is being run (either KDE or Gnome) and resolve it appropriately.

Variables and Magic Folders

Every Magic Folder has an associated InstallAnywhere variable. These variables are first initialized when the installer starts up. Changing the value of a Magic Folder variable will change the installation destination for the Magic Folder. This technique can be used for any of the folders. For example, changing the value of $USER_INSTALL_DIR$ through Install-Anywhere will change where all the files inside the install folder that

Magic Folder will install. With three exceptions, these variables are initialized at install time and will not change, except through using custom code or the Set InstallAnywhere Variable action. The exceptions are as follows:

- **$USER_INSTALL_DIR$:** This variable is initialized to the default value determined in the **Project** task in the advanced designer. If the end-user selects a different folder, then its value can change at the **Choose Install Folder** step.
- **$USER_SHORTCUTS$:** This variable is initialized to the default value determined by the **Platforms** task in Advanced mode. If the end-user selects a different location, then its value can change at the **Choose Alias, Link, Shortcut Folder** installation step.
- **$JAVA_HOME$:** This variable is initialized to the default value determined by the **Platforms** task in Advanced mode. If the end-user selects a different location, then its value can change at the **Choose Alias, Link, Shortcut Folder** install step.

  Installer without JVM: This defaults to the value of the Java property java.home. If the end-user selects a JVM, then its value can change at the **Choose Java Virtual Machine** step.

  Installer with JVM: This defaults to the value $USER_INSTALL_DIR$/jre. If the end-user selects a JVM already on his machine, then it can change when the $USER_INSTALL_DIR$ changes or at the **Choose Java Virtual Machine** step.

NOTE Variables can't be set to themselves. For example, if you wanted to append /test to USER_MAGIC_FOLDER_1, you can't set USER_MAGIC_FOLDER_1 = $USER_MAGIC_FOLDER_1$$/$test. You can't have either direct or indirect recursion with InstallAnywhere variables as this will cause an infinite loop.

SpeedFolders

Using SpeedFolders will dramatically increase installation speed and memory efficiency. Similar to folders that are added to a project using the Add Files method, SpeedFolders represent a container of other folders and files that are to be installed on the destination computer. SpeedFolders are a pointer to a particular folder, as opposed to a traditional folder, in which every item is a separate action. However, unlike normal folders, SpeedFolders and the contents they represent are treated as a single action, rather than each item representing an individual item. This combining of items lowers memory requirements and speeds up the installation.

SpeedFolders are excellent for use in an automated build environment. The contents of a SpeedFolder are determined at build time. At the time the installer is built, all of the contents of the folder on the build system (excepting items that have been marked to filter out) are added to the installer recursively. SpeedFolders are used to specify that a folder and all of its contents and subfolders on the development system are to be automatically updated and included in the installer at the time the project is built. Standard folders (non-SpeedFolders) require developers to add or remove any files at build time that are present or absent since the last installer build or an error will occur.

SpeedFolders have filters that allow inclusion or exclusion of files that meet particular naming criteria. Individual files or folders in a Speed-Folder cannot be assigned to different components; nor can SpeedFolders be converted into traditional directories, or traditional directories into SpeedFolders. To convert one type to the other, you must delete the one and replace it with the other type of folder.

Project File

InstallAnywhere stores every project in its own XML file. These XML-based project files can be checked in and out of source control systems, and can be modified with text and XML editors. For added flexibility, project files may also be modified using XSL transformations, providing the ability to modify referenced file paths, or other attributes. Several XML and XSL tools to work on the XML project file can be found in the InstallAnywhere application folder, inside `resource/extras/XML Project File Tools`.

Manifest Files

InstallAnywhere uses a manifest file to identify the files that will be put in the installer. Manifest files allow you to build installers directly from a list of files without needing to open and modify entire project files within InstallAnywhere. Useful when groups of developers are working on a project, manifest files can be used to combine files. Development groups only need to supply a list of files, rather than to provide partially built options within InstallAnywhere (although that capability is also available through the use of merge modules and templates).

Developers can allow builds to succeed even if files referenced in the manifest file cannot be found. This flexibility allows for a single manifest file to identify all portions of a development project, promoting parallel development of software projects.

Manifest files' ability to set UNIX file permissions gives the developer fine-grained control over the files that will be written to UNIX target platforms.

CHAPTER 5
Basic Installer Development Strategies

- **Installation Planning**
- **Installation Goals**
- **InstallAnywhere Installation Planning Worksheet**

Installation Planning

Occasionally, you'll imagine that an installation will be simple. You think you'll put the files to disk in their specified location, and the application will just work. However, this does not usually turn out to be the case. In today's world of systems integration, installation stacks, suite installers, and client-server-application development, you are far more likely to run into a very complex installation scenario—one requiring multiple steps, multiple products, and intricate configuration steps.

The idea behind using a fully featured installer such as InstallAnywhere is to minimize the impact that this sort of complexity will have on your customers and your end-users.

As such, it's important to plan your installation process carefully and determine your installation needs prior to beginning development.

Installation Goals

When planning your installation process, consider the goals and targets of your installation.

- Does the installer need to allow a nontechnical end-user to install a complex product, or must it be highly flexible so that expert users can use it in a number of environments?
- What platforms and architectures will your deployment project target?

To help you plan your installation process, the Installation Planning Worksheet can be used to structure and manage your installation development project. A worksheet template can be found on page 41.

InstallAnywhere Installation Planning Worksheet

Product name: _____ Product version: _____

Target Platforms
- ❏ Mac OS X   ❏ Linux
- ❏ Windows   ❏ Solaris
- ❏ AIX   ❏ Other UNIX: _____
- ❏ HP-UX   ❏ Other Java-enabled platforms:

Installer Target
- ❏ Technical end-user
- ❏ Nontechnical end-user

Deployment Media
- ❏ Web
- ❏ CD-ROM/DVD
- ❏ Merge module

Application Type
- ❏ Native application
- ❏ Java application
- ❏ NET

Java-Specific Options
Java Virtual Machine(s) version required:

Installation Needs
Location(s) on target system where files are to be installed:
- ❏ Mac OS X   ❏ Linux
- ❏ Windows   ❏ Solaris
- ❏ AIX   ❏ Other UNIX: _____
- ❏ HP-UX   ❏ Other Java-enabled platforms:

Configurations That Must Be Made on the Target Platform
_____
_____
_____

Information That Must Be Collected from the End-User
_____
_____
_____

Team Development Options
Will more than one developer manage this project? ❏ Yes ❏ No
If yes, then what source paths will be defined for file maintenance?

Name: *Description:*
_____   _____
_____   _____
_____   _____
_____   _____

Uninstall Options
Will this installation require any special uninstall options? ❏ Yes ❏ No
If yes, specify uninstall options:
Pre-uninstall:

Post-uninstall:

CHAPTER 6

An Introduction to the Advanced Designer

- **Defining Installer Projects and the Product Registry**
- **File Settings—Timestamps and Overwrite Behavior**
- **Platforms**
- **Locales**
- **Rules before the Pre-Install Task**
- **Creating Debug Output**
- **Virtual Machines**

THE INSTALLANYWHERE ADVANCED DESIGNER has an intuitive, graphical interface that allows developers to manage all aspects of their installer project. All of the features of InstallAnywhere are available in this easy-to-use, integrated development environment.

To access the InstallAnywhere advanced designer, click the **Advanced Designer** button after selecting a project file or creating a new project.

The advanced designer is divided into tasks represented by tabs found along the left-hand side of the window. Each tab represents tasks and settings specific to each installation project.

- **Project:** Settings related to your specific project, including general settings, file settings, and localization settings
- **Installer UI:** Settings for adjusting the look and feel of the installer by adding background images, billboards, and other graphical components
- **Organization:** Settings related to the management of install sets, features, components, and merge modules
- **Files:** The manage file installation tree and install time actions
- **Pre-Install:** An ordered sequence of panels and actions that occur before file installation
- **Post-Install:** An ordered sequence of panels and actions that occur after file installation
- **Pre-Uninstall:** An ordered sequence of panels and actions that occur before file uninstallation
- **Post-Uninstall:** An ordered sequence of panels and actions that occur after file uninstallation
- **Build:** Settings related to the management of build settings, including the bundling of JVMs

Each **Advanced Designer** task contains subtabs that offer greater fine-tuning of InstallAnywhere's features. For an example, go through Exercise 6.1.

Exercise 6.1 Building an Installer with the Advanced Designer

In this exercise we will rebuild the previous OfficeSuite Installer using the advanced designer. The advanced designer offers a much wider range of configuration over InstallAnywhere's many options than the Project Wizard allows.

1. Creating a new project
   a. Launch InstallAnywhere.

      On the first screen, the **Create New Project** option should already be selected.
   b. Select the Basic Project template.

      This template should already be selected
   c. Click **Save As** to save and name the project.

      The **Save New Project As** dialog appears. InstallAnywhere will use this name as the name of the product in the installer project.
   d. Select the **Advanced Designer** button.

      This selection will open the newly created project file in the InstallAnywhere advanced designer. The advanced designer will open to the **Project | Info** task. This task sets the basic installer options such as the name of the product, the installer title, and the installer name. The installer name will be the name of the executable file that InstallAnywhere creates. This tab also sets the location for the building of the installer and the settings for the generation of installation logs.
   e. Complete the Installer **Title** and **Product Name** fields.

      For now, we will skip the **Installer UI**, **Organization**, and **Files** tasks.
2. Pre-install actions
   a. Select the **Pre-Install** task.

      The **Pre-Install** task sets the panels and action that occur prior to the installation of files. By default, a new InstallAnywhere project contains the following panels.

      Introduction: This panel allows developers to introduce the product or installation process.

Choose Install Folder: This panel allows the end-user to choose the installation location for the product.

Choose Alias, Link, Shortcut Folder: This panel allows the end-user to specify the location for any Mac OS aliases, Windows shortcuts, and UNIX symlinks (used as shortcuts) that will be installed.

Pre-Install Summary: This panel provides the end-user with a summary of various installation settings prior to the installation of files.

Actions in the **Pre-Install** task will occur in the order set in the task list. In a default project, an **Introduction** panel will be followed by a **Choose Install Folder** panel, followed by a **Choose Alias, Link, Shortcut Folder** panel, and so on. The order of panels and actions can be manipulated using the arrow buttons to the middle right of the advanced designer screen.

The behavior and content of panels can be modified by highlighting each panel. The dialog along the bottom half of the advanced designer will change to reflect the panel selected. In InstallAnywhere's vocabulary, this dialog is known as a customizer and is available for each action and panel in the installer.

3. Defining the installation tasks

   a. Select the **Files** task from the far left side of the advanced designer.

   The **Files** task defines the files to install, the folder location in which to install those files, and the order in which the tasks need to happen as the files are being installed.

   By default, the InstallAnywhere **Files** task has a folder called `Uninstall $PRODUCT_NAME$`, which contains any InstallAnywhere uninstaller actions and a Comment action with instructions pertaining to the uninstaller.

   Actions (including, but not limited to, the installation of files) in the **Files** task list occur in order, with actions at the top of the installation occurring first.

Exercise 6.1 Building an Installer with the Advanced Designer

HINT The advanced designer implements a drag-and-drop interface in many tabs and tasks. In the **Files** task, actions and files can be moved by selecting and dragging them. A dark underline appears in the location where the file or action will be placed.

TIP Leave the Uninstaller Creation in its default place in the installation (although the folder structure can be changed). For organizational purposes, it's generally best to have the Uninstaller Creation action first.

Because the advanced tutorial mainly replicates the tasks for the OfficeSuite installer from the Project Wizard, those same files will be added.

   b. Add files.

   i. Use the **File Chooser** to browse to the OfficeSuite Source Files folder found in the InstallAnywhere installation directory. The folder can also be dragged and dropped into the **Files** task.

   ii. Add the OfficeSuite 2000 folder and its contents.

   After they are added, the files will be displayed in the file installation tree in the advanced designer window.

   File trees may be expanded or contracted within the InstallAnywhere advanced designer **Files** task by clicking on the "+" or "–" boxes at the apex of the tree branches. An object may be moved up and down or into and out of subfolders in the file tree by highlighting the object and using the right, left, up, and down arrows (or dragging and dropping the files into the correct locations) found at the middle right of the **Files** task screen.

4. Adding a LaunchAnywhere executable (LAX) to the **Files** task

   a. Select the **Add Launcher** button.

   An LAX is a unique native executable, created by InstallAnywhere, that is used to launch a Java application. While the InstallAnywhere wizard specifically asks you to select a main class and automatically creates a single launcher, the advanced designer allows developers to add as many launchers as they would like.

There are two ways to add a LaunchAnywhere launcher to an InstallAnywhere project file. The **Create LaunchAnywhere for Java Application** option may be selected from the **Add Action** palette or can be added by clicking the **Add Launcher** button on the middle control bar in the advanced designer.

　　i. Highlight the User Install folder in the advanced designer and click the **Add Launcher** button.

　　ii. Click **OK**.

　　When adding a launcher, InstallAnywhere will automatically introspect into the added files (including introspecting into Java archive [JAR] and or ZIP files) to find class files with main methods specified.

　　iii. Select **com.acme.OfficeSuite** as the main class for the application.

　　Because OfficeSuite is a simple project, we're presented with only the `com.acme.OfficeSuite` class.

b. Click **OK** to continue.

NOTE The **Add Launcher** button has not only added the launcher to the file structure, but also created a shortcut, link, or alias action in the **Shortcuts' Destination Folder** Magic Folder. This location is variable and will be specified by the **Choose Alias, Link, and Shortcut** panel in the pre-install section.

c. Customize the launcher.

The appearance the launcher will have as a shortcut can now be customized. Highlight the launcher. The customizer along the lower portion of the advanced designer screen will change to reflect the options for the Create LaunchAnywhere for Java Application action.

In the lower-middle right of the customizer (below the **Arguments** field) is a set of buttons that control the icon associated with the launcher. The default icons are a teal tile with a coffee cup and a rocket ship.

　　i. Click **Change** to alter the icon.

　　ii. In the **Choose Icon** dialog, click **Choose GIF File**.

Exercise 6.1 Building an Installer with the Advanced Designer

iii. Select a GIF or JPG file to use as an icon. For this tutorial, use the OfficeSuite Icon file in the Images and Docs folder within the OfficeSuite Source Files folder.

NOTE Interlaced GIF files cannot be used with InstallAnywhere. The conversion process does not support these files, and their use can result in blank icons.

For Mac OS X, provide an ICNS file (created with iconbuilder—part of the Mac OS X Developer Tools).

---

d. Set the InstallAnywhere classpath.

InstallAnywhere maintains a general classpath that is used to create launchers for the Java application.

i. In the InstallAnywhere advanced designer, click the **Set Classpath** button.

A blue CP icon will appear on folders and archives that the process has added to the classpath.

ii. Select the **Project | Java** tab along the left side of the advanced designer window to view the classpath as determined by the Set Classpath action.

Because OfficeSuite is a simple product, we'll have only the main OfficeSuite 2000 folder (which contains loose class files). If our example project contained JAR or ZIP files containing classes, they would also have been added. If a file has been added mistakenly on the classpath, it can be removed at this point or by highlighting that file in the installation tree and unchecking the **In Classpath** option box in the customizer for that file.

5. Post-install actions

The **Post-Install** task list specifies actions and panels to occur after the installation of files. Like **Pre-Install**, the **Post-Install** step is ordered with the top actions occurring first.

By default, InstallAnywhere has added two actions to the InstallAnywhere project.

- **Panel: Install Complete**. This panel appears when the installation has completed successfully. This action is determined by the status of the $INSTALL_SUCCESS$ variable. This panel will display only if $INSTALL_SUCCESS$ does not contain an error condition.

- **Restart Windows**. This action restarts a Windows system if the installer determines that it is necessary.

InstallAnywhere installations are controlled primarily by InstallAnywhere rules. As an example of an InstallAnywhere rule, highlight the Restart Windows action in the OfficeSuite project. In the customizer in the lower portion of the screen, select the **Rules** tab.

The InstallAnywhere rules customizer will appear in the lower portion of the advanced designer. The rules set on the Restart Windows action are simple rules set to compare InstallAnywhere variables. InstallAnywhere rules are Boolean and allow the file, panel, or action to be installed, displayed, or run only if the rule resolves to true.

a. Click the **Add Action** button to open the action palette.

The action palette is divided by tabs that vary based on the task that is active at the time the palette is called.

b. Select **Execute Target File** found under the **General** tab.

The Execute Target File action is used to execute files that are included as part of the installation, and consequently it is available only in the install and post-install portion of the installation. (The Execute Target File action is not available at pre-install because files cannot be executed that are not installed yet!)

c. Click **Add**, or double-click on the action to add it.

The palette will remain open so additional actions may be added.

d. Add a name for the action in the customizer in the lower portion of the screen.

Naming the action will help identify it in the visual tree.

e. To select the target, click the **Choose Target** button.

The **Choose an Action** dialog represents the file installation tree specified in the **Files** task. File(s) can be executed in this stage. To execute the just-installed OfficeSuite application, choose the launcher for that application.

NOTE Choose the actual OfficeSuite launcher, not the shortcut (which should share the same icon). Shortcuts, especially on Windows and Mac OS systems, are pointers and are not inherently executable. InstallAnywhere will not execute a shortcut.

Customizer Options

By using the **Command Line** field modifications can be made to the command line used to execute the file, such as adding a handler or an argument to the execution.

NOTE Do not remove or modify the $EXECUTE_FILE_TARGET$ entry, as this represents the file to execute. To specify a handler, prepend an executable path; to specify an argument, append a file path. These paths must be absolute; however, the paths can include InstallAnywhere variables.

The user experience for this action can be tailored by using the **Options** fields.

The option to suspend the installation until a process is complete is particularly useful in cases where a later step in the installation depends on the execution. There is also a subtask that allows developers to specify an indeterminate progress bar with a message. This task can be used if the execution may take some time (for example, an execute that installs another product or that configures a database or other application).

The **Show Please Wait** panel option will display a message panel to the user while the execution is occurring.

The **Suppress First Window** option allows developers to suppress the first window on Microsoft Windows platforms. This option is particularly useful in suppressing the appearance of the cmd.exe window when executing batch files or command-line executables.

NOTE If the **Execute Action** panel was added at a location other than the bottom of the **Post-Install** task, move it now. Either utilize the up and down arrows, or drag the action to the bottom of the task list.

6. Building the installer

    The InstallAnywhere **Build** task allows the options that will be used to build the installer(s) to be set. In this task, you can set platforms for the build, configuration options for bundled virtual machines, and platform optimization and installer type.

TIP For early testing, build only for the development platform. Each additional platform adds to the time required to build, cycling through run-rebuild-run-rebuild stages. A faster build will make the development process easier.

    On the **Build Targets** tab in the **Build** task, select the platform(s). Selecting **With VM** will bundle the installer with a VM. **With VM** is only selectable for platforms that have a VM pack. VM packs should be placed in the `<InstallAnywhere>/resource/installer_vms` folder, and InstallAnywhere should be restarted to refresh the available VM packs.

    The **Build** task also includes the **Distribution** and **Build Log** tabs.

    The **Distribution** tab allows developers to set options for the type of installers to build and the optimizations for each installer. As the installer being built in this tutorial doesn't contain any platform-specific files, it will not need to be optimized at this point. However, if the installer did include platform-specific files, these files would be optimized based on the application of the Check Platform rules.

    The **Build Log** tab displays the XML log of previous builds.

    a. Click **Build Project** to build the OfficeSuite installer. The **Build Information** dialog will appear.

    b. Click the blue arrow on the lower left of that dialog to see the build details console.

       When the build is complete, there will be a notification (in this case, the build should take a minute or less).

7. Testing

    After the build process is complete, try the installer by selecting either the **Try Web Install** or **Try Installer** button. For the purposes of this exercise, use the **Try Web Install** button to launch our browser and the InstallAnywhere Web Install Page generated by the build process.

a. Click **Try Web Install**. The Web Install Page will load and should request a security access.
b. Grant this access to allow the Web Install Applet to run the InstallAnywhere installer.

   The Web installer can now be launched with just one click.
c. Click the **Start Installer for Windows** button below the image. The applet will check for sufficient disk space, download the installer, and execute it.
d. Run the installer.

   After the **Install Complete** panel, the installer should launch OfficeSuite. The OfficeSuite icon can now be selected from the Windows **Start** menu to run the installed product.

Defining Installer Projects and the Product Registry

Product Registry

The product registry is essentially a product configuration database that keeps track of features and components of products for the operating system. The product registry accomplishes tasks such as associating filename extensions with applications. InstallAnywhere makes it easy to enter vendor and product information in the product registry to uniquely identify products.

NOTE Correctly setting the product ID and version is critical to using the Find Component in Registry action. By checking the product ID, InstallAnywhere finds the locations of components in the registry.

Product ID and vendor information is entered in the **Project | Description** subtask.

Installer Identification and Version

Installers—just like the software products they are installing—need to be given names and versions. Just as names and versions help track changes in a software product, InstallAnywhere helps uniquely identify versions of installers. InstallAnywhere also provides an installation log, which details the files installed and the actions executed by the installer. The developer defines whether to create an installation log, how to format the log, whether it should be created in plain text or XML format, and whether the installation log should be removed if the application is uninstalled.

> **NOTE** To set the installation log install location, set the InstallAnywhere variable $INSTALL_LOG_DESTINATION$.

The **Project | Info** task defines basic information about the installer to be created, displays information about the InstallAnywhere installer project, and enables the developer to make decisions about the installer installation log.

File Settings—Timestamps and Overwrite Behavior

When installing software, be it a new product or a newer version of a product, it is possible to overwrite files that already exist on the target system. InstallAnywhere uses timestamps to uniquely identify files that have the same name. InstallAnywhere also allows the developer to set the type of overwrite behavior—whether to prompt the end-user or overwrite the older file.

> **NOTE** When installing to Windows operating systems, files may be in use. When the **Replace In-Use Files after Restart** option is selected, the installer action will detect if files being installed are overwriting files that are in use. If files are in use, InstallAnywhere will register these files with the Windows product registry so they can be correctly installed when the system is restarted.

Timestamps, in-use file behavior, and overwrite behavior are defined in the **File Settings** subtask.

Installed File Timestamps

The **File Modification Timestamp Behavior** section enables developers to timestamp installed files in three different ways.

1. **Preserve Timestamp:** This selection maintains the default timestamp on the file, that is, the time that file was last modified as shown by the operating system where the file was created or saved. For example, the file would show the time it was last modified and not when it was installed.
2. **Install Timestamp:** This selection sets the creation property and the file modification property to the time that the files were installed on the target system. Using this option all of the installed files will have the same creation and file modification properties.
3. **Specify Timestamp:** This selection enables developers to place a specific timestamp on installed files. Specific date- and timestamps may be selected from the scroll lists.

NOTE The files' timestamp property may be set to both before and after the current date.

Java 2 Virtual Machines handle timestamps properly. Prior JVMs may not handle timestamps properly.

InstallAnywhere displays all timestamps in the system's local time zone. Behind the scenes, InstallAnywhere automatically maintains those timestamps in Greenwich Mean Time (GMT), but the timestamps display in the local time zone.

Default Overwrite Behavior

When the installation contains files that also exist in the installation location(s) on the target system, the installer must know how to determine whether to overwrite files. Files are considered to be the same when they have the same name and the same path. The decision as to whether to overwrite or not install the files depends on the timestamps of the files on the target computer and the timestamp of the installation files.

The default behavior is to overwrite older files and to prompt the user if the files on the destination computer are newer.

The options for determining overwrite behavior may be prompted or set as a default (see Table 6.1).

Table 6.1 Overwrite Options

Overwrite Option	Select This Option To ...
Always overwrite	Install files without giving the user the choice whether to overwrite files that currently exist on the computer.
Never overwrite	Leave existing files untouched on the user's computer rather than overwrite them with files that are being installed. The user is given no option.
Overwrite if older, do not install if newer	Overwrite existing files on the user's computer that are the same as files that are being installed if the installed files are newer (have a later timestamp) than the existing files. The user is given no option.
Overwrite if older, prompt if newer	Overwrite existing files on the user's computer that are the same as files that are being installed, without giving the user the option, if the installed files are newer (have a later timestamp) than the existing files. Prompt the user if the installed files are older than the existing files on the user's computer.
Prompt if older, do not install if newer	Prompt the user if the existing files on the user's computer are older than the installation files. If the existing files are newer, there will not be a prompt, and the installation files will not be installed.
Always prompt user	Prompt the user whenever an installation file exists on the target computer.

Platforms

While InstallAnywhere runs on any Java-enabled platform, features such as default install folders and default link folders (UNIX), default shortcut folders (Windows), and default alias folders should be defined separately for each target operating system.

The options are simple for Windows: just locate the default install and shortcut folders. Mac OS X adds defining default permissions for files and folders that will be created on the target system. The developer can also enable installer authentication (providing the end-user the correct permissions to install if not running as a privileged user) and the ability to set which VM versions. InstallAnywhere adds RedHat Package Management (RPM) settings for Linux installations. RPM is a package of installation tools that InstallAnywhere installers will use in the Linux environment and other UNIX environments. The RPM feature enables the installer to interact with and make entries into the RPM database.

Locales

The **Locales** subtask defines the languages for which the installer will be created. A locale is enabled when it is checked.

All enabled locales will generate a locale file that will be placed in a folder in the same directory as the InstallAnywhere project file. To customize a locale, customize this file. For more information about locales and localization, please see Chapter 21.

Rules before the Pre-Install Task

Some rules should be evaluated before any installation tasks, even **Pre-Install** tasks, occur. These rules, such as checking if the target system is a proper platform for this installation or if the user is logged into the root or has the necessary permissions to perform the installation, can be added in the **Project | Rules** subtask.

Creating Debug Output

Installer debug output information can be useful for tracking down issues in an installer. InstallAnywhere developers can enable debug output and select whether it should be sent to a file or to a live console.

Installer Debug Output

If the **Send stderr to** or **Send stdout to** fields are left blank, the output of the installer will be discarded. To send the output to a live console to monitor the output, enter "console" in the text field. To send the information to a file, enter the filename.

Virtual Machines

With InstallAnywhere developers can define a valid list of JVMs their installer can use. This option can be used to select VMs that have been fully tested. LaunchAnywhere searches for VMs sequentially based on VM type (Java 1 JRE, Java 2 JRE, JDK, and so on). Valid VM types are listed in the LaunchAnywhere executable's `lax.nl.valid.vm.list` property.

LaunchAnywhere uses the following approaches on each platform:

- **Windows:** first search on the system path, then the system Registry.
- **UNIX:** search the system path.
- **Mac OS X:** LaunchAnywhere will use the VM specified in the **Project | Platforms | Mac OS X** task.

InstallAnywhere developers can also set the heap size for the VMs.

NOTE Change the heap size when experiencing out-of-memory conditions. With large installations that have many files to install, the heap size may need to be increased.

Optional Installer Arguments

To support JVM configuration options that are not available through the InstallAnywhere advanced designer, specify additional command-line parameters to pass to the JVM used by the installer through the use of the **Optional Installer Arguments | Additional Arguments** field.

Java

The **Project | Java** subtask enables developers to fine-tune the classpath settings and decide whether to install the bundled JVM. Developers may choose not to install a VM, to install the VM only while performing the installation, or to leave the VM on the target system. If developers choose to install the VM, the VM install folder pull-down list provides a variety of locations.

Quick Quiz

1. Which rule is used to determine which "Install Complete" message to display?
    A. Check Platform
    B. Compare InstallAnywhere Variables
    C. Compare Time Stamps

2. Which two indicators show the classpath to be used for your Launch-Anywhere launched application?

    A. A list in the **Classpath** task

    B. An indicator on the file/folder icon

    C. A beeping tone when mousing over the file

3. When would you use the **Suppress First Window** option on an Execute Target File action?

    A. When executing a Windows batch file

    B. When running a subinstaller

    C. When running a UNIX shell script

Quick Quiz answers are located in Appendix J.

CHAPTER 7
Build Options

- **Generic UNIX Build**
- **VM Packs**
- **Distribution**

WITH THREE DIFFERENT BUILD OUTPUTS, InstallAnywhere users can build installers for deployment over the Web, on a CD, or through a merge module. Templates—a specialized merge module for maintaining look and feel, as well as retaining standardized installation panels, such as the **License Agreement** or **Choose Install Folder** panels, or even files—are also created in the **Build** task.

In the **Build** task developers define the target operating system for the installer, as well as the form for distributing the installer. In **Build | Build Targets**, operating systems are defined. Developers also define whether to provide a JVM with the installer to provide greater ease of use for the end-user.

Generic UNIX Build

While InstallAnywhere provides options for many flavors of UNIX, it also allows the creation of other flavors. To create an installer for a flavor of UNIX that is not on the list of platforms:

1. In the text field below the **Solaris** option, type the name of the UNIX flavor.
2. Select a VM from the list to bundle with the new UNIX flavor.

NOTE The **Open Select Target** text field may also be used to differentiate between two variations of the same installer.

VM Packs

Zero G provides VM packs on its Web site. The **Download Additional VM Packs** button in **Build | Build Targets** brings up the VM packs section of Zero G's Web site.

VM packs are stored as .vm (ZIP/JAR) files, which contain the archive of a JVM and a vm.properties file. These VM packs need to be stored as resources in the ../resources/installer_vms directory. The selected bundled VM will be saved on a project-by-project basis.

Distribution

In the **Distribution** subtask developers define the form for the installer to be distributed. Developers can build and optimize an installer on one or more CD-ROM disks, for use over the Web, or to be launched from an HTML file.

The **Distribution** subtask also enables developers to build and optimize merge modules and templates.

Web Installers
The Web installer is a single executable file that contains all of the necessary installation logic. Building the Web installer also generates an HTML page and embedded Java applet to make downloading the installer over the Web easy. Select **Optimize Installer Size by Platform** to minimize the size of the final installers by excluding platform-specific resources (this is determined by evaluating Check Platform rules). The developer also has the option to select in which language to build the target Web page.

CD-ROM/DVD Installers
CD-ROM/DVD installers consist of multiple files to be burnt onto one or more CDs or DVDs. They can also be placed on network volumes to provide easier access to large installers. The output of this build process can be directly burned onto disk.

InstallAnywhere CD-ROM/DVDs installers can span multiple CD-ROMs/DVDs. By default, the installer will automatically segment the installer into a new disk if the size of the installer grows to 650MB. To control when InstallAnywhere will span to new disks, configure your disk names by pressing the **Change Disk Name or Space** button. This allows the developer to set the size for each disk, as well as its name. The name will be displayed during the install process when the installer asks for the next disk in a set.

Burning CD-ROM Installers
The directory structure for CD-ROM installers is

```
Disk1/ InstallerData.1/
    |- Platform1/
    |- Plaftorm2/
Disk2/ InstallerData.2/
    |- InstallerResources
```

Optimizing CD-ROM installers causes them to output in a different structure:

```
Platform1/ Disk1/
    |- InstallerData.1/
Disk2/
    |- InstallerData.2/
Platform2/ Disk1/
    |- InstallerData.1/
Disk2/
    |- InstallerData.2/
```

When burning CDs or DVDs, the developer needs to make sure that the folders Disk1, Disk2, and so on, are burned as is to the disk. Burning only the contents of these folders will cause installers to work incorrectly. The directory structure for the disk-burning application should look as follows:

```
<ISO CD NAME>
    |- Disk1
    |-..Disk2
```

Merge Modules and Templates

Developers can also build merge modules. Merge modules allow you to create installers that can be integrated easily into other InstallAnywhere installers. More information on merge modules and templates is available in Chapter 17.

Build Log

The **Build Log** window displays an XML log of the build once an installer project is successfully built. Click **Refresh Log** to display the current log. Click **Delete Log** to remove the log.

CHAPTER 8

Basic Installer Customization

- **Customizing Your InstallAnywhere Installer's Look and Feel**
- **Introducing Conditional Logic**

INSTALLANYWHERE INSTALLERS are almost infinitely customizable. You control how the install looks, as well as the tasks it will accomplish. You have complete control over what (if anything) appears on the end-user's screen, in what order the actions will occur, where files are to be installed, how each panel looks in a graphical installer, what messages appear to the end-user.... The options go on and on.

In this chapter, we'll cover some of the myriad customization options for your installer project, beginning with customizing the appearance of the installer and progressing to customizing installer flow. We commence with our first complex installer project.

Customizing Your InstallAnywhere Installer's Look and Feel

One of the keys to a professional-looking installer is the appearance of the installer itself. Most developers want their installers to reflect the image of their product or company. InstallAnywhere gives you the ability to customize your installer to provide end-users with an installation experience that matches your product's graphics, your target audience, and/or your organizational image and branding.

Exercise 8.1 Exploring Look and Feel

InstallAnywhere provides many options for altering the look and feel of the installer. You can add splash screens, display a list of steps or an image along the left side of the installer panel, add a background image that will display behind the steps, or add billboards and graphics (even animated graphics) that display in the large right-hand display of the installer.

Installer UI Modes

Defined by the **Allowable UI Modes**, InstallAnywhere installers can run in several different modes defined by the end-user interface.

- **AWT:** The classic InstallAnywhere interface, this mode results in a simple gray installation interface. AWT mode is compatible with Java 1 VMs, including Microsoft JView.

- **Swing:** Swing is the newer end-user interface provided by the Java 2 specifications. InstallAnywhere's Swing installer interface provides a rich end-user experience, including background graphics, rendered HTML, and alpha transparency for graphics used in the installer. The InstallAnywhere installer itself is an example of a Swing installer.
- **Console:** Console mode provides a TTY, or terminal-style, interface that can allow an interactive installation on a system lacking a graphical end-user interface. (Please note that you may still need to set a display and/or have Xwindows running.)
- **Silent:** Silent installers are, as the name implies, silent installers that require and provide no end-user interaction. Silent installers can either run without any input or accept data from a properties file containing the values for specific InstallAnywhere variables used to control the installation.

Splash Screens

InstallAnywhere installers present a splash screen at the initial launch of the installer. This screen is displayed for a few seconds while installer resources are extracted and the installer environment is set up. The splash screen is an ideal introduction to your product and an opportunity to set its mood and image. The splash screen will also appear on the HTML page generated for the InstallAnywhere Web Install Applet.

Background Images

InstallAnywhere has the ability to add customized background images to your installer. This feature allows you to create a truly unique installer by superimposing the left-hand installer steps or image screen and the right-hand informational or interactive rectangle upon a background image.

GUI Panel Additions

The **Additions to GUI Installer Panels** option allows developers to display a list of steps or an image along the left side of the installer's panel.

Billboards

Billboards are graphics that the installer will display during the installation of files. You can use files to convey a marketing message, a description of your product, or simply something fun for your end-user to see as the file installation is occurring. Each billboard you add will be displayed for an even amount of time, based on actions within the installation. If you have very few files and many billboards, each will only be displayed for a short time.

One of the more interesting features of the Billboard action is the support included for animated GIF files. This allows you to add animations to your billboard, providing your end-user with a rich media experience during installation.

Help

Help is available to the users of the InstallAnywhere installer. Help files may be written in either HTML or plain text. With HTML you use HTML tags to define formatting. With plain text there is no formatting. Help may be associated with a panel, or the same Help text may be displayed regardless of the panel being shown to the end-user.

Exploring the Look and Feel Task

The **Look and Feel** task includes several subtasks defined in the tabs across the top of the task. Each of these tasks controls a specific portion of the installer.

1. Open the OfficeSuite project you created earlier and browse to the **Project | Look and Feel | General UI Settings** task.

   The **Installer UI | Look and Feel** subtask contains three tabs that enable developers to configure the look and feel of the installer and to customize many graphic elements and progress panels within it. Within these three tabs are different preview buttons that will display the look and feel of the installer with the current settings.

   The **Installer UI | Look and Feel | General UI Settings** tab sets general look and feel settings for the installer. Developers select whether the installer will work in GUI, Console, or Silent mode. (An installer may support all the modes at the same time.) The preferred graphics mode, whether AWT (built with Java's Abstract Window Toolkit) or Swing (an addition to AWT), can also be set. Swing offers the ability to display a background image, such as a company logo, in the installer. The specific background image can also be defined in this tab of the **Installer UI** task.

2. Set the UI modes.
    a. In the **Allowable UI Modes** section, select **AWT** and **Swing**.
    b. In the **Preferred GUI Mode** section, select **Swing**.

    If we wanted a Silent or Console installer, we could enable these modes here.

    The **Preferred GUI Mode** option sets which mode the installer will prefer. The **Swing** option will only be available if the virtual machine against which the installer is running is Swing compliant. If **AWT** is chosen as the preferred mode, the installer will run in AWT mode when a graphical mode is available.

3. Explore splash screens.
    a. In the **Startup Splash Screen Image** section, click the **Preview** button to see an example of the splash screen.

    InstallAnywhere installers present a splash screen at the initial launch of the installer. This screen is displayed for a few seconds while the installer prepares the wizard.

    b. Click **Choose** to select an image for the splash screen.

    Several splash images can be found in the Images and Docs folder.

    The splash screen will also appear on the HTML page generated for the InstallAnywhere Web Install Applet. It can be a GIF, PNG, or JPEG file of any size, although the preferred size is 470 × 265 pixels.

4. Select a background.
    a. In the **Installer Background Image** section, select **Preview**.
    b. In the **Installer Background Image** section, click **Choose**.
    c. Select a background graphic of your liking.
    d. In the **Installer Background Image** section, select **Preview**.

The InstallAnywhere installation includes a number of background images, which are free for your use (and notably without royalties). These images are located in the graphics/background folder within the InstallAnywhere installation.

The background image is behind the entire GUI image, behind both the left area (which can have install steps) and the right informational rectangle. The background image you choose will appear in every panel in your installer. Background images are only supported in Swing GUI installers.

5. Make additions to the GUI installer panels.

   a. In the **Additions to GUI Installer Panels** section, select **Add images or a list of installer steps** on the left side of the installer panel.

      While selecting **Add images or a list of installer steps**, watch the remaining two tabs of the **Installer UI | Look and Feel** task. As the option is selected, the **Installer Panel Additions** and **Install Progress Panel** tabs will become active.

      If **Additions to GUI Installer Panels** is not selected, the **Installer Panel Additions** or **Install Progress Panel** tabs will not be accessible because there will be no additional progress panels to modify. These additional panels are either images or labels.

   b. Select the **Installer Panel Additions** tab.

      The **Look and Feel | Installer Panel Additions** tab allows developers to customize installer panels for the left-hand-side install-progress-steps rectangle.

   c. In the **Types of Additions to Installer Panels**, select **Images**.

      If **Images** is selected, no install labels will be displayed. Selecting **Images** provides the ability to select a default image in the **Default Installer/Uninstaller Panel Image** section of the **Installer Panel Additions** tab. When **Images** is selected, the default image may be overridden by specifying an image in the **Install Progress Panel** tab. The developer may also choose not to display an image or to use the same image as the previous panel.

      Later we will show that you can also put a background image behind steps in the left-hand-side install-progress-steps-rectangle.

   d. Click **Preview**.

e. In **Types of Additions to Installer Panels**, select **List of Installer Steps**.

Selecting **List of Installer Steps** provides labels that can be customized.

If **List of Installer Steps** is selected in the **Look and Feel | Installer Panel Additions** tab, the **Installer Steps Background Image** option will be available, if **Use This Image as the Background behind the List of Installer Steps** is selected. The **Installer Steps Background Image** option enables developers to select a specific image to display in the rectangle on the left-hand side, where installation step labels will be displayed.

When using Swing, a transparent image can be displayed on top of the background image selected in the **Look and Feel | General UI Settings** tab.

NOTE The size of the install progress pane is 380 × 270 pixels. Installer dimensions may change slightly by platform to display text and different fonts better.

The bottom pane of the **Installer Panel Additions** allows developers to view and alter the installation steps labels. The buttons to the right enable developers to add or remove labels or to change the order of the labels. Developers can edit the text string that is displayed. The **Auto Populate...** button adds an installer panel for every panel action added to the **Pre-Install** and **Post-Install** tasks.

f. Alter the order of steps.

Using the arrows allows you to change the order of the steps.

g. Edit labels.

To change a label, select the installer step whose label you want to change and click the **Edit label** button. For instance, "Pre-Installation Summary" can be changed to "Summary."

h. Change icons.

Choose Icons... enables developers to alter the small square graphics to the left of the text labels. The default icons are double arrows for the current step or steps to be completed and a check mark for installation steps that have been completed.

6. Select **Look and Feel | Billboards**.

   Billboards are images that appear in the large right-hand pane of the installer while files are being installed. Billboards generally convey a marketing message, a description of the product, or simply something fun for the end-user to see as the installation is occurring.

   a. In the **Billboard** section near the bottom of the window, click **Preview**.
   b. Click the **Add Billboard** button near the center of the screen.
   c. In the `InstallAnywhere 6 Enterprise\OfficeSuiteSourceFiles\ImagesandDocs` folder, select **billboard1.gif**.

      There are several billboard graphics available in the Images and Docs directory within the OfficeSuite Source Files folder. In this case, we advise adding two billboards to the installation (if you add more than two, the appearance of the panels will be too short due to the small number of files in this installation).

      Billboards can be GIF, PNG, or JPEG files, and should be 587 × 312 pixels in size.

NOTE The size of the billboard panel is 587 × 312 pixels. Installer dimensions may change slightly by platform to display text and different fonts better.

---

   d. Click **Choose**.
   e. Select **billboard2.gif**.
   f. Click **Preview**.

      Each billboard added will be displayed for an even amount of time, based on actions within the installation. If an installation has very few files and many billboards, each billboard will only be displayed for a short time. Several billboard graphics may be added for larger (and longer) installations. For small installations, like the tutorial OfficeSuite example, only one billboard will show. Billboards may also be assigned to features and will only be displayed if the features they are associated with are installed.

      When adding multiple billboards, the billboards will display in the order they are shown in the **Project | Billboards | Billboard List**.

7. Explore Help options.
    a. Browse to **Installer UI | Help**.
    b. In the top section, select **Enable installer help**.
    c. In **Help Text Format**, select **HTML**.
    d. In **Help Context**, select **Use the same help text for all panels**.
    e. In the **Title** text field, enter "Sample Help Text."
    f. In the **Help Text** text field, enter
       `<b>OfficeSuite</b> Help<p> This is an <i>example</i> of HTML Help.`
    g. Click **Preview**.
    h. Click **Close**.
8. Rebuild the project.
    a. Click **Build**.
    b. Click **Build Project** to build the OfficeSuite installer.
    c. Click the blue arrow on the lower left of that dialog to see the build details console.
9. Test the Web applet page customization.
10. Test the installer customizations.

Introducing Conditional Logic

InstallAnywhere uses variable-based Boolean rules to control most aspects of installer behavior.

In the following segment, we'll cover basic implementation of these rules and of some of the methods by which the end-user interacts with the rules-based architecture.

InstallAnywhere rules can be applied to any action within the InstallAnywhere installer, as well as to organizational units such as install sets, features, and components (all of which we will discuss a little later in this chapter).

The rules logic allows you to create simple and complex logic systems that determine what actions will occur. The rules can be structured based on end-user input or on conditions determined by the installer.

There are a handful of preset rules included in InstallAnywhere.

- **Check File/Folder Attributes:** This rule allows you to check the attributes of a file or directory that already exists on the target system. The rule allows you to check if the object exists, whether it is a file or a folder/directory, and whether it is readable and/or writable.
- **Check If File/Folder Exists:** This rule applies to individual file/folder install actions. It will check to see if the file or folder to which it is attached already exists in the specified install location. You can choose to install either if it does, or does not, exist at that location.
- **Check Platform:** This rule allows you to specify actions or files to be run/installed only on specific platforms. The platform is determined by the JVM and reported to the installer.
- **Check End-User Chosen Language:** You can use this rule to make installation decisions based on the locale chosen by the end-user at installation time.
- **Check File Modification Timestamp:** This rule allows you to compare the timestamp of an existing target file in order to make an overwrite decision.
- **Compare InstallAnywhere Variables:** This rule allows you to make a simple string comparison of any InstallAnywhere variable. You can check if a variable equals, does not equal, contains, or does not contain a value.
- **Evaluate Custom Rule:** Custom rules are built using the specifications outlined in the InstallAnywhere API and can be tailored to fit the needs of your installation. More concerning custom and API development will be covered later in Chapter 20.
- **Match Regular Expression:** This rule allows you to compare a string or InstallAnywhere variable to a regular expression of your choosing. Regular expressions (`regexp`) are an industry-standard method of expressing a variable string. You can find considerable information on regular expressions, including archives of useful expressions and Web applications that can validate your expression, on the World Wide Web.

Exercise 8.2 Using Installer Rules

InstallAnywhere rules can be implemented in a number of actions within the installer. However, the first set of rules evaluated in the installer is the Installer rules. These rules, set in the **Project | Rules** task, allow you to control the complete installer based on rules.

For example, let's consider that our OfficeSuite product is designed to run only on the following systems: Windows NT Generation Systems, including NT, 2000, and XP, but not Windows 95, 98, or ME; on Mac OS X, and on Linux.

Add this condition to the OfficeSuite installer.

1. Add the rule.
    a. Open the **Project | Rules** task.
    b. Click **Add Rule**.
    c. Select **Check Platform**.
    d. Click **Add**.
2. Set the condition for the rule.
    a. In the customizer for the Check Platform rule, select **Windows NT**, **Windows 2000**, **Windows XP**, **Mac OS X**, and **Linux** from the left-hand (Do Not Perform On) column.
       You can hold down the CTRL or Apple keys to select multiple items.
    b. Move the selected items to the right (Perform On) column by clicking the arrow.
3. In the customizer below the **Check Platform** section, modify the message that will appear if an end-user attempts to run the installer on a platform other than those you've specified.
4. Build and run the installer.
   If you are running on a platform other than those that we've specified, the installer should run normally.
5. Return to the project, and remove the platform you are working on at the moment. Rebuild and rerun the installer. You should see the message you entered indicating that the platform was disallowed.

> **NOTE** Before continuing, be sure to add the rule back in. This will allow your installer to run properly in the next exercise.

Exercise 8.3 Using Rules to Control Visual Elements

Often, you'll want certain panels and/or other visual elements to appear only under certain conditions. For example, notes explaining errata on Windows shouldn't appear on Mac OS X. Like the installer rules, you can use rules to control visual elements in the **Pre-Install** and **Post-Install** tasks. In this next set of exercises, we'll introduce some elements of visual control and introduce a few of the available panels and other actions.

1. Click **Pre-Install task** from the task list along the left-hand side of the InstallAnywhere advanced designer.
2. Click **Add Action** near the middle of the screen.

    This step will open the action palette, which has several tabs for differing types of actions.
3. Select the **Panels** tab on the palette and add the following panels to your project.
    - **License Agreement:** This panel allows you to display a license agreement to your end-user. The end-user must choose to accept the agreement in order to continue. You can set the default state of the radio buttons (accept or decline) and choose a file to use for a license agreement. You'll find a `License.txt` file in the Images and Docs folder within OfficeSuite Source Files that can be used for this installer. The **License Agreement** panel can also utilize HTML files, which gives you a degree of control over the text formatting and allows you to link to external documents.
    - **Display Message:** This panel allows you to simply display a text message to the end-user during the installation. This can be useful for conveying information about installation choices that the end-user has made. This panel is also particularly useful in debugging installer issues having to do with InstallAnywhere variables. You can add **Display Message** panels with variables resolved to test variable values you are using in rules.

Place any text of your choosing on the **Display Message** panel; however, try including several InstallAnywhere variables, using the $VARIABLE$ notation so that they are resolved.

Example:

This installer is running on a $prop.os.name$ $prop.os.version$ system named $prop.computername$ and is running against a $prop.java.vendor$ $prop.java.version$ VM.

> **NOTE** This panel allows you to display a text or HTML file without the radio buttons found on the **License Agreement** panel. It is particularly useful for displaying readme or errata-type documents.

You can choose to place these panels in any order or location within the **Pre-Install**, although for authenticity's sake, we'll recommend that you place them after the **Introduction** panel and before the **Choose Install Folder** panel.

4. Add rules to actions and/or panel actions.

   We've now created a set of install panels that will appear in the **Pre-Install** section of the installer. Now, let's add a rule to one of the panels.

   a. Select **Display Message**.
   b. In the **Title** text bar, name the display message "Running as root" so it will be easily recognized if other display messages are used.
   c. In the textbox **Enter message to be displayed during installation**, enter "Display only if running as root."
   d. In the customizer, click **Rules**.
   e. Click **Add Rule**.
   f. Select **Compare InstallAnywhere Variables**, then click **Add**.
   g. Create the following rule:

      Install Only If:
      | Operand 1 | | Operand 2 |
      $prop.user.name$ equals   root

      Can you tell the purpose of this rule? This rule should restrict the first **Display Message** panel so that it appears only if the end-user name for the end-user running the installer is root.

h. Create another similar rule:

Install Only If:

Operand 1		Operand 2
$prop.user.name$	does not equal	root

The second panel will display only if the end-user is not root. Generally, this type of rule would only be used to display panels or execute actions for administrative end-users on UNIX systems.

Notice the "R" that appears in the upper right corner of the panel icon in the advanced designer. This visual identifier serves to indicate that a rule has been applied to the action.

5. Build and run the new installer project.

Notice the addition of the new panels. If you added the rule to your **Display Message** panel, you'll not see that panel. Try removing that rule and rerunning. The panel should now appear.

The example we've just considered is, of course, oversimplified. However, the concepts are important to understanding the basic behavior of InstallAnywhere functionality. By now, you should have a basic understanding of InstallAnywhere variables and a basic understanding of InstallAnywhere rules. In the next segment, we'll be building a more complex installer, integrating end-user input with the concepts covered here.

Exercise 8.4 Managing Installer Flow Based on End-User Input

In many cases the path that an end-user will take through an installer depends on the choices made in different steps within the installation procedure. InstallAnywhere provides methods to gather input from end-users, which you can leverage to control your installation.

In this first example, we'll return to an action we added to our OfficeSuite installer, the Execute action added in the **Post-Install** task.

Generally, it's nice to ask the end-user if they would like to launch the application when the installation is complete. In order to add this functionality, we'll need both a method to ask if the end-user would like to launch the application and a method by which we can control that action.

In previous sections, we've seen the rules methods that can be used to prevent the installer from displaying certain panels, and we've learned a little about the InstallAnywhere variable architecture that is used to store information within the installer.

In this exercise, we'll put the two together in a useful manner.

Step One: Retrieving End-User Input

1. Open the **Post-Install** task of the project.

   Later we'll actually create some new projects, but for now we'll continue to use and abuse our OfficeSuite installer.

2. Open the action palette and from the **Panels** tab, click **Panel: Get User Input—Simple**.

   The **Get User Input—Simple** panel allows you to retrieve a single type of information from the end-user and store it in a single InstallAnywhere variable for later use. The panel allows input to be entered via text fields, choice menus, pop-up menus, radio buttons, or check boxes.

3. Define and configure the panel.

   a. In the **Title** field of the customizer for the **Get User Input—Simple** panel, enter "Launch."

   b. In the **Prompt** text field, enter "Would you like to Launch OfficeSuite?"

   As we only want to ask a yes or no question, we'll utilize the **Radio Buttons** option as the input method.

   c. Choose **Radio Buttons** from the pull-down menu on the middle right of the customizer.

   Now, we'll configure the panel to present our options.

   d. Click the **Configure** button, then click **Add**.

   Clicking the Configure button will open a dialog where you can add labels for the buttons and set their default states.

   e. A field will appear in the dialog. In the left-hand portion of the field, type your message. For this example, we'll use "Yes, launch OfficeSuite now."

Make sure the word "Yes" is capitalized. The capitalization of the message is important because the string from the label will be stored exactly as you enter it in the Results variable—the variable that stores the results of the end-users input.

    f. Now click twice in the **Default Value** field to the right, then choose **Selected**.

4. Create the "No" message for the panel.
    a. Click **Add**.
    b. In the **Label** column, enter "No, I'll open OfficeSuite later, thanks."

       Be sure that "No" is capitalized in your message.
    c. Click **Set Variable**.
5. Set the Results variable to `$LAUNCH_APPLICATION$`.

   The default Results variable is `$USER_INPUT_RESULTS$`; however, you can change the variable to fit your needs or your naming scheme.
6. Click the **Preview** button. You should see two radio buttons.
7. Before continuing, make sure that you've placed the **Get End-User Input** panel in the post-install tree prior to the Execute Target File action.

Step Two: Applying the End-User's Choice

Now, to control the Execute Target File action we added earlier, we'll add a rule to that action. We want the action to occur only if the end-user has selected the **Yes** option. Because that information is stored in the variable we selected in the **Get User Input—Simple** panel, we'll use a Compare InstallAnywhere Variables rule.

1. Add the Compare InstallAnywhere Variables rule by selecting the **Execute Target File** action and choosing the **Rules** tab from the customizer in the lower portion of the window.

   Use **Add Rule** to add the Compare InstallAnywhere Variables rule. We'll add the following rule:

   Install Only If:

Operand 1		Operand 2
$LAUNCH_APPLICATION$	contains	Yes

If you used a variable other than $LAUNCH_APPLICATION$ in the Results variable in the **Get User Input—Simple** panel, use that variable here.

> **TIP** Although it is only strictly necessary when retrieving variables, using the $ notation when setting variables as well is a good idea. This makes it easier to keep variables and literal values straight.

2. Rebuild and relaunch the installer.

   You should be able to choose whether or not to launch the application. If the application launches, even when you've chosen **No**, check your rule to ensure that you are correctly comparing the variable and that the case of the value is correct.

Quick Quiz

1. Which InstallAnywhere rule would you use to verify an entry that a user had made in a text field (for example, checking to see if they have entered a valid telephone number)?
   A. Check Platform
   B. Compare InstallAnywhere Variable
   C. Match Regular Expression

2. What notation is used in InstallAnywhere to indicate that a variable's value, as opposed to its literal name, should be returned?
   A. #Variable#
   B. $VARIABLE$
   C. $Variable

3. If the logged-in username is Jim, what effect will the following rule have on a panel?

   Install Only If:
Operand 1		Operand 2
$prop.user.name$	equals	jim

   A. The panel will display.
   B. The panel will not display.

Quick Quiz answers are located in Appendix J.

CHAPTER 9
Installer Organization

- **Install Sets, Features, and Components**
- **Organizing Features and Components**
- **Adding Components**
- **Assigning Files to Components**
- **Removing Empty Components**
- **Integrating Components Already Installed on Target Systems**
- **Adding Features**

SO FAR, WE'VE WORKED EXCLUSIVELY with a very simple file set, a single product with a single install option. Although it would be nice if all installations were this easy, it would also generally negate the need for installer software. Most installations are complex and offer the user the choice of multiple options, multiple products, and even more options within those multiple product installations. InstallAnywhere provides three logical groupings for managing product installation options—install sets, features, and components.

Install Sets, Features, and Components

Install sets, features, and components are among the most important concepts to understand when using the InstallAnywhere installer development environment. InstallAnywhere provides levels of granularity for end-user installation options. Install sets and features may be selected by the end-user.

Install sets are groupings of features such as Typical Install or Minimal Install. Features are meant to identify specific units of functionality of your product. Although both install sets and features are made up of files, there is not necessarily a direct correlation between these larger organizational groupings and the files.

Components are groupings of the specific files and actions of your product and are invisible to the end-user. A component may also include a group of registry changes or other elements needed to make a feature work properly. Components are used for the organized sharing of resources and versioning; they are uniquely identified and are the organization tool of the installer developer, not the installer user. A developer could create a component for each feature in the application, a component for shared libraries used by all of the features, and a component for the Help system.

Although developers may assign files, folders, and actions directly to product features, it is best to think of features as groupings of components. Install sets such as Typical Install or Minimal Install are groupings of features. You should address the interaction between the three levels when planning the options to present to the end-user.

InstallAnywhere's organization features both allow you to manage the installation from a developer standpoint and offer your users the maximum number of installation options.

Install Sets

Install sets are the simplest and broadest organizational concept within InstallAnywhere. Install sets are sets of product features that represent high-level, easily selectable, installation options. End-users can choose only one install set. These sets are generally options such as Typical and Minimal, or Client only and Client and Server. End-users select their desired install set using the **Choose Install Sets** panel or console. Install sets are made up of features.

Features

Features are a logical grouping of capabilities in a product. Features are effective if developers want to give their end-users fine-grained choices. Features are meant to identify distinct parts of the product so the end-user may choose whether or not to install them. It is up to the developer to define the logical grouping of components into features by assigning components to the features.

Features may be hierarchical, and you can include as many as you desire, but must include at least one. One example of features in a hierarchy would be a **Documentation** subfeature and a **Samples** subfeature added beneath the main Help feature.

Several features make up each install set, and each feature can belong to one or more install sets. End-users select features as an option from the **Choose Install Sets** panel or console. Features are visible to the end-user only when the user chooses to customize an install set.

Files can be assigned directly to features, or you can assign components to features. InstallAnywhere actually creates components for you if you assign files directly to features.

End-users can uninstall specific features if desired.

Components

Components are the smallest piece of an installation handled by the installer. From a developer's perspective they are the building blocks of applications or features. End-users never see or interact with components.

There are many advantages to having fine-grained control over components. Common components may be shared between multiple installers, multiple versions of a product, or multiple products. For example, two products in a suite could have several shared components.

Components are uniquely identified so developers may update a specific component or use the Find Component in Registry action to locate a particular component. Components are versioned, as well as having unique IDs, so that a search for a particular version of a component on a system can ascertain whether the latest version has been installed.

Several components make up each feature, and each component can belong to one or more feature. Components are made up of files and actions. Although you can assign files and actions to components, you can also assign files and actions directly to features and let InstallAnywhere automatically create the components.

A file or action may belong to one component only. All installers must have at least one component and can have as many as are needed.

The InstallAnywhere uninstaller is component-based and can provide feature-level uninstallation functionality.

NOTE For most installations, you will not need to manipulate the components in any way. Components are automatically generated based on the way that you've assigned files to features and install sets.

The Organization Task

The **Organization** task enables developers to arrange install sets, product features, components, and merge modules (merge modules will be discussed in depth in Chapter 17). Install sets and features allow for levels of installation options for the end-user of the installer. Components are the smallest widget that can be selected by a feature set. Install sets are groupings of features and are an organizational tool for the developer of the installer. Components may be much more than files; they can be sophisticated actions required to install and run applications or features properly.

There is an interaction between the **Install Sets**, **Features**, and **Components** subtasks, as well as the **Files** task. If an install set is added in the **Organization | Install Sets** task, features can be assigned to that install set in **Organization | Features**. If a feature is added in **Organization | Features**, components can be assigned to that feature in **Organization | Components**. If a component is added in **Organization | Components**, files and/or actions can be assigned to that component after they are added in the **Files** task.

Install Sets

The **Organization | Install Sets** subtask allows developers to add, name, remove, or order install sets in the installer. In the **Install Set List** developers define which install set(s) to use as the default option to provide to the end-user. Features are assigned to install sets in the **Organization | Features** subtask.

When the installer requests install set information, each install set is represented by a graphic element. The **Choose Image...** button enables developers to select the graphic element.

Rules may be associated with an install set, and that association is created by selecting **Rules** in the customizer and adding rules. The rules for install sets are evaluated before the install set is installed. If the rules on the install set evaluate to `false`, the install set will not be displayed.

Features

The **Organization | Features** subtask enables developers to add, name, remove, or order features.

Rules may be associated with a feature set, and that association is created by selecting **Rules** in the customizer and adding rules. The rules for feature sets are evaluated before the feature set is installed. If the rules on the feature evaluate to `false`, the feature will not be displayed.

Components

The key file must be present in all subsequent versions of the component. It is used to define the component's location when the Find Component in Registry action is used.

The **Organization | Components** subtask enables developers to add, name, remove, order, identify, and version components.

Rules may be associated with component sets, and that association is created by selecting **Rules** in the customizer and adding rules. The rules for component sets are evaluated before the component set is installed.

Organizing Features and Components

Components are the lowest level of organization in an installer. Each product must have at least one component, but most installers will by default contain at least two components as the uninstaller is considered a component of its own.

InstallAnywhere's component architecture is designed to allow developers to plan for future releases, suite installers, and other uses of their software elements in their deployment plans.

InstallAnywhere will automatically create components as you add files to your project and assign them to features. This approach, while working well for most projects, does not give you the most flexibility. To realize the ultimate benefits of componentized software, you should manually manage the creation of components.

Best Practices for Components

When using components, first determine and organize which components to add. Keep the following in mind.

- Make unique components for files that will need to be updated separately. For example, a Help feature may have both a user guide and Javadocs. However, the user guide may be updated more frequently than the Javadocs. Make the two items separate components so a unique User Guide component may be added that can be versioned and updated individually.

- Components should make logical sense. When building a suite installer, keep in mind the pieces of applications that are shared between different products. When componentizing a product for versioning purposes, designate the version of the component in the **Organization | Component | Properties** task when the component is added.

NOTE If you are using components, we recommend that you not modify files and features using the **Files** task. If you modify which files are assigned to a particular feature using this option, components will be modified automatically.

Best Practices for Features

Features are effective if you want to provide end-users fine-grained control over what they install. For example, you might have a Main Application feature, a Shared Libraries feature, and a Help feature. To make sure end-users can choose which features get installed, enable the **Choose Install Sets** panel action via the **Pre-Install** task in the advanced designer. Enable the **Feature Level Uninstall** option in the Create Uninstaller action.

A few things you should know about features:

- Features are logical groupings of components.
- Feature designation arranges your components by function.
- Features may be hierarchical.
- You can create as many features as you wish, but every project needs at least one.
- Features are visible to the end-user.

You'll also want to ensure that your features are as independent as possible, each being as close to an individual package as possible. However, keep in mind that features do not include dependencies, so if multiple features share dependent file sets, those files must be added to each feature (this is merely organizational and does not in any way affect the size of your installation).

Best Practices for Install Sets

The InstallAnywhere **Choose Install Sets** panel will only display approximately four features with complete descriptions. You should design your installation with a minimal number of options, or so that rules eliminate invalid install sets prior to the display of the option panel.

Exercise 9.1 Using InstallAnywhere's Basic Installer Organization

While we'll cover component architecture later in the book, we've advanced enough to delve into the basics of installer organization.

In this exercise, we'll extend our OfficeSuite installer to employ Install-Anywhere features and install sets.

1. If it's not already open, open your OfficeSuite project in the Install-Anywhere advanced designer.
2. Click on **Files**.

    Depending on what files you added when initially creating the project, you probably have either a directory called OfficeSuite Source Files or one called OfficeSuite 2000.

3. If you added the entire OfficeSuite Source Files directory, you can skip onto the next step. If not, we're now going to add some auxiliary files so that we have a little more to work with in the installer.

    a. Click the **Add Files** button.

    b. Use the file chooser to select the Images and Docs directory from within the OfficeSuite Source Files directory. Add this directory and its contents to your installer.

4. If you originally added the entire OfficeSuite Source Files directory, we'll make a little change that will improve the "cleanliness" of the project and make it easier to organize. Using either the left and right arrows or the drag-and-drop functionality, move the OfficeSuite 2000 and Images and Docs folders into the root of your installation—the `$USER_INSTALL_DIR$`.

5. Remove the OfficeSuite Source Files directory by highlighting it and clicking **Remove**.

Exercise 9.1 Using InstallAnywhere's Basic Installer Organization

The OfficeSuite Source Files directory should now be empty.

You should now have three separate directories under the root of your installation: OfficeSuite 2000, Images and Docs, and Uninstaller Data.

6. Rename the OfficeSuite 2000 and Images and Docs folders. For this example, use the names Program and Data For OfficeSuite and Images and Docs.

> **NOTE** InstallAnywhere allows you to rename resources independently of the source directories and files. Simply highlight the file you need to rename and alter the entry in the **Name** field. This allows you to use multiple instances of the same file, but with different names. It also allows you to name files dynamically when necessary, using InstallAnywhere variables in the **Name** field in the InstallAnywhere advanced designer.

7. Browse to the **Organization | Install Sets** task.

   A default InstallAnywhere project contains two install sets—Typical and Minimal. We'll add a third called Documentation Only.

> **NOTE** The customizer available for the **Files** task allows you to set an image and description to appear on the **Choose Install Sets** panel. The **Choose Install Sets** panel presents your end-user with large radio-style buttons with a description of the installation option. At this stage, you should add descriptions of the Typical (All features), Minimal (Application only), and Documentation Only (Only the documentation) install sets.

8. Select **Typical** as the default by clicking in the check boxes to the right of **Install Set Names** in the panel above the customizer.

   Now, we're ready to assign features to the install sets. In this simple example, we only have two features: Application and Help.

9. Navigate to the **Organization | Features** task.

   Notice that two default features—Application and Help—have been created as part of the default project. As these meet our needs, we'll not have to add any additional features; however, the process by which they are added is identical to that used for install sets.

10. Add a description for the features we'll use in this example.

    Now, we'll assign the features to the install sets. We've defined three distinct sets; two have only one feature, and one has both of the features.

> **NOTE** The check boxes along the right-hand side of the install tree within the **Files** task are used to assign files, folders, and actions to features within the task.

　　a. Using the check boxes to the right of the panel, select **Typical** and **Minimal** for the Application feature.

　　b. Select **Typical** and **Documentation** for the Help feature, making sure to leave out Minimal.

11. Assign files to features in the **Files** task.

　　a. Browse to the **Files** task.

　　b. Assign the entire contents of the OfficeSuite 2000 folder to the Application feature.

　　c. Assign the entire contents of the Images and Docs folder to the Help feature.

Now, we have all the files and actions assigned properly, and our organization is complete. However, we've still not presented a method to our end-user by which to alter the choice of install sets (in its current configuration, our installer will simply use the default install set).

12. In order to offer our user a choice, we'll need to add a **Choose Install** panel to the **Pre-Install** task.

　　a. Browse back to the **Pre-Install** task, where we'll add the panel.

　　This panel is, of course, a built-in option in InstallAnywhere.

　　b. Open the **Add Action** palette and from the **Panels** tab, choose **Panel: Choose Install Sets**.

　　c. Use the arrows or the drag-and-drop functionality to move the panel to a location after the introduction, but before the user selects an installation location.

> **NOTE** The **Choose Install Sets** panel has several options that directly affect the options the user is presented with. The check box **Allow end-user to customize installer via the Choose Product Features panel** will allow the user to choose individual features to install. Although it is not strictly necessary in an installation as simple as our current example, we suggest engaging this option so that you may see the results.

13. We're now ready to build our first organized installer.

    a. Browse to the **Build** task.

    b. Build the installer.

    The option **Show Product Features without the Choose Install Sets panel** allows you to present only the features to your user, creating a highly flexible installer. For this example, do not engage this option.

    When running the installer, note the **Choose Product features** panel. Select the **Custom Install Set** so that you can see the results of selecting the check box **Allow end-user to customize installer via the Choose Product Features panel**.

Adding Components

Components are managed in the **Organization | Components** task. Each component is created with a long name, a short name, and a unique ID. The version and key file may be specified. Key files are single files that identify the component. A key file should always be included in a component.

Assigning Files to Components

To assign files to a component, use the **Assign Files to Components** option in the **Files** task.

Removing Empty Components

Sometimes components are no longer needed or do not have any files assigned to them. To remove empty components from the project, click **Clean Components** in the **Organization | Components** task.

Integrating Components Already Installed on Target Systems

If the installer needs a component that should already be installed on the target system, use the Find Component in Registry action to locate that component. This action searches for the component by using the Universal Unique Identifier (UUID) specified for the component. The component's location can then be used as an installation location by the installer.

The installer can compare versions and locate the highest version found or search for the key file.

Adding Features

Features are managed in the **Organization | Features** task. You can add and remove features, as well as assign features to install sets.

Quick Quiz

1. To which basic InstallAnywhere organization element are files assigned?

    A. Install sets

    B. Features

2. In which InstallAnywhere advanced designer task are files assigned to features?

    A. The **Features** task

    B. The **Components** task

    C. The **Files** task

Quick Quiz answers are located in Appendix J.

CHAPTER 10

Introduction to Advanced Actions and Panel Actions

- Actions
- List of Actions

THIS CHAPTER COVERS THE USE AND MISUSE of some of InstallAnywhere's more advanced and more useful installer actions.

InstallAnywhere actions represent operations that will be performed by the installer or uninstaller. Actions may be as simple as installing files or displaying a panel or as sophisticated as executing custom code during the installation process.

Actions

Actions may only be added while working in the advanced designer. Actions may be added to the tasks that represent real-time operations being accomplished by the installer: **Pre-Install**, **Files**, **Post-Install**, **Pre-Uninstall**, and **Post-Uninstall**.

Actions are executed in the order that they appear in the task from top to bottom. They may be reordered with the up and down arrows. The left and right arrows move actions into and out of folders.

Once an action has been added, its customizer will appear in the bottom half of the advanced designer. Developers modify the action in the customizer. The Properties area enables developers to add file locations and variables to the action, as well as to detail how they would like the action to run. The Rules area enables developers to add specific rules to an action. Once an action has a rule added to it, its icon will display a small "R," so developers will be able to see that a rule is associated with it. This icon badge may help test or modify an installer if there is a long list of actions.

Action Availability by Task

Some actions are only available to some tasks. The **Choose an Action** dialog will only present actions that are appropriate for the task within which the developer is working. For example, **Add Action** from within the **Files** task will not provide any actions that require user input.

For the **Files** task, the **Choose an Action** dialog will have one tab for install tasks and one for general tasks. Actions under the **General** tab are available from all tasks. The **Pre-Install**, **Post-Install**, and **Uninstall** tasks have other actions listed under the **Panels**, **Consoles**, and **Plug-ins** tabs.

> **NOTE** The **Plug-ins** tab will appear when a custom code plug-in has been added.

Not all InstallAnywhere actions are available in each stage of the installation. For example, very few actions pertaining to installed files are available in the pre-install section (although there are, of course, exceptions.) This chapter will cover some useful actions, as well as give an accounting of all actions available in each step.

General Actions

General actions perform tasks related to installer performance or act on your target system.

Pre-Install/Uninstall and Post-Install/Uninstall Actions

Pre-install/uninstall actions are executed before files actions, which are executed before post-install/uninstall actions. Pre-install actions are generally actions that determine what to install on the target system, or even if the installation should occur. Actions added from the **Files** task define what will occur on the target system, like creating folders, expanding archives, or moving files. Post-install actions are generally taken after files are installed, like showing the readme file or launching the application that was just installed. Actions that occur within pre-install or post-install will not be uninstalled.

> **NOTE** An action executed in pre-install or post-install may be executed more than once if an end-user clicks **Previous** and then **Next** repeatedly. This could cause several errors for actions that modify files, such as Modify Text File—Single File or Register Windows Service. Zero G recommends executing these types of actions during the actual installation (within the **Files** task) to prevent this type of error.

The **Pre-Install** task sets up those actions that will occur prior to the installation of files. In general, this is the portion of the installation in which most configuration options are offered. Most developers choose to require that information be input at this stage and automate later configurations based on that input. This allows your user to make one bank of entries in a long install process, then to leave the installation relatively unattended during the actual install.

Exercise 10.1 Using Panels in Pre-Install

Add the following panels to your installation and rebuild to investigate their appearance and configuration options.

1. Add a **Choose File** panel.

   This panel requests that the user select a file, either by typing in the full pathname or by browsing. The panel may require the user to browse to select the file. You name the InstallAnywhere variable the panel returns by entering it into the **Selected File** field. The directory where the file is located will also be returned to the variable named by the **Parent Folder** field.

2. Add a **Choose Folder** panel.

   This panel requests that the user select a folder, much in the same way the **Choose File** panel works. The panel returns a variable you name in the **Selected Folder** field. You may also check to see if you have write permissions for the chosen folder.

3. Add a **Choose Java Virtual Machine** panel.

   This panel searches for a JVM on the target system. The panel may also prompt the user to install a VM.

4. Add a **Find File/Folder** panel.

   The **Find File/Folder** panel conducts searches on the target system, depending on a number of criteria that the developer may define. The InstallAnywhere variable the panel returns is named in the **Results Variable** field.

5. Add a **Get Password** panel.

   The **Get Password** panel requests a password from the user. The password may then be validated, compared against an index that allows different passwords to unlock different features, or saved in a variable.

> **NOTE** The **Get Password** panel can be configured either to simply store a masked entry or to confirm against a file. For this exercise, use the `password.txt` file in the Images and Docs directory included with OfficeSuite.

6. Add a **Display Message** panel to exhibit the Results variables from each of your previous panels.
7. Build and run your installer.

Console installs and their associated actions will be covered in Chapter 13.

Exercise 10.2 Using Files Task Actions

1. Browse to the **Files** task.
2. Add an Install SpeedFolder action.
   a. Click **Add Action**.
   b. Click the **Install** tab.
   c. Select **Install SpeedFolder**.
   d. Click **Add**.
3. Add a Set System Environment Variable action.

   Variable name: `$PRODUCT_NAME$_DIR`
   Set value to: `$USER_INSTALL_DIR$`
   When setting this variable: Append to existing value
   Set this variable for: Current user

4. Add a Set Windows Registry—Single Entry action.
   a. Click the **General** tab.
   b. Select **Set Windows Registry—Single Entry**.
   c. In the customizer define the registry entry as follows:

      Comment: "Set Windows Registry Test"
      Registry key: `-HKEY_LOCAL_MACHINE\SOFTWARE\$PRODUCT_NAME$`
      Value name: `InstallDirectory`
      Data type: `String`
      Data: `$USER_INSTALL_DIR$`
      Uninstall options: Remove if value has not changed.

5. Add Show Message Dialog action. Display the following text:

    Variable name: `$PRODUCT_NAME$_DIR`
    Value: `$USER_INSTALL_DIR$`

6. Add an Execute Script/Batch File action. Enter the following commands:

    ```
    @echo off
    echo enter script
    mkdir $DESKTOP$$/$TestDir
    mkdir $DESKTOP$$/$TestDir
    ```

7. Add another Show Message Dialog action. This time display the following text:

    ```
    STDOUT: $EXECUTE_STDOUT$
    STDERR: $EXECUTE_STDERR$
    EXITCODE: $EXECUTE_EXITCODE$
    ```

8. Rebuild and run your installer.

    Note the files installed by the SpeedFolder, the changes made to the system registry, and the Environment variable created. The changes on the target system should reflect all of the changes you have made to the project.

9. To add an action to an installer, click **Add Action**.

    The **Add Action** button is present wherever actions are available. Clicking **Add Action** will display the **Choose an Action** dialog.

Quick Quiz

1. Where is the Expand Archive action available?

    A. Pre-install

    B. Post-install

    C. Install

    D. All of the above

2. Where would you place an action that requires an uninstall equivalent?

    A. Pre-install

    B. Post-install

    C. Install

    D. All of the above

3. Why can't you add an uninstaller to your new project?

   A. There is already an uninstaller in the default project.

   B. You've deleted your mojo file.

   C. Mikey, the IT guy, doesn't like you.

Quick Quiz answers are located in Appendix J.

List of Actions

Install Actions

InstallAnywhere comes with action request operations that will be performed by the installer and the uninstaller. Table 10.1 lists the actions available to the installer.

Table 10.1 Install Actions

Action	Editions	Description
Copy File	E	Copy a file from one location to another location on the end-user's system.
Copy Folder	E	Copy a folder from one location to another on the end-user's system.
Create Alias, Link, Shortcut	E S	Create an alias (Mac OS X), symbolic link (UNIX and Linux), or shortcut (Windows).
Create Folder	E S	Create a new folder on the end-user's system. If the folder already exists, it will not be deleted.
Create LaunchAnywhere for Java Apps	E S	Create a launcher to start the installed Java application. See the expanded section on LaunchAnywhere below for more information.
Create Uninstaller	E S	Create the uninstaller and several additional files needed by the uninstaller. Zero G recommends that the uninstaller be installed into its own folder.
Delete File	E	Delete a file from the end-user's system.
Delete Folder	E	Delete a folder from the end-user's system.
Expand Archive	E S	Expand a ZIP file (.zip, .jar, .war, .ear) or decode a Mac binary file (.bin) on the end-user's system.
Install Archive	E S	Install a ZIP file (.zip, .jar) from the installer onto the end-user's system. This action appears automatically when a ZIP file is added.

Table 10.1 Install Actions (Continued)

Action	Editions	Description
Install File	E S	Install a file from the installer onto the end-user's system. This action appears automatically when files are added.
Install from Manifest	E	Install all of the files and folders specified in the manifest file on the end-user's system. See the expanded section on manifest files below for more information.
Install HP-UX Depot	E	Install and uninstall HP-UX depot files through the Install HP-UX Depot action. The developer needs to specify the package name within the depot file, which can contain multiple packages. In order to install multiple packages in the same depot, add one action for every package you want to install. This will not increase the size of the installer.
Install Linux RPM	E	Install and uninstall Linux RPMs through the Install Linux RPM action. These RPMs can either be bundled with the installer or preexisting on the system. If the RPM is relocatable and the **Relocatable** check box is set in the action customizer, the RPM will be installed to its location in the file tree. Additionally, the RPM can be set to ignore dependencies (similar to the --nodeps option for the command-line RPM tool) and to force the installation (--force).
Install Merge Module	E	Install a merge module as if the merge module were run as a separate silent installer.
Install PowerUpdate Client	E S	Create a PowerUpdate Check for Updates client for the installed application. This requires a downloaded client ZIP from a PowerUpdate server.
Install Solaris Package	E	Install and uninstall Solaris package files through the Install Solaris Package action. These packages can either be bundled with the installer or preexisting on the system. The developer must enter the name of the package. Additionally, InstallAnywhere supports bundling admin and response files for the packages with the installer. For more information on these files, consult the man pages for pkgadd(1), pkgask(1), and admin(4).
Install SpeedFolder	E S	Dynamically pick up files at build-time from a folder. All files will be installed as one, single, fast operation. (Tip: Use SpeedFolders for large installations with many files or builds that occur automatically.)
Move File	E	Move or rename a file from one location to another on the end-user's system.
Move Folder	E	Move or rename a folder from one location to another on the end-user's system.
Register Windows Service	E	Start, stop, or pause a Windows service on the end-user's system.

Table 10.1 Install Actions (Continued)

Action	Editions	Description
Set System Environment Variable	E	Set Environment variables on the end-user's system. This is compatible with Windows and UNIX only. UNIX Bash, sh, ksh, zsh, csh, tcsh shells are supported.
Set Windows Registry—Multiple Entries	E	Set multiple Windows registry keys, data, and values on the end-user's system.
Set Windows Registry—Single Entry	E S	Set an individual Windows registry key, data, and value on the end-user's system.

General Actions

General actions occur transparently to the end-user and do not require any user input. Table 10.2 lists the available panel actions in InstallAnywhere.

Table 10.2 General Actions

Action	Editions	Description
Add Comment	E S	This action is designed to allow developers to add a simple comment to the installer.
Add Jump Label	E	Use this action to branch off the installation conditionally. By applying InstallAnywhere rules, developers may jump end-users to a specific part of the installation, depending on the specifics of their system or install. Use this action in conjunction with the Jump to Target action. This action is available during the install sequence, but not within the files.
Execute ANT Script	E	This action allows developers to execute scripts designed for the Apache Jakarta Project's ANT application. If this action is selected, ANT will be bundled with the application. Only developers familiar with ANT should use this action. For more information, go to http://ant.apache.org.
Execute Command	E	This action allows developers to execute a command as they would at any command-line interpreter. This action is useful for executing applications that are already installed on the system. This command line is entered just as the system's command line would be.
Execute Custom Code	E S	This action allows developers to extend InstallAnywhere's functionality. InstallAnywhere's API is purely Java-based and allows developers to do nearly anything that is possible in Java. The Execute Custom Code action represents the noninteractive interface for this API.

Table 10.2 General Actions (Continued)

Action	Editions	Description
Execute Script/ Batch File	E	This action allows developers to enter the text to a script or batch file, which will then be executed from within the installation.
Execute Target File	E S	This action launches an executable or opens a document that is included in the installer. If the target is a document with the appropriate application associations set up, then it will be opened in the correct application. This action is available only during and after file installation.
Find Component in Registry	E	This action discovers whether a component exists on a system through the cross-platform registry; it also finds existing component versions, their locations, and if there are multiple instances of a particular component on the destination system.
Get Windows Registry Entry	E	This action allows developers access to information stored in the Windows registry. It allows developers to retrieve or check for the existence of a key or value and store that information in InstallAnywhere variables to be used in the installation.
Jump to Target	E	Related to the Add Jump Label discussed above, this action allows developers to jump to a specific point in an installation. When controlled by InstallAnywhere rules, this action gives developers a conditional method of moving nonlinearly through an install. This action is available during the **Files** and **Sequence** tasks.
Launch Default Browser	E S	This action allows developers to launch users' default Web browsers with specified arguments. It can open a URL or a file on the system. This action is available during the **Sequence** tasks.
Modify Text File— In Archive	E	This action allow developers to alter text files found in Zip-format archives.
Modify Text File— Multiple Files	E	This action allow developers to alter multiple text files. It can also be used to properly change line endings for a large number of files.
Modify Text File— Single File	E	This action allow developers to the contents of a single file.
Output Debug Information	E S	The InstallAnywhere installer includes comprehensive debugging. By running the installer in Debug mode, developers can diagnose many issues. This action allows developers to output specific information either to the console or to a file. Developers can output the entire contents of the InstallAnywhere variable manager, the install tree, Java properties, and other information related to the installation.

Table 10.2 General Actions (Continued)

Action	Editions	Description
Output Text to Console	E S	This action outputs specified text to the debug console, which is useful for measuring the progress of a noninteractive installer in Silent or Console mode or the progress of a noninteractive portion of the installation.
Perform XSL Transform	E	This action allows developers to specify an Extensible Stylesheet Language Transform (XSLT) and target. Predefined XSLTs can be found in the <InstallAnywhere>\resource\extras\presets directory.
Perform XSL Transform—In Archive	E	This action works the same as the Perform XSL Transform action, but does so for files in an archive. This action is useful for configuring Web applications in WAR, EAR, and JAR files.
Restart Windows	E S	This action will restart a Windows system. The system will reboot as soon as this action is reached, so use it carefully and only in conjunction with rules.
Set InstallAnywhere Variable— Multiple Variables	E S	The root of any InstallAnywhere installation, these actions allow developers to specify values for, or to create, InstallAnywhere variables. These actions are used throughout the installation and can control nearly any aspect of the installation.
Set InstallAnywhere Variable—Single Variable	E S	See Set InstallAnywhere Variable—Multiple Variables.
Show Message Dialog	E	This action creates a modal dialog that requests end-user input. The message dialog will appear over the currently displayed panel and can be used to force the end-user to return to the previous panel, exit the installer, or input information. When controlled by rules, this action can be used as a data verification tool.
Start, Stop, Pause Windows Service	E	If the application is interacting with a Windows service, the installer may need to manage that service. This action, when the installer is run with sufficient privileges, allows the installer to stop, start, or pause registered Windows services.

Panel Actions

Panel actions are requests for the user's input, which appear in the Graphical Installer Wizard. Table 10.3 lists the available panel actions in InstallAnywhere.

Table 10.3 Panel Actions

Action	Editions	Description
Choose Alias, Link, Shortcut	E S	Added as part of the default project, this panel allows the end-user to choose an installation location for shortcuts (Windows), aliases (Mac), and links (UNIX).
Choose Features to Uninstall	E S	This panel allows the end-user to select the features he or she wants to uninstall.
Choose File	E	This panel allows installers to request that the user select a file based on certain criteria and set its result as an InstallAnywhere variable. The variable can then be used later in the install.
Choose Folder	E	This panel allows developers to request that the user select a folder based on certain criteria and set its result as an InstallAnywhere variable that can be used later in the install.
Choose Install Folder	E S	Part of the default project, this panel allows the user to choose the primary installation folder. It is not necessary that this panel be included, as without it, the installer will select the default specified in the **Project | Platforms** task.
Choose Install Set	E S	This panel allows developers to request that the end-user choose an install set or features to install.
Choose Java VM	E S	This panel allows developers to have the end-user select the JVM to be used for any installed LaunchAnywhere launchers. Developers can specify the type of VM that the end-user should select, and the panel will search the system for an appropriate VM.
Choose Uninstall Type	E S	This panel allows the end-user to select whether to install all or part of the application.
Custom Code Panel	E	InstallAnywhere's Custom Code API allows developers to create custom panels where necessary.
Disk Space Check	E S	This panel performs a disk space check on the installation destination system based on the end-user's chosen install location and features. If there is not enough disk space to perform the install, then the installer will prompt the end-user to free the required disk space or choose another install location. This panel is automatically added before files are installed and does not appear in the list.
Display Message	E S	This panel allows developers simply to display a text message to the end-user during the installation. This can be useful for conveying information about installation choices that the end-user has made. This panel is also particularly useful in debugging installer issues having to do with InstallAnywhere variables.

Table 10.3 Panel Actions (Continued)

Action	Editions	Description
Find File/Folder	E	This panel implements a search process that, depending on specifications made by the developer, will search portions of the file system for a specific named file or a file matching a certain pattern. The end-user can also choose a matching file.
Get Password	E	This panel allows developers to request a password from the end-user. Developers can choose to validate the password against a list of specified passwords (enabling the Index feature that allows different passwords to effectively unlock different features) or they can simply store the entered password in a variable (as when requesting a password to be used in a configuration routine).
Get Serial Number	E	This panel implements InstallAnywhere's built-in serial number verification and creation routines. It allows developers to add serial number functionality to the installer. Developers can choose to generate any number of serial numbers for any number of products. Serial numbers can represent unique products or sets of products. As a result, this action allows developers to create rules that can manage all aspects of the installation based on rights granted by the serial number the end-user has entered.
Get User Input—Advanced	E	The older, smarter, and more capable brother of the **Get User Input** panel, this panel allows developers to get input from the user by using multiple input types and setting multiple variables. This action can use radio buttons, check boxes, text fields, and menus—all on the same panel.
Get User Input—Simple	E	This panel allows developers to request input from the end-user.
Important Note	E S	This panel allows developers to display a text or HTML file without the radio buttons found on the **License Agreement** panel. It is particularly useful for displaying readme or errata-type documents.
Install Complete	E S	This panel displays information about the installation's status to the end-user. It also optionally displays if a restart is needed on a Windows system. It is available only after files have been installed.
Introduction	E S	Part of the default project, this panel offers an introduction to the installation.
License Agreement	E S	This panel allows developers to display a license agreement to the end-user. The end-user must choose to accept the agreement to continue. Developers can set the default state of the radio buttons (accept or decline) and choose a file to use for a license agreement. The **License Agreement** panel can also use HTML files, which gives developers a degree of control over text formatting and allows them to link to external documents.

Table 10.3 Panel Actions (Continued)

Action	Editions	Description
Pre-Install Summary	E S	This panel summarizes information collected and evaluated prior to the installation of files. It allows the developer to customize what information is presented. It is included in the default InstallAnywhere project.
Scrolling Message	E	This panel allows developers to enter long text in a message panel that includes scroll bars. This is particularly useful for instructions.
Uninstall Complete	E S	This panel displays the information that the uninstaller has completed.
Uninstaller Introduction	E S	This panel offers an introduction to the uninstaller.

Console Actions

Console actions (commonly called consoles) are the means for requesting installer end-user input when using a command-line interface (see Table 10.4). When the end-user selects a console installation, console actions will be used instead of panel actions.

Table 10.4 Console Actions

Action	Editions	Description
Choose Features to Uninstall	E	This console allows the end-user to select the features to uninstall.
Choose Install Folder	E	This console chooses the primary installation location.
Choose Install Sets	E	This console allows developers to request that the end-user choose an install set or features to install.
Choose Java VM	E	This console allows developers to have the end-user select the JVM to be used for any installed LaunchAnywhere launchers. Developers can specify the type of VM that the end-user should select, and the panel will search the system for an appropriate VM.
Choose Link Folder	E	This console allows the user to determine where to install UNIX links.
Choose Uninstall Type	E	This console allows the end-user to select whether to install all or part of the application.
Custom Code	E	InstallAnywhere's Custom Code API allows developers to create custom consoles where necessary.

Table 10.4 Console Actions (Continued)

Action	Editions	Description
Display Message	E	This console allows developers simply to display a text message to the end-user during the installation.
Get Password	E	This console allows developers to request a password from the end-user.
Get Serial Number	E	This console allows end-users to generate a list of serial numbers, as well as request them from the end-user.
Get User Input	E	This console allows developers to request input from the end-user.
Install Complete	E	This console displays information about the installation's status to the end-user. It is available only after files have been installed.
Install Failed	E	This console should be displayed when a console installer has generated an error.
License Agreement	E	This console allows developers to display a license agreement to the end-user.
Pre-Install Summary	E	This console summarizes information collected and evaluated prior to the installation of files.
Ready to Install	E	This console alerts the end-user that the installer is about to install files.
Show Message Console 'Dialog'	E	This console displays a message dialog to the end-user.
Uninstall Complete	E	This console displays the information that the uninstaller has completed.
Uninstaller Introduction	E	This console offers an introduction to the uninstaller.

Common Properties

Table 10.5 contains common properties found in action customizers in InstallAnywhere.

Table 10.5 Common Properties

Property	Description
Comment	Sets the name of the action in the visual tree
Do not uninstall	Tells an action to not attempt to undo the results of the action at uninstall time
If file already exists on end-user's system	Overrides the default behavior for how to resolve conflicts between installed files and preexisting files

Table 10.5 Common Properties (Continued)

Property	Description
In classpath	Puts the item on the classpath for all LaunchAnywhere executables installed
Installed file/existing file	Determines whether the file is being installed or already exists on the end-user's system
Override default UNIX/Mac OS X permissions	Sets the file permissions to a specific value for this action
Path	Shows the path where the action will be installed
Show indeterminate dialog	Brings up an indeterminate progress bar to show progress to the end-user while an external process is executing
Source	Shows the path where the item currently exists on the developer's system (displays the source path if source paths are being used)
Store process' exit code in	Sets the value of the InstallAnywhere variable to the process' exit code
Store process' `stderr` in	Sets the value of the InstallAnywhere variable to the process' standard error
Store process' `stdout` in	Sets the value of the InstallAnywhere variable to the process' standard out
Suspend installation until process completes	Pauses the installer until the launched process completes

Panel Action Settings

Panel actions (commonly called panels) are the means for requesting user input through a graphical interface.

Graphic installers may show the installation steps through a set of labels, or words that represent the step. Installers may also display specific images for the steps. When **Images** is selected in the **Installer UI | Look and Feel | Installer Panel Additions | Type of Additions to Installer Panels** task, the customizer for the panel in the **Pre-Install** and **Post-Install** tasks will enable the use of the **Image Settings** tab. If **List of Installer Steps** is selected, the **Label Settings** tab will be enabled.

> **NOTE** These settings are unavailable to panel actions in the uninstaller. Panel actions in the uninstaller use the default values set in the **Installer UI | Look and Feel** task.

Image Settings

Use panel image settings to choose a specific image to display on the chosen panel. Developers may choose to use the default panel image, display an image specific to that panel, or display no image at all.

Label Settings

The **Label Settings** tab in the customizer enables developers to preview labels and icon images. The labels are highlighted and marked as the installation progresses. The installer build process will autopopulate the list based on the panel titles.

NOTE Using the **Installer UI | Look and Feel** task's **Installer Panel Additions** tab and the **Label Settings** tab found on each individual panel's customizer, developers can assign multiple panels to the same label. Thus, if there are numerous steps or if the installer has several panels for the same step, the interface can be adjusted as needed.

To control label order or to edit the content of the label, in the **Installer UI | Look and Feel** task's **Installer Panel Additions** tab, use the arrows and other control buttons found to the left of the list of panels.

Help

Selecting **Enable installer help** in the **Installer UI | Help** subtask provides a Help feature for the installer program. Developers may set a single Help message, which they can define in this window. To customize Help for each installer screen, select **Use different help** for each text panel. Add the customized Help in the **Help** tab of the action customizer at the bottom of the **Pre-Install** and **Post-Install** tasks.

Selecting **HTML** allows greater formatting control of the message, but not the title bar. To change formatting, use HTML formatting tags, such as

```
<B>MyHelp</B> <I>Information</I>
```

which displays as **MyHelp** Information.

Additional Action Information
LaunchAnywhere
A LaunchAnywhere executable, or LAX, is a file used to launch a Java application on any LaunchAnywhere-compatible platform (all Windows and UNIX platforms and on Mac OS X). LaunchAnywhere enables end-users to double-click on an icon (Windows or Mac OS X) or type a single command (UNIX) to start a Java application. The LAX is also in charge of configuring the Java application environment by setting the classpath; redirecting standard out and standard error; passing in system properties, Environment variables, and command-line parameters; and many other options.

The launcher looks at a configuration file, <MyLauncherName>.lax, to determine how the launcher runs. This LAX file is created during the installation and is placed in the same location as the launcher.

A list of LAX properties is located in Appendix I.

Manifest Files
Manifest files are text files that specify a list of files and directories. The manifest file has a certain format (listed below), which specifies the file's source, its destination (which is relative to the location of the action in the visual tree of the **Files** task), and, optionally, which UNIX file permission it should have and if it should be placed on the classpath. At build time, this file is analyzed, and its contents are placed into the installer.

Manifest File Format
For files:

```
F,[SOURCEPATH]relative_path_to_source_file,./
  relative_path_to_destination_file
F,absolute_path_to_source_file,./relative_path_to_destination_file
```

To put files on the classpath:

```
F,absolute_path_to_source_file,./relative_path_to_destination_file,cp
```

To set a file's permissions on UNIX:

```
F,[SOURCEPATH]relative_path_to_source_file,./
  relative_path_to_destination_file,755
```

For directories:

```
D,[SOURCEPATH]relative_path_to_source_dir[/],./
  relative_path_to_destination_dir[/]
D,absolute_path_to_source_dir[/],./
  relative_path_to_destination_dir[/]
```

Examples:

```
F,$IA_HOME$/path/to/source/file.txt,./destination/path/
  thisfile.txt
F,/absolute/path/to/source/file.txt,./destination/path/
  thisfile.txt,cp,655
D,$IA_HOME$/path/to/dir,./destination/path/dir
D,/absolute/path/to/dir,./destination/path/dir
```

CHAPTER 11

Managing Installation Locations with Magic Folders

- Magic Folders and InstallAnywhere Variables
- InstallAnywhere-Provided Magic Folders

Magic Folders and InstallAnywhere Variables

Magic Folders represent a specific location, such as the user selected installation directory, the desktop, or the location for library files. At install time, the installer determines which operating system it is running on and sets the Magic Folders to the correct absolute paths. Many Magic Folders are platform-specific, and many are predefined by InstallAnywhere to standard locations across InstallAnywhere-supported platforms.

Every Magic Folder has an associated InstallAnywhere variable. These variables are first initialized when the installer begins. Changing the value of a Magic Folder variable will change the destination to which the Magic Folder installs. Changing the value of the $USER_INSTALL_DIR$ through InstallAnywhere will change where the files will install.

With the three following exceptions, these variables are initialized at install time and will not change, except through using custom code or the Set InstallAnywhere Variable action:

- **USER_INSTALL_DIR$:** This is initialized to the default value determined in the **Platforms** task in the Advanced Designer. Its value can change at the **Choose Install Folder** step if the end-user selects a different folder.

- **USER_SHORTCUTS$:** This is initialized to the default value determined by the **Platforms** task in the Advanced Designer. Its value can change at the **Create Alias, Link, Shortcut Folder** install step if the end-user selects a different location.

- **JAVA_HOME$:**

    Installer without VM: Defaults to the value of the Java property java.home. Its value can change at the **Choose Java Virtual Machine** step if the end-user selects a VM.

    Installer with VM: Defaults to the value specified in the **Project | Java** task. It can change when the $USER_INSTALL_DIR$ changes, or at the **Choose Java Virtual Machine** step if the end-user selects a VM already on his or her machine.

> **NOTE** Variables cannot be set to themselves. For example to append/test to USER_MAGIC_FOLDER_1, the developer cannot set USER_MAGIC_FOLDER_1 = $USER_MAGIC_FOLDER_1$$/$test. InstallAnywhere does not allow either direct or indirect recursion with InstallAnywhere variables. This condition will cause an error.

InstallAnywhere defines a number of Magic Folders as defaults, mostly those representing common installation locations. One of the keys to understanding Magic Folders is to understand that they resolve to different locations based on the configuration of the target system.

For example:

The Magic Folder system drive root ($SYSTEM_DRIVE_ROOT$) resolves, on UNIX, Linux, and Mac OS X, to C:\ (or the root of the drive containing the WINNT or Windows directory).

Other Magic Folders are reserved, but are defined by actions in the installer, or actions taken by the end-user. These Magic Folders are important to the operation of the installer.

One such Magic Folder is the **User Install Dir** ($USER_INSTALL_DIR$), the directory that represents the root of the installation as specified by the developer or as chosen by the user. This directory structure is not defined by the installer, but is defined on a project-by-project basis.

Another such Magic Folder type is the User Magic Folder. While InstallAnywhere defines many installation paths via predefined Magic Folders, Zero G cannot have accounted for all possible installation needs when implementing the technology. As such, the User Magic Folder is introduced. These variable-based installation paths are designed to allow you to define a path manually or using any of InstallAnywhere's dynamic installation tools. You can create your own User Magic Folders by setting the associated variables and then simply adding your resources to that Magic Folder in the install step.

Exercise 11.1 Magic Folders

In this exercise, we'll implement a new installer project that serves to demonstrate the use and flexibility of the InstallAnywhere Magic Folders architecture.

1. Open InstallAnywhere and create a new project in the advanced designer.

   Yes, at least for the moment, OfficeSuite will be retired.

2. On your desktop (or in a location where you can easily find them), create the following files (they need not have any content):

   ```
   Desktop.txt
   SystemDriveRoot.txt
   Home.txt
   Temp.txt
   Programs.txt
   System.txt
   MagicOne.txt
   MagicTwo.txt
   ```

3. Add all files you've just created to your installer project.

4. Browse to the **Files** task.

   For each file, we'll be choosing a Magic Folder that will result in the file being installed to a location that matches the filename. This will allow us to see the installation process in action and to see how the Magic Folders resolve.

5. Set Magic Folder destinations for each file.

   a. For the `Desktop.txt` file, highlight the file and in the customizer use the pull-down menu to select **Desktop Folder**.

   b. Highlight `SystemDriveRoot.txt` and select **System Drive Root**.

   c. Highlight the `Home.txt` file and select **Home Directory**.

   d. Repeat, selecting the matching destination pathname, until reaching the MagicOne and MagicTwo files. For these files, select `USER_MAGIC_FOLDER_1` and `USER_MAGIC_FOLDER_2`, respectively.

6. Define the User Magic Folders that we've used.

   As the folders must be defined before they're installed, we'll define them in the pre-install section of the installer.

a. Browse to the **Pre-Install** task.

   As we're only exploring the Magic Folders in this installer, we can remove all the panels from pre-install. This will allow our installer to run more quickly and without interaction.

   Now, to define the User Magic Folders, we need to define the InstallAnywhere variables that define them.

b. Add a Set InstallAnywhere Variable action by clicking **Add Action**, then in the **General** tab chose **Set InstallAnywhere Variable—Single Variable**.

   This action will define the $USER_MAGIC_FOLDER_1$ variable and, as such, define the location for the MagicOne.txt file.

c. Select a location where you have write permissions and enter that path as the value for the file.

7. Add another Set InstallAnywhere Variable action, which we'll use to define $USER_MAGIC_FOLDER_2$.

   For this variable, try using one of the Magic Folder variables to help define the path. The variables used in Magic Folders are described in Appendix B. We suggest using something like $SYSTEM_DRIVE_ROOT$$/$MagicFolder. The $/$ will resolve to the proper "/", "\", or ":" depending on the system used. It is one of the standard InstallAnywhere variables, and we suggest using it in place of the system-specific file separators.

8. Build and run your installer.

   After execution, you'll want to check each file location that you've specified with a Magic Folder to see if the file was correctly installed. The Desktop.txt file should appear on your desktop. The other files will appear in the locations that have been specified. The only tricky one here is the Home.txt file. This should appear in the user's home directory, which is highly variable. On most Windows systems this will be in C:\Documents and Settings\USERNAME, and of course on UNIX and derivative systems, it will be ~$USER.

InstallAnywhere-Provided Magic Folders

InstallAnywhere uses Magic Folders to define installation locations. Table 11.1 lists the Magic Folders you can use with InstallAnywhere.

Table 11.1 Magic Folders

Folder Name	InstallAnywhere Variable	Destination
User Installation Directory	$USER_INSTALL_DIR$	This is the installation folder as specified by the end-user. Developers can specify a default value for this variable in the **Project Info** screen in the Advanced Designer by choosing a location in the Default Install Folder area of the screen.
Programs Folder (Platform Default)	$PROGRAMS_DIR$	This is the default application directory on the destination system (the Program Files folder on Windows, the Applications folder on Mac OS, and the logged-in end-user's home account on UNIX).
Shortcuts	$USER_SHORTCUTS$	This is the folder specified by the end-user as the shortcuts/links/aliases location. The value of this location can be changed by the end-user if the Choose Alias, Link, Shortcut Folder action is turned on in the installer. Developers can specify a default value for this variable on a per-platform basis by selecting the **Platforms** task in the Advanced Designer.
System	$SYSTEM$	This variable represents the system folder on the target machine. On Windows 95/98, this resolves to <WINDOWS>\System. On Windows NT/2000, this resolves to <WINDOWS>\System32. On the Mac OS, this resolves to the System folder. On UNIX, this resolves to /usr/local/bin.
Desktop	$DESKTOP$	This variable represents the desktop on the target machine. This folder only resolves on Windows, Linux, and Mac OS systems.
Temp Directory	$TEMP_DIR$	This variable represents the temp directory on the target machine. When running the pure Java installer on Windows, $TEMP_DIR$ will resolve to the user's home directory.
Startup	$STARTUP$	This is the automatic start-up folder for items that are launched automatically during operating system boot up. This folder only resolves on Windows and Mac OS systems.
Installation Drive Root	$INSTALL_DRIVE_ROOT$	This is the root directory on the volume where the installation is taking place.
Home Directory	$USER_HOME$	This is the home directory of the end-user running the installer. This variable works with all platforms except Mac OS. For users who have already included the variable $UNIX_USER_HOME$, this variable will continue to function with the same definition as $USER_HOME$.

Table 11.1 Magic Folders (Continued)

Folder Name	InstallAnywhere Variable	Destination
System Drive Root	$SYSTEM_DRIVE_ROOT$	This is the root directory of the system drive.
Java Home	$JAVA_HOME$	This is the home directory of the JVM to be used.
Windows	$WIN_WINDOWS$	This is the Windows directory (Windows 95/98/Me/XP/NT/2000 computers only).
Start Menu	WIN_START_MENU	This is the Windows Start Menu directory (Windows 95/98/Me/XP/NT/2000 computers only).
Quick Launch Bar	$WIN_QUICK_LAUNCH_BAR$	This is the Quick Launch Bar on Windows. On Windows 2000 and XP, the location is relative to the UserProfile Environment variable. On Windows 98 and Me, it's relative to the Windows directory.
Do Not Install	$DO_NOT_INSTALL$	This doesn't install the file on the target platform. It is used for files (typically localized license agreements and graphics) that are used during installation, but don't need to remain on the target system.
USER_MAGIC_FOLDER_#	$USER_MAGIC_FOLDER_#$	These variables are user-defined destination install Magic Folders. They install to whichever directories their variable names have been set. To set these variables, use the Set InstallAnywhere Variable action. Note: For UNIX, if the leading "/" is not included in the path before the Magic Folder location, the result is `<directory in which installer double-clicked>/USER_MAGIC_FOLDER_#` because the operating system assumes that any path not preceded by a "/" is below the current directory.
Programs Menu	$WIN_PROGRAMS_MENU$	This is the Windows **Programs** menu (in the **Start** menu) (Windows 95/98/Me/XP/NT/2000 computers only).
All Users Start Menu	$WIN_COMMON_START_MENU$	This is the Windows All Users Start Menu directory (Windows NT/2000 computers only). On Win 9x computers this resolves to the same value as WIN_START_MENU.
All Users Programs Menu	$WIN_COMMON_PROGRAMS_MENU$	This is the Windows **All Users Programs** menu (in the **Start** menu) (Windows NT/2000/XP computers only). On Win 9x computers this resolves to the same value as $WIN_PROGRAMS_MENU$.

Table 11.1 Magic Folders (Continued)

Folder Name	InstallAnywhere Variable	Destination
All Users Startup	$WIN_COMMON_STARTUP$	This is the Windows All Users Startup folder (in the **Start** menu) (Windows NT/2000/XP computers only). On Win 9x computers this resolves to the same value as $STARTUP$.
All Users Desktop	$WIN_COMMON_DESKTOP$	This is the Windows Common Desktop folder (Windows NT/2000/XP computers only). On Win 9x computers this resolves to the same value as $DESKTOP$.
Fonts	$FONTS$	This is the Fonts directory (on both Windows and Mac OS computers only): $WIN_WINDOWS$\Fonts on Windows; $SYSTEM$:Fonts on Mac OS.
Apple Menu Items	MAC_APPLE_MENU	This is the Apple Menu Items folder (Mac OS computers only).
Control Panels	$MAC_CONTROL_PANELS$	This is the Control Panels folder (Mac OS computers only).
Extensions	$MAC_EXTENSIONS$	This is the Extensions folder (Mac OS computers only).
Preferences	$MAC_PREFERENCES$	This is the Preferences folder (Mac OS computers only): $SYSTEM$:Preferences.
Clean-up at Startup	$MAC_CHEWABLE$	This is the Clean at Startup folder (Mac OS computers only): $SYSTEM_DRIVE_ROOT$:Cleanup At Startup.
User Applications	$MACX_USER_APPLICATIONS$	This is the User Applications directory of the end-user running the installer (Mac OS X only).
The Dock	$MACX_DOCK$	This is the Mac OS X Dock—for shortcuts only. Files cannot be installed to the Dock.
/usr/local/bin	$UNIX_USR_LOCAL_BIN$	This is the /usr/local/bin directory (UNIX computers only).
/opt	$UNIX_OPT$	This is the /opt directory (UNIX computers only).
/usr/bin	$UNIX_USR_BIN$	This is the /usr/bin directory (UNIX computers only).

NOTE Developer-defined Magic Folders are not available in the Standard Edition.

CHAPTER 12

Applying Basic and Intermediate Development Concepts

- Concept Review
- Debugging InstallAnywhere Installers

THIS CHAPTER WILL CONSIST OF a single unstructured exercise where we will utilize much of what we've discussed up until this point. After completion of an installer project, we will test and debug the installer utilizing InstallAnywhere's built-in debugging features.

Concept Review

You will build a single installer utilizing each of the concepts, actions, and panels listed. The idea is to create an installer that you plan and create using a number of InstallAnywhere development concepts.

1. Build an Installer with the following guidelines.
    - **Magic Folders:** Your installer should include at least one Magic Folder other than the core `USER_INSTALL_DIR` and `SHORTCUTS`.
    - **LaunchAnywhere:** Your installer must contain at least one LaunchAnywhere launcher.
    - **InstallAnywhere variables:** Your installer should display an understanding and reasonable management of InstallAnywhere variables.
    - **InstallAnywhere rules:** You should implement rules that control installer behavior and install path options.
    - **Actions and panels:** Your installer should implement the following actions and panels:
        - Panel: Choose Alias, Link, or Shortcut
        - Panel: Choose File or Choose Folder
        - Panel: Choose Install Folder
        - Panel: Display Message
        - Panel: Get Password
        - Panel: Get User Input—Simple
        - Panel: Install Failed
        - Panel: Install Success
        - Panel: Install Summary
        - Panel: Introduction
        - Panel: Show License Agreement

- **InstallAnywhere actions:** Your installer should implement the following InstallAnywhere actions:
    - Add Comment
    - Create Alias, Link, or Shortcut
    - Create LaunchAnywhere for Java Application
    - Execute Command
    - Execute Target File
    - Get Windows Registry
    - Install File
    - Install Folder
    - Install Uninstaller
    - Output Text to Console
    - Set InstallAnywhere Variable
    - Set Windows Registry Entry—Single
    - Show Message Dialog
2. When you have completed your installer project, test your installer. Does it meet your expectations?

Debugging InstallAnywhere Installers

Using the installer we've just constructed, we'll explore some of InstallAnywhere's built-in debugging features. There are several methods available to debug InstallAnywhere installers. Deciding which method to use depends in part on the installer development cycle—during installer development or later if an end-user has a problem with the installer.

Most InstallAnywhere installers utilize Zero G Software's LaunchAnywhere technology. Along with many convenient features for end-users (double-click-able launchers, native-like user experience) LaunchAnywhere launchers provide a host of built-in debugging features.

During Installer Development

InstallAnywhere provides a project-specific Debugging feature that will allow you to create a debug file for each installer. To activate the project-specific Debugging feature, do the following:

1. In the InstallAnywhere advanced designer, select **Project | Config**.

   From here you'll see two fields within the **Installer Debug Output** section. In these fields, you can enter a path to the text file where the installer will place output when run. Both entries should point to the same file. These paths should be absolute and can be managed using Java paths, rather than the system-specific paths. This will allow you use one entry for multiple platforms.

2. Set the output files:

   Send `stderr` to: `/tmp/outputfile.txt`

   Send `stdout` to: `/tmp/outputfile.txt`

   These settings will direct the output to `/tmp/outputfile.txt` on a UNIX or derivative system and to `C:\tmp\outputfile.txt` on a Windows system. You'll need to make sure that the directory `/tmp` or `c:\tmp` exists on the target system in order for the output file to be created. The file itself (in this example `outputfile.txt`) will contain most, if not all, information needed to debug InstallAnywhere installations.

> **NOTE** Because these files will not be uninstalled, we recommend that this feature be deactivated prior to the final build of your product installer. However, some developers have chosen to leave the output intact to make debugging any issue that arises post-development easier.

After Development

Post-development suggestions should help when debugging a customer problem or with other post-development issues.

Debugging a Win32 Installer

To view or capture the debug output from a Win32 installer, hold down the <CTRL> key immediately after launching the installer and until a console window appears. Before exiting the installer, copy the console output to a text file for later review.

On some Windows NT systems, run the installer once with the <CTRL> key down, resetting the scroll back buffer for the console window, then quit and run the installation again.

If there are problems capturing the console output, try a slightly more convoluted method (this will often be the case on Win9x because of the console's limited ability to capture output). First launch the installer and allow it to extract the necessary files. Once it reaches the **Preparing to Install...** window, when given the opportunity to choose a language or to go to the Windows temp directory, look for a temp folder that starts with an "I" followed by many numeric digits (e.g., I1063988642). Be sure it is the most recent directory by sorting the directories by their "modified" date. Open the directory; there should be a file called `sea_loc`. Delete this file. Now go back to the installer, click **OK**, and at the first opportunity, cancel the installation.

Now go back to the directory inside the temp directory, where the file `sea_loc` was deleted. There should be another directory called Windows; open it. There should be an `.exe` file (most likely `install.exe`). There should also be another file with the same name, except it will have a `.lax` extension. Open it with a plain-text editor and edit the lines as follows:

```
lax.stderr.redirect=  AND lax.stdout.redirect=
```

to be:

```
lax.stderr.redirect=output.txt AND
    lax.stdout.redirect= output.txt
```

After these changes have been made, save the file and launch the `.exe`. When the installation is complete, there should be an `output.txt` file in the same directory as the `.lax` file. The `output.txt` file will contain the same information as that generated to the console.

Debugging a UNIX/Linux Installer

To capture the debug output from the UNIX command-line, developers need to perform the following: Enter one of the following (based on which shell) at the command line prior to executing the installer:

```
export LAX_DEBUG=true    or    setenv LAX_DEBUG true
or     LAX_DEBUG=true    or    set LAX_DEBUG
```
or whatever would be appropriate for the UNIX shell.

Then run the installer. This will redirect the debug output to the console window you are currently in, and this output will help debug the installer.

If you would like to redirect the output to a file, you'll need to set `LAX_DEBUG=file`. Once you launch the installer, a file called `jx.log` containing debug output will be generated in the directory containing the installer.

Debugging a Mac OS X Installer

InstallAnywhere utilizes the standard output layers in Mac OS X to display output. To gather debugging output from an OS X installer, launch `console.app`. This output is found in `/Applications/Utilities`. To retain this information, cut and paste it from the console window to a file.

Debugging a Pure Java Installer

The method for debugging the Pure Java or other platforms' installers is as follows:

1. Place a file named `ia_debug` (lower case) in the same directory as the JAR, which contains the installer. Placing this file here will not direct the output to this file, but its existence will redirect the output to the console.
2. Set the general settings to create output prior to building the installer.
3. Set the output in **Project | Config** as described above.

Debugging LaunchAnywhere Launched Executables

Because InstallAnywhere installers use LaunchAnywhere executables, the above procedures are also useful for debugging installed applications that make use of the LaunchAnywhere Java launcher technology. Generally, however, it's quite simple to alter the LAX file to allow the launcher to always generate output. This behavior can then be changed upon qualification and final release.

To generate debug output:

1. In the InstallAnywhere advanced designer, highlight the launcher.
3. Click the **Edit Properties** button.
4. Alter the values for the following variables:

   lax.stderr.redirect= AND lax.stdout.redirect=

   to be:

   lax.stderr.redirect=output.txt AND
       lax.stdout.redirect= output.txt

5. After a normal installation, edit the LAX file as described in the preceding instructions.
6. This procedure will have to be repeated for each installation.

NOTE For UNIX, set LAX_DEBUG=true. For Mac OS X, open the Console.app.

Reviewing Debug Information

InstallAnywhere debug output will generally appear as in the following sample (truncated):

```
InstallAnywhere 6 Enterprise Build 2262
Wed Dec 10 17:13:04 PST 2003
Current Total Java heap = 24575 kB
Current Free Java heap = 22581 kB
No arguments.
java.class.path = C:\Program Files\InstallAnywhere 6
Enterprise\resource C:\Program Files\InstallAnywhere 6
Enterprise\resource\swingall.jar C:\Program Files\InstallAnywhere 6
Enterprise\resource\compiler.zip C:\Program Files\InstallAnywhere 6
Enterprise\IAClasses.zip C:\Program Files\InstallAnywhere 6
Enterprise\lax.jar C:\program files\installanywhere 6
enterprise\jre\lib\rt.jar
ZGUtil.CLASS_PATH = C:\Program Files\InstallAnywhere 6
Enterprise\resource C:\Program Files\InstallAnywhere 6
Enterprise\resource\swingall.jar
C:\Program Files\InstallAnywhere 6
Enterprise\resource\compiler.zip
C:\Program Files\InstallAnywhere 6
Enterprise\IAClasses.zip C:\Program Files\InstallAnywhere 6
Enterprise\lax.jar
```

```
java.version = 1.3.1
java.vendor = Sun Microsystems Inc.
java.home = c:\program files\InstallAnywhere 6
enterprise\jre\bin\..
java.class.version = 45.3
```

The debug information will show vital information such as the VM in use, the VM version, the locale, the system architecture, operating system, and other features.

Using Output Debug Information Actions

InstallAnywhere offers an Output Debug Information action. This action outputs information stored by, or available to, the installer. This information can be either directed to the standard output, or it can be directed to a file for later review. While all the options available in Output Debug Information have useful purposes, the most useful for troubleshooting are the **Print InstallAnywhere Variables** and **Print Java Properties** options. Both of these options allow easy access to those variables most often used in rules formulation. If developers are experiencing errors related to rules (or, for example, an action is not occurring that should occur), use Output Debug Information to verify the values that InstallAnywhere has perceived for each of the variables and Java properties used by the InstallAnywhere rules.

Debugging Using Display Message Panel

Often, it's desirable to debug some portions of an installation during installer development. One simple feature of InstallAnywhere Enterprise Edition allows developers to add a **Display Message** panel that can display specific InstallAnywhere variable values.

For example:

1. Add a rule that states, `Install Only If $prop.os.name$=Solaris`.
2. The install continues, and the action assigned this rule does not execute.
3. So, add a **Display Message** panel. The message is "The `prop.os.name` is: `$prop.os.name$`."

When the install is run, the value of `prop.os.name` is SunOS, not Solaris; the rule can be reformulated to match the proper name.

CHAPTER 13

Advanced Installer Concepts

- **Console Installers**
- **Silent Installers**

IN CONTEMPORARY INFORMATION systems environments, end-users are likely to find a number of heterogeneous systems. They'll be working with different platforms, different operating environments, and different interaction environments. InstallAnywhere does its best to help you meet the needs of these end-users by presenting installer options that can run in any number of environments.

In enterprise-level environments it's not uncommon for end-users to install applications to servers and other remote systems. In these cases, a rich GUI, such as that provided by InstallAnywhere's standard installer modes, is not always desirable. You may find that your end-users will need a command-line-interface mode installer or even silent installations that require no end-user interaction.

In the InstallAnywhere Enterprise Edition, you'll find support for both Console- and Silent-mode installations. Console mode provides your end-user with a text-only interface similar to that found in ANSI terminal applications. Silent mode provides an automated noninteractive installation mode, which can either run entirely from the defaults set by you, the user, use intelligent logic to determine installation parameters, or read configuration information from a simple response file.

These modes provide enormous flexibility in your installation, allowing you to give end-users a choice of the mode that best meets their needs.

Console Installers

Console-mode installers allow your end-users a nongraphical user interface structured to allow interaction through text only. InstallAnywhere does not automatically provide console alternatives for panels you have added to your installer. You must provide consoles for each panel that you have included.

Console mode is intended to add support for nongraphical environments such as those common on so-called headless UNIX systems. It is not intended for, and does not support, running on Windows systems, although it can be connected to a Windows host via an SSH or TELNET session.

Exercise 13.1 Building a Console-Enabled Installer (Return of OfficeSuite)

In general, InstallAnywhere console actions provide parity with panels provided in the graphical modes. In the next exercise, we'll discuss building console installers and use some of the consoles to reproduce one of our earlier installers.

Console mode mimics the default GUI steps provided by InstallAnywhere and uses standard input and output. The biggest advantage to Console mode is that UNIX developers no longer need X-windows (X11) to run their installers.

Console mode allows text to be output to the console line-by-line. It does not allow for any formatting, clearing of the screen, or positioning of the cursor.

```
+----------------------------------------------------------+
| CHOOSE ALIAS, LINK, SHORTCUT FOLDER                      |
|                                                          |
| Where would you like to create application shortcuts?    |
|                                                          |
| 1) In the Start Menu                                     |
| 2) On the Desktop                                        |
| 3) Don't create shortcuts                                |
|----------------------------------------------------------|
| Please make a selection [1, 2, or 3], and then           |
| press ENTER.                                             |
|----------------------------------------------------------|
```

To trigger a console installer from the command line, type the following command:

```
installername -i console
```

Exercise 13.1 Building a Console-Enabled Installer (Return of OfficeSuite)

NOTE In this exercise we'll build a console-enabled version of our OfficeSuite installer.

1. Open InstallAnywhere and create a new project named OfficeSuite-Console.

2. Open the InstallAnywhere advanced designer.
3. Set up the project similarly to the previous OfficeSuite installer.
   a. Add the OfficeSuite 2000 and Images and Docs directories from the OfficeSuite Source Files directory within your InstallAnywhere installation.
   b. Set up your features, and install sets so that the user is presented with at least two, and preferably three, installation options.
   c. Add the necessary panels in pre-install to enable the users' choice of installation options (**Choose Install Sets**).
   d. Add launchers and set up the classpath for OfficeSuite.
4. Set up the installer to allow the user to use Console mode. In **Installer UI | Look and Feel | General UI Settings**, enable **Console** in the **Allowable UI Modes** section.
5. Switch to the **Pre-Install** task. Click **Add Action**, and select the **Consoles** tab. Add the following console actions:

   ```
   Console: Introduction
   Console: Choose Install Sets
   Console: Choose Install Folder
   Console: Choose Link Folder
   Console: Pre-Install Summary
   Console: Ready to Install
   ```

> **NOTE** While you can insert the consoles anywhere in the install, as long as their order represents what you would like, it's generally best to insert them paired with their graphical equivalent. This helps keep your flow and organization even.

6. Browse to the **Post-Install** section and insert the following consoles:

   ```
   Console: Install Complete
   Console: Install Failed
   ```

7. Add rules to the Install Complete and Install Failed actions so that the appropriate action will display based on the value of the InstallAnywhere variable $INSTALL_SUCCESS$.
8. Rebuild your installer, choosing Linux as one of your target platforms. Ask your IT person for address log-on information to a Linux system where you will test the installer.

9. Ftp the installer to your test system. Run the installer using the following command:

   `sh ./<installername>.bin -i console`

   The -i option tells the installer to default to the mode specified. In most cases, this is necessary, as InstallAnywhere will make an attempt to attach to a graphical environment, unless otherwise directed. You can, however, set default modes by removing the option for an installer to run in graphical mode.

Silent Installers

Silent mode, which enables an installer to run without any user interaction, is fully supported on all UNIX platforms. A near-Silent mode is possible on Windows, and Mac OS X. InstallAnywhere and end-user-defined variables may be set through command-line parameters or a properties file.

To trigger a silent installer from the command line, type the following command:

`installername -i silent`

You may also call a properties file from the command line as follows:

`installername -f <properties file>`

You may use the direct or the relative path to the properties file.

NOTE InstallAnywhere variables may be incorporated into these values, and they will be resolved at install time.

Using Response Files and Silent Installers

Silent mode is an InstallAnywhere UI mode useful for enterprise class systems. In Silent mode, InstallAnywhere has no end-user interaction and runs either on the defaults provided by the developer or by providing a response file from which the installer retrieves the values for various InstallAnywhere variables used to control the install.

The installer automatically checks the directory in which it resides for a file called `installer.properties` or `<installername>.properties`. You can also indicate a properties file for the installer to use by specifying the following command-line switch:

```
-f /path/to/properties file
```

This file utilizes a simple `key=value` format.

For example, the console installer we've previously built has effectively one real option—the installation directory. The properties file might look as follows:

```
INSTALLER_UI=silent
USER_INSTALL_DIR=<select directory>
```

The `INSTALLER_UI` variable allows you to specify the installer mode in the properties file, negating the need to use the −i silent command-line switch.

Exercise 13.2 Building a Silent-Mode Installer

1. Open InstallAnywhere and create a new project.
2. Set up the project.
   a. Create your install files and launcher.
   b. Set the classpath.
3. In **Installer UI | Look and Feel | General UI Settings**, enable Silent in the **Allowable UI Modes** section.
4. Build your installer.
5. Create a properties file called `installer.properties` with the following contents:

   ```
   INSTALLER_UI=silent
   USER_INSTALL_DIR=<select directory>
   ```

6. Place your properties file in the same directory as your executable.
7. Run the installer.
8. Verify the output results. Did the installer install where you expected?

CHAPTER 14
Uninstaller Issues

- **About Uninstaller**
- **Feature Uninstall**
- **Uninstaller for Multiple Products**

DESIGNING YOUR UNINSTALLER is as important as properly designing your installer. Most simple projects will not require much uninstaller customization. However, if you are installing multiple projects, using merge modules, or installing server applications, you may wish to add additional functionality to your uninstaller. In InstallAnywhere 6.0, you can now customize the uninstaller in the same way you can customize the installer.

About Uninstaller

InstallAnywhere automatically creates an uninstaller for the project, which can be removed manually. The InstallAnywhere uninstaller removes all files and actions that occur during the **Files** task of the installation. Actions added in other phases of the installation cannot be removed using the uninstaller and should be accounted for in the install phase.

The uninstaller is much like the installer. It is a collection of panels, consoles, and actions. It keeps track of what the installer has done and contains a record of every action run during install time. All pre-uninstall panels, actions, and consoles run first. Then the uninstall functionality of actions in the **Files** task are called. Lastly, post-uninstall actions are run.

Feature Uninstall

Each installer project has one uninstaller. All features are registered with the uninstaller through a local registry. If the **Choose Feature** panel is included in the uninstaller, the user will be offered the option to uninstall only certain features.

A feature-level uninstall enables end-users to choose specific features to uninstall. If an end-user opts to uninstall a feature that shares a component with a feature not to be uninstalled, the uninstaller recognizes this conflict and does not uninstall the shared component.

Uninstaller for Multiple Products

Each uninstaller is tied to a certain product. It does this through its product ID (found in the **Project | Description** task). In order to have one uninstaller function for a group of separate products, it is necessary that every project have the same product ID. Each separate product should then be "demoted" to a feature. The uninstallers for these separate projects must also share the same uninstaller name and installer location. For example:

Product:	Acme Office Suite (ID: 97338341-1ec9-11b2-90e2-a43171489d33)
Installer 1:	Acme Word Processor and Acme Spreadsheet
Product ID:	97338341-1ec9-11b2-90e2-a43171489d33
Features:	Acme Word Processor and Acme Spreadsheet
Installer 2:	Acme Slide Show
Product ID:	97338341-1ec9-11b2-90e2-a43171489d33
Features:	Acme Slide Show
End Result:	One uninstaller for all three features

CHAPTER 15

Source and Resource Management in InstallAnywhere

- **How Source Paths Work**
- **Managing Source Files**
- **The Resource Manager**

IN TODAY'S SOFTWARE DEVELOPMENT environment, it's very rare that a developer works in a vacuum, alone in a dark room, coding away at a project that he or she will be responsible for from the planning stages to deployment. Development is done by tightly integrated teams, often working in parallel. A core team tweaks the product while those responsible for release and deployment work at creating the deployment packages.

Source paths allow developers to reference file resources using variable paths, instead of absolute paths. This allows you to share a project file with other team members, even when the file resources are located on different paths on other team members' development systems. With source paths, you can even use the same project file on different types of operating systems. For example, you can share a project between UNIX and Windows.

How Source Paths Work

Source paths will automatically be substituted for the most complete path possible. For example, say you have the two following source paths defined:

$SOURCEPATH1$ = D:\temp\dir\foo

$SOURCEPATH2$ = D:\temp

When you add a file such as D:\temp\dir\foo\hello.txt, the file will be referenced by $SOURCEPATH1$/hello.txt because $SOURCEPATH1$ has the most complete path match available.

If a team member opens this project and the source path is not defined, a dialog will appear asking him or her to locate and redefine the source path.

In any project, there are several predefined source paths that cannot be changed or edited:

- IA_HOME is the location on the system where InstallAnywhere is running. A common location might be c:\Program Files\InstallAnywhere.
- $IA_PROJECT$ is the location on the system of the InstallAnywhere project.
- $USER_HOME$ is the User Home folder.

Adding Source Paths

Source paths can be added through the use of Source Path variables in one of two different ways.

1. Go to InstallAnywhere's Preferences area.
    a. Choose **Edit | Preferences**.
    b. Select the **Source Paths** tab.
    c. Click **Add**.
    d. Type the Source Path variable name, such as "Resource," in the table. Do not type dollar signs ($) around the pathname. They will be added automatically when it is used.
    e. Click under **Folder** in the table. A button labeled **Choose Folder** will appear. Click this button to select the target location for the Source Path variable (for example, `c:\resources\test.txt`).
2. Set the System Environment variables.
    a. Access the Environment variables. On Windows, right-click on **My Computer** on the Desktop, choose **Properties**, choose **Advanced**, and click **Environment Variables**. On UNIX or Mac OS X, modify the proper shell configuration file or set the variable directly using the shell.
    b. Add an Environment variable for the source path, prepended with the IA_PATH_ tag. For example, to set the variable SOURCE_PATH, set the Environment variable to IA_PATH_SOURCE_PATH.

Updating the Location of Files and Resources

When the location of a file or folder has changed, simply change the folder location listed for the source path. By changing the source path to the new location, InstallAnywhere will update the references to the resources automatically.

If you open a project and InstallAnywhere cannot find the resources because they either have moved or no longer exist, you will be asked to locate the resource or remove the resource from the project. If you want to open a project without updating the location of the resource, change the **Project Loading** preference found on the **General Settings** tab after setting **Edit | Preferences** to **Never**. Projects will be opened without checking the location of each resource. Instead, resources will be checked only when you build.

With this in mind, InstallAnywhere introduced features designed to help you manage resources shared between developers—from file resources included in the installer, to project files themselves, to individual component packages that can be merged into a single larger installer or suite installer.

Managing Source Files

Normally, InstallAnywhere uses absolute paths to reference your product's included files and other resources added to your installer. This means that, by default, your installer must be built with all files in the same location as when they were added to the project. This is enforced by a component of the InstallAnywhere designer called the InstallAnywhere resource manager.

The Resource Manager

The resource manager helps you keep track of files that are needed for your installation and will prompt you to find those files or add them to the project if they are missing. In its default mode, the resource manager checks to see if necessary files are present when projects are loaded, saved, or built; however, this behavior can be altered under Preferences. Open **Edit | Preferences** or click the **About InstallAnywhere** button on the initial screens, then select the **Preferences** button from that screen. This will take you to the InstallAnywhere **Preferences Control** panel. From this panel you can manage many of the features of InstallAnywhere, including the behavior of the resource manager.

Resource manager settings can be found on the **General Settings** tab within the **Preferences** panel. The two settings here that affect resource manager behavior are

- **Project loading:** Check **always** or **never** to determine if the resource manager should check for specified resources when the project is loaded. If **never** is selected, the InstallAnywhere advanced designer will allow you to work with a project file regardless of whether the resources specified in the project are present at their specified locations.
- **Command-line builds:** This option affects the way that Install-Anywhere's resource manager will treat resources missing when a command-line build is executed. By default, the build will fail, requiring you to add or return the resources to their specified locations. Selecting **Continue without the missing files** will allow the installer to build without the files.

Adding Source Path Management Capability to Your Installer Project

InstallAnywhere enables team development while working on installers. Use this feature to share an installer project across your entire development team, working with common source control management (SCM) tools. Instead of having to map the entire project to one machine, InstallAnywhere leverages Source Path Management variables so that developers can work on the same project file in disparate computing environments.

Source paths resolve to the most complete value:

If $TEMP$ = D:\temp\dir\fred

And TMP = D:\temp

The file D:\temp\dir\fred\hello.txt becomes $TEMP$\hello.txt and not TMP\dir\fred \hello.txt.

Enabling/Disabling Source Paths

To enable or disable any of these source paths, click **Edit | Preferences | Source Paths** and select which option you would like.

Default Source Paths

There are three default source paths in any project that cannot be changed or edited:

- `$IA_HOME$` is the location on your system where you are running InstallAnywhere. A common location might be `c:\Program Files\InstallAnywhere`.
- `$IA_PROJECT$` is the location on your system of you InstallAnywhere project.
- `$USER_HOME$` is the User Home directory on all platforms except the classic Mac OS.

Adding Source Paths

Source paths can be added through the use of variables.

1. Go to the **Edit** menu.
   a. Choose **Edit | Preferences** and then select the **Source Paths** tab.
   b. Click **Add**.
   c. Type the access pathname, such as "Resource," in the textbox.
   d. Type the folder path in the space allotted (for example, `c:\resources\test.txt`).

NOTE Do not type dollar signs ($) around source paths when you add them into Preferences.

2. Modify the `PathManager.properties` file.
   a. Go to `InstallAnywhere\resource\preferences` and open the `PathManager.properties` file.
   b. Add any number of source paths and precede each one with the IA_PATH tag; the Resource example would look like `$IA_PATH_RESOURCE$`.
3. Set the System Environment variables.
   a. Access your Environment variables. On Windows, right-click on **My Computer** on the Desktop, choose **Properties**, choose **Advanced**, and click **Environment Variables**.

b. Add source paths. These are stored in the same format as the source paths created in the Preferences area of InstallAnywhere.

Using Source Paths in Your Project
Go to the **Files** task and add the file `test.txt` that is in your Resources directory.

Switching Access Path Locations
When the location of a file or folder is changed, simply change the location where you have listed your source paths. By pointing your source path to the new location, your installer will update its resources automatically.

Exercise 15.1 Creating Source Paths
Add the following user-defined source path and enable the following default source paths.

1. **OFFICE_SOURCE (user-defined):** Point this source path to the following directory.

   `<InstallAnywhere root>/OfficeSuiteSourceFiles`

2. **IA_PROJECT_DIR (predefined):** This will point to the directory in which your project file resides.

Managing Resources in the InstallAnywhere Project File
While not recommended as a best practice per se, it is possible to manage resources directly from the project file itself.

InstallAnywhere versions after InstallAnywhere 5.0 utilize a new XML project file format (previous versions of the software utilize a binary format based on a Java class file).

As the `.xml_iap` file is essentially a plain-text file, it is possible to manipulate it directly. The file can be managed using simple search and replace techniques, or using more advanced functions such as `sed` or `awk` scripts or even an Extensible Stylesheet Language Transform, or XSLT.

Quick Quiz

1. Which of the following are valid ways to set source paths?
   A. Using the **Edit** menu (in the advanced designer)
   B. Modifying the `PathManager.properties` file
   C. Setting System Environment variables
   D. All of the above

2. What must be prepended to an Environment variable to make it a valid source path?
   A. `IA_SOURCE_`
   B. `IA_PATH_`
   C. `SOURCE_PATH_`

Quick Quiz answers are located in Appendix J.

CHAPTER 16
Advanced Interface Options

- **Installer Panel Additions**

IN EARLIER SECTIONS of this book, we discussed some basic interface customizations. In this chapter, we'll discuss advanced modifications to both the flow of the installer interface and to the graphical interface itself.

Installer Panel Additions

InstallAnywhere allows you to modify the appearance of the installer panels to convey information to your user or to present a branded image for your product (or both, should you so desire).

We've already discussed customizing the background and splash screen images for an installer. You can also customize the appearance of the area on the left-hand side of an installer panel. This area can contain a consistent image, an image that differs for each panel, a list of installer steps that serves as a progress indicator, or a combination of images and labels.

Panel Images

In **Project | Look and Feel | Installer Panel Additions**, you can customize the appearance of the left-side panel. You can choose whether the addition will include images or a list of installer steps. You can also opt to include borders and background images.

Panel Labels

This task also allows you to specify the order in which labels will appear and the icon image (such as an arrow) that will appear beside them. These labels are highlighted and marked as the installation progresses. You can allow the installer build process to autopopulate the list based on the panel titles you've entered, or you can manually assign panels to a label in the settings found in each panel's customizer. To control label order or to edit the content of a label, use the arrows and other control buttons found to the left of the list of panels.

NOTE Using the **Project | Look and Feel | Installer Panel Additions** tab and the **Label Settings** tab found on each individual panel's customizer, you can assign multiple panels to the same label. Thus, if you have numerous steps or if your installer may have several panels for the same step, you can tweak the interface to meet your needs.

Advanced Installer Interface Actions

In previous segments we covered the use and implementations of the **Get User Input** panel and mentioned the **Advanced Get User Input** panel. Here, we'll discuss the features of the **Advanced Get User Input** panel in more depth.

The **Get User Input—Advanced** panel, unlike its little brother, **Get User Input—Simple**, allows you to create panels that include more than one type of data and store that information in more than one variable.

This allows you, for example, to create a panel that collects registration information using the following:

- Text fields for first name, last name, company, street, address, and Zip/postal code
- Pop-up menu for state/province and country
- Check boxes for preferred contact method

The **Advanced Get User Input** panel interface is complex. Each element is added based on type, then configured individually. If the elements added require more space than the graphic panel allows, the panel will add a scrollbar. You can use the **Preview** button to see the layout of your fields.

Using Jump Actions and Logic

Within a specific task, InstallAnywhere allows you to jump back and forth based on a combination of jump actions, jump labels, and InstallAnywhere rules.

You can create conditions where end-users must repeat a task or meet certain criteria before they can progress with the installation. You can also allow end-users to skip over a large portion of the configuration options if they merely want to accept all of your defaults.

Jump actions are created by inserting jump labels at places in the install that you want to be able to jump to. These labels function much like

HTML target or anchors. In the location where you would like the jump to occur, place a jump action. This action (you'll need to add conditional rules to it or your end-user will constantly be jumping) allows you to jump to the target specified.

Exercise 16.1 Creating Installer Logic Using Jump Labels and Actions

In this exercise, we'll use the advanced features that we've implemented so far in this segment.

Create an installer that does the following:

1. Retrieves information from an end-user. The **Input** panel should use at least three input types.
2. Presents the information to the end-user for verification. If the end-user does not accept the information, it returns them to the **Input** panel.
3. Writes the collected information to a file.
4. Offers the end-user the option to enter more information.
5. Returns to the initial **Input** panel if the end-user chooses to enter more info.
6. Modifies the labels so that your configuration process shares one label.

Quick Quiz

1. What happens if your **Get User Input** panel fields exceed the allotted space?
    A. The panel scrolls.
    B. The information splits into two panels.
    C. The installer deletes everything it cannot display.
2. Multiple labels can be assigned to the same action or panel.
    A. True
    B. False

Quick Quiz answers are located in Appendix J.

CHAPTER 17

Advanced Organizational Concepts

- **Integrating the Find Component in Registry Action**
- **Merge Modules and Templates**
- **Importing a Design-Time Merge Module**

Integrating the Find Component in Registry Action

If your installer uses a component already installed on your target system or one that already should be, you can use InstallAnywhere's Find Component in Registry (referring to the InstallAnywhere registry, not the Windows registry) action to locate that component. You can then utilize that component in your installation or use that installation location as a path within your installation.

This action allows you to find an existing component using the Universal Unique Identifier, or UUID, specified for the component. You can then request that the installer find only the highest version, that it compare versions, or that it search for the key file. The action sorts the count of components found, the versions found, and the locations found in variables specified by you.

Merge Modules and Templates

Merge modules allow for the easy creation of suite installers, subinstallers, and templates, delivering reusability from project to project, within development teams, across the enterprise, or from third-party providers.

A suite installer is an installer for a suite of applications. Each application in a suite may be collected in a merge module so that they may be easily added to a different mix of applications.

Templates are generally used as starting points for installer projects. Installer items that remain unchanged, such as the **License Agreement** panel, would be saved in an InstallAnywhere template. You may also want to create a template to maintain the look and feel of your installer projects.

Merge Modules

Merge modules are essentially installer subprojects that can be created independently of one another and later merged. Like an installer, a merge module is a reusable collection of installation functionality, complete with features, components, panels, actions, and files. However, a merge module cannot be installed on its own; instead, developers use merge modules when they want to include the functionality of one installer within another installer.

Merge modules provide the following benefits and solutions to complex installation requirements:

- You can combine several merge modules from different products to create a suite installer.
- Independent development teams in different locations can create merge modules for different software components. A release engineer can combine those merge modules into a single product installer.
- You can create self-contained units of installer functionality for reuse in future installer projects. For instance, if the same software component needs to be in several different installers, build it into a merge module and make it available to all of the installer developers.
- You can save common installer functionality, such as **License Agreement** panels and **Custom User Input** panels, into merge modules to simplify future installer project creation.
- You can combine merge modules from third-party software packages to build complex software solutions without having to figure out how to install each individual package.

NOTE Zero G provides many third-party merge modules on its Web site. See www.ZeroG.com to download them.

- You can use a merge module as the starting point for a new installer project. These merge modules are referred to as templates and are covered in the "Templates" section below.
- You can build any installer project into a merge module, and you can use any merge module within any other installer project.
- Merge modules are created as an option through the installer build process. Because merge modules contain all of the resources for a project, building them is just like building an installer. They can be built automatically when the installer is built, or they can be built

explicitly from the advanced designer (check the **Build Merge Module** option on the **Build** task under the **Distribution** tab) or from the command line (use the +merge option).

Merge modules can be merged into an existing installer in one of two ways:

1. In the **Organization | Modules** task, click **Import Merge Module** to merge a merge module into the current installer. All of the merge module's features, components, files, actions, and panels (optionally) will be combined into the current project, allowing developers to further customize any settings.
2. Merge modules can also be installed as self-contained subinstaller units without merging them into the current project. This is useful if developers do not know what a merge module will contain or if they will not be modifying any settings. Merge modules added in this manner are run as silent subinstallers.

Merge modules can be integrated with a project in one of two ways:

1. Use the Install Merge Module action and select **Bundle Merge Module at Build Time** if the merge module is available when you are ready to build the installer. These merge modules will be included in the actual generated installer.
2. Use the Install Merge Module action and select **Locate Merge Module at Install Time** to have the installer install a merge module that is available at install time, but external to the installer. The merge module can be stored on either the end-user's system or CD-ROM. If the location is a folder that contains several merge modules, they will all be installed.

Other important things to know about merge modules include the following:

- **Read-only option:** Merge modules can be locked to prevent them from being opened, used as templates, or merged into an installer. Read-only merge modules can only be installed as self-contained installer units.

- **Optimize merge module size by platform option:** Separate merge modules will be created for each platform. Each will contain only the resources needed for that specific platform. Do not use this option if merge modules will be imported into another installer. Importing a merge module requires a nonoptimized merge module.
- **Advertised variables:** These InstallAnywhere variables must be set before a merge module can be installed using the Install Merge Module action. On the **Build** task, under the **Distribution** tab, click **Edit Advertised Variables** to add variables, set default values, and add comments. Use advertised variables to inform master installers of settings required for a merge module's configuration.
- **InstallAnywhere variables:** These can be passed to the merge module when using the Install Merge Module action. Only selected variables will be passed to the merge module. By default, any advertised variable set by the merge module (advertised variables are set when the module is built) will be automatically passed in. Specific variables can also be passed in through the customizer of the merge module. For example, if the Magic Folder variable $IA_PROJECT_DIR$ was advertised by the merge module, it will be passed in. If the variable $OTHER_VARIABLE$ was not advertised, but was set in the customizer of the Install Merge Module action, it, too, would be passed in.

Templates

A template is the starting point for every new installer project. A template can be a simple empty project, or it can contain everything a regular project would contain, such as license agreements, custom graphics and billboards, and even files.

A template is simply a merge module that has been placed within the iatemplates folder inside the InstallAnywhere installation folder. When you create a new project, you have the option of starting from a template. When you start from a template, a copy of the template is created and saved.

Templates are great for large installer teams, where you want everyone to have a consistent starting point, or for starting a new project based upon an older one.

Merge Module Types

Design-Time Merge Modules

Use design-time merge modules to integrate a merge module into your main installer project. Once a merge module has been imported, it is fully integrated into your master project file; all files, actions, and panels will appear as if they were a part of your main installer project. Merged projects may be added and removed; however, any changes that are made once they've been imported will be lost if you remove a merged project from the suite.

For example, if you import a merge module into your master installer and then modify a few panels, when you save the project, those changes will be saved. If you remove the imported merge module from the suite, all of those changes will be lost, regardless of how many times your main installer project is saved.

Design-time merge modules display all panels you add to the project. They are the only merge module type that is not run silently.

> **NOTE** Only nonoptimized merge modules may be imported as design-time merge modules.

Build-Time Merge Modules

A build-time merge module is included in your installer at build time and installed by the master installer. Unlike install-time merge modules, build-time merge modules are included with the master installer when you build the installer project. At install time, the master installer will install the build-time merge module. To specify that the merge module be build-time, select the option labeled **Bundle Merge Module at Build Time** from the Install Merge Module action customizer and pick a merge module with the **Choose Merge Module** button.

Build-time merge modules are packaged along with the master installer project in one .iap_xml file. Build-time suite installers can build a number of separate installers into a single executable. In this scenario, a single master installer runs a number of merge modules silently during the installation process. The master installer is responsible for the user interface and for passing properties files to the merge modules so that they run with the correct configuration information. The merge modules may also advertise specific properties they require to operate properly.

Install-Time Merge Modules

The main installer executes install-time merge modules at install time. They are external to the main installer project. At install time, the master installer looks for the merge module at the specified path and launches whatever merge module it finds there. If the install-time merge module path points to a directory, then all merge modules contained in that directory will be installed. This enables you to update suite installers without having to update the master installer package

To specify that the merge module will be an install-time merge module, select the **Locate Merge Module at Install Time** option from the Install Merge Module action customizer and then enter a path in the text field next to it.

NOTE Merge modules cannot be authenticated. If you need authentication for a merge module, add it to your main installer project. Then, the merge module will inherit this setting during the installation.

Creating Merge Modules and Templates

You create merge modules and templates in much the same way as regular installers. Add any panels, actions, and rules just as you would for a typical installer project, then before building the **Build | Distribution | Merge Module/Template Option**, select **Build Merge Module/Template**. Once merge modules are built, they have almost the same contents as a regular installer project, except they don't contain an `IAClasses.zip` file or a launcher.

Build Options

When you have an InstallAnywhere project ready to be made into a merge module, go to the **Build | Distribution | Merge Module/Template Option**. Select **Build Merge Module/Template**. Build options are used to optimize the size of the merge module, define whether it is to be read-only, and edit the advertised variables for the merge module.

Merge Module Size
Merge modules will contain an approximation of their required size (based on the largest amount of space any given module could need), but you may override this size with your own calculation by setting an advertised variable. The variable $DISK_SPACE_REQUIRED$ may be set to override the automatic approximation.

Creating Merge Modules as Read-Only
You have the option of designating merge modules as read-only. This option protects their integrity; they can only be added to an installer project through the Install Merge Module action. A read-only module cannot be integrated with the main installer project using the **Project | Modules** task.

Advertised Variables
The Advertised Variables area lists all variables in a merge module installer project. The main installer project can pass InstallAnywhere variables to a merge module at install time. The merge module will then use these variables as regular InstallAnywhere variables.

To add your own variables to be passed to a merge module, go to the customizer for the Install Merge Module action in the designer, and click **Edit Variables** to add some variables.

There may be cases, however, when the merge module cannot run without some variables having already been set. Those variables should be advertised so the merge module can be configured easily. To do this, click **Edit Advertised Variables** on the **Build Settings** tab and set up your variables.

Now, if you go to the main installer project, add a merge module, and look at the settings for variables that will be passed to the merge module, you will see that the names of advertised variables have been added to your list and some may have been set to default values. Change the values as you like, and these will be passed to the merge module at install time.

Adding Advertised Variables

To add advertised variables, go to the **Build** task and then select **Build Settings**. Click **Edit Advertised Variables**. The **Edit Advertised Variables** dialog appears.

NOTE In the **Edit Advertised Variables** dialog, list all variables to be set in the installer project.

The variable name is the same as that defined for the merge module. The value is the corresponding value in the main installer project. For example, if you included the common Magic Folder $IA_PROJECT_DIR$ in your merge module, and you wanted that to correspond with the value of $IA_PROJECT_DIR$ in the main installer project, the variable name and value would both be $IA_PROJECT_DIR$.

NOTE Variables in InstallAnywhere must be expressed with dollar signs ($) on either side.

Adding Merge Modules

To add a merge module, go to the **Files** task and click **Add Action**. Select **Install Merge Module**, and click **Add**. For information on the merge module action customizer, please see the "Merge Module Customizer" section below.

Importing a Design-Time Merge Module

To import a merge module, perform the following steps:

1. Choose **Organization | Modules** and then click **Import Merge Module**.
2. Navigate to a <productname>.iam_zip file, select it, and click **Open**. The **Import Settings** dialog appears.
3. Select the tasks you'd like to import. You can import just the **Files** task panels and actions (the default choice) or any combination of pre-install, files, and post-install panels and actions.

> **NOTE** Merging pre-install actions will result in duplicate actions. We recommend that you not merge the **Pre-Install** task for this reason, or if you do, that you take care to clean up any duplicate actions.

4. Choose how to import the product features of this merge module.

   If you choose to import each feature as a top-level feature, each will be given equal weight hierarchically. If you choose to import each feature as the child of a new feature, a new feature will be created titled **<MergeModuleName>**, with all of the merge module features appearing below it hierarchically.

5. Click **OK**.

   The merged project appears on the **Suite** tab. The panels and actions you have merged should appear in their respective tasks, with an added "M" badge on their icons to identify their merge module status.

Merge Module Customizer

The merge module customizer will be populated automatically with the information about the merge module. You may add comments or notes in the textbox provided.

Exercise 17.1 Creating Merge Modules

1. Create a merge module that can be used to install OfficeSuite as a part of a larger install.
2. Create an OfficeSuite installer without graphical elements.
3. Set up the advertised variables so that the user can access the Office-Suite install options from the master installer.
4. Build your OfficeSuite merge module.
5. Build a "fake" master installer to pass information to your OfficeSuite Installer as a subinstaller.
6. Import your OfficeSuite merge module into a master project.

Quick Quiz

1. Which merge module type will allow you to modify your files in the advanced designer?
   A. Design-time
   B. Build-time
   C. Install-time

2. Which merge module type will be included in the master uninstaller?
   A. Design-time
   B. Build-time
   C. Install-time

3. Which types of merge modules can be used in a silent installer?
   A. Design-time
   B. Build-time
   C. Install-time
   D. All of the above

4. Which answers are reasons to use an installer template?
   A. To have an installer project that contains standard panels, graphics, and files
   B. To maintain the look and feel of installers
   C. To create an installer for a suite of applications
   D. All of the above

Quick Quiz answers are located in Appendix J.

CHAPTER 18

Integrating InstallAnywhere with Automated Build Environments

- **InstallAnywhere Command-Line Build Facility**
- **Build Tools**
- **Exit Codes**
- **ANT Build Integration**

INSTALLANYWHERE'S CURRENT DISTRIBUTIONS include a number of features that can be utilized to integrate your deployment project into an automated build environment or process. This includes the ability to build your project from a headless system, make some modifications to the project without utilizing the InstallAnywhere advanced designer, and add a task that will allow you to integrate InstallAnywhere with the Apache Jakarta Project's ANT Java build tool.

InstallAnywhere Command-Line Build Facility

The InstallAnywhere Enterprise and Standard editions include functionality that allows you to perform command-line builds. This allows you to build your completed project without instantiating InstallAnywhere's graphical advanced designer interface.

The command-line build facility comes in the form of a second executable called `build` (`Build.exe` on Windows systems). This executable takes the full path to an InstallAnywhere `.iap_xml` file as an argument and, by default, will simply build the installer as specified in the project file.

For example, to build the OfficeSuite Installer that we've been developing throughout this book, you might use a command line similar to the following:

```
C:> "C:\Program Files\InstallAnywhere 6 Enterprise\build.exe" "C:\OfficeSuite\OfficeSuite.iap_xml"
```

In this case, the installer build will occur with the settings stored in the project file from the last build or save of the project.

There are times at which you may want to build an installer with different settings than those stored in the project file. Obviously, you could simply open the project file, make the changes, and build the project. However, the `build` executable also accepts additional parameters that allow you to make a number of changes to the build settings of the installer.

Build Tools

A build properties file template named `Build.properties` can be found in your InstallAnywhere application folder inside `resource/build`. Table 18.1 lists some build tool options.

Table 18.1 Build Tool Options (Part 1)

Option	Description
-v	Print InstallAnywhere product version C:\Program Files\InstallAnywhere 6 Enterprise>build.exe -v InstallAnywhere 6 Enterprise
-p	Use the specified build properties file (more information on the Build.properties can be found in Table 18.2)
+	Add platform to build
-	Remove platform from build

The arguments listed in Table 18.2 modify the add (+) and remove (−) platforms arguments.

Table 18.2 Build Tool Options (Part 2)

Option	Description
a,A	AIX without VM option
av,AV	AIX with VM option
h,H	HP-UX without VM option
hv,HV	HP-UX with VM option
j,J,o,O	Pure Java option
l,L	Linux without VM option
lv,LV	Linux with VM option
s,S	Solaris without VM option
sv,SV	Solaris with VM option
u,U	Generic UNIX without VM option
n,N	Named UNIX without VM option
nv,NV	Named UNIX with VM option

Table 18.2 Build Tool Options (Part 2) (Continued)

Option	Description
w,W	Windows without VM option
wv,WV	Windows with VM option
x,X	Mac OS X without VM option
web	Build Web installers
cd	Build CD-ROM installers
opt	Optimize by platform
merge	Build merge modules

Exit Codes

The command-line build tool returns an exit code based upon the results of the build as shown in Tables 18.3 to 18.9.

Table 18.3 Resource-Related Exit Codes

Code	Status
cancelled1	Missing resources; build abort cancelled by preferences

Table 18.4 Project File–Related Exit Codes

Code	Status
101	Project load error
102	Project copy load error
103	Project file not found
104	Project file is read-only
199	Project file unknown error

Table 18.5 Command Line Options–Related Exit Codes

Code	Status
200	Illegal build flag
201	Insufficient build flag

Table 18.6 VM Pack–Related Exit Codes

Code	Status
300	VM Pack replaced
301	VM Pack not found
302	VM Pack illegal format
399	VM Pack unknown error

Table 18.7 File Write Errors

Code	Status
400	File write not found
401	File write busy
402	File write protected
403	File write error
499	File write unknown error

Table 18.8 File Read Errors

Code	Status
500	File read not found
501	File read busy
502	File read protected
503	File read error
599	File read unknown error

Table 18.9 Other Errors

Code	Status
-1	Other error/unknown error
0	No errors; build completed successfully without errors or warnings
666	Insufficient rights in directory
799	Unknown internal error

Examples

To build installers for `MyProduct` project with the previously saved build settings, use the following:

`build MyProduct.iap_xml`

To build installers for `MyProduct` project overriding the saved build settings for that project with a build properties file, use the following:

`build MyProduct.iap_xml -p Build.properties`

To build installers for `MyProduct` project overriding the build platforms and building for Mac OS X and Linux only (turning all others off), use the following:

`build MyProduct.iap_xml +x +l -s -j -w -u`

ANT Build Integration

ANT is a powerful, Java-based build tool developed by the Apache Foundation's Jakarta Project. It can be used to control complex build tasks in Java and other development environments. ANT manages specific actions though tasks that can either be part of the core ANT distribution or available as extensions.

InstallAnywhere comes with an **ANT** task to build installers from ANT. The InstallAnywhere **ANT** task is located in your InstallAnywhere application folder inside `resource`, then inside `build`. Add `iaant.jar` to your classpath when executing ANT to access the InstallAnywhere **ANT** task.

ANT uses an XML file to specify the order of tasks for your build process. More information on ANT can be found on the Apache Foundation's Jakarta Project Web site.

Task Name and Class

The InstallAnywhere **ANT** task is specified as follows:

```
<taskdef name="buildinstaller" classname=
"com.zerog.ia.integration.ant.InstallAnywhereAntTask"/>
```

This task can be found inside the `iaant.jar` file in your InstallAnywhere application folder, inside `resource`, then inside `build`.

Parameters

After defining the task, specify any parameters necessary for the build settings:

```
<buildinstaller
  IAlocation="C:\Program Files\InstallAnywhere 6 Enterprise"
  IAProjectFile="C:\Projects\myproject.iap_xml"
  additionalparameter=value
/>
```

Replace the `IAlocation` with the absolute path to your own InstallAnywhere application folder. If InstallAnywhere cannot be found, ANT will search for it in one of the default locations or look in the registry to find where InstallAnywhere was installed.

Specify the path and filename of the project to build in the `IAProjectFile` parameter.

All other properties are optional. The parameters closely match the properties found in the build properties file described above. Table 18.10 shows the available parameters.

Table 18.10 Platform Target Parameters

Attribute	Description	Required
IAProjectFile	Specifies the location of the InstallAnywhere project that you want to build	Yes
IALocation	Specifies the location where InstallAnywhere is installed	No*
propertiesfile	Specifies the location of a `Build.properties` file you can use (if used, all other attributes are ignored)	No
failonerror	Stops the build process if the command exits with a return code other than 0 (defaults to `false`)	No

* If `IALocation` is not specified, the task will search for a copy of InstallAnywhere to run against. If InstallAnywhere is not installed in one of the default locations, then the task will check the InstallAnywhere product registry for a valid location.]

NOTE Remember, in order for the InstallAnywhere **ANT** task to work, you will need to add `iaant.jar` to $ANT_HOME/lib.

Tables 18.11 to 18.13 list the various platform, build, and installer options available.

Table 18.11 Platform Options

Option	Value
BuildLinuxWithVM	true/false
BuildLinuxWithoutVM	true/false
LinuxVMPackLocation	Path
BuildHPUXWithVM	true/false
BuildHPUXWithoutVM	true/false
HPUXVMPackLocation	Path
BuildAIXWithVM	true/false
BuildAIXWithoutVM	true/false
AIXVMPackLocation	Path
BuildSolarisWithVM	true/false
BuildSolarisWithoutVM	true/false
SolarisVMPackLocation	Path
BuildNamedUNIXWithVM	true/false
BuildNamedUNIXWithoutVM	true/false
NamedUNIXVMPackLocation	Path
NamedUNIXTitle	Path
BuildWindowsWithVM	true/false
BuildWindowsWithoutVM	true/false
WindowsVMPackLocation	Path
BuildMacOSX	true/false
BuildPureJava	true/false

ANT Build Integration

Table 18.12 Build Options

Option	Value
BuildCDROMInstaller	true/false
BuildWebInstaller	true/false
BuildMergeModule	true/false
BuildReadOnlyMergeModule	true/false
BuildOutputLocation	Path
OptimizeCDROMInstaller	true/false
OptimizeWebInstaller	true/false
OptimizeMergeModule	true/false
AutoPopulateLabels	true/false
AutoCleanComponents	true/false

Table 18.13 Installer Options

Option	Value
InstallerStdErrRedirect	Path
InstallerStdoutRedirect	Path
InstallerValidVMList	String
InstallerInitialHeapSize	Integer
InstallerMaxHeapSize	Integer
UNIXDefaultUI	Silent/Console/GUI

Examples

```
<taskdef name="buildinstaller" classname=
"com.zerog.ia.integration.ant.InstallAnywhereAntTask"/>
<buildinstaller

  IAlocation="C:\Program Files\InstallAnywhere 6 Enterprise"

  IAProjectFile="C:\Projects\myproject.iap_xml"

  BuildLinuxWithVM="true"
  BuildMacOSX="true"
  BuildWebInstallers="true"
  OptimizeWebInstallers="true"
  InstallerStdErrRedirect="C:\console.txt"
  />
```

CHAPTER 19
Custom Code

- **Writing Custom Code**

THE MAJORITY OF TASKS NEEDED TO DEPLOY the application can be handled using InstallAnywhere's built-in actions and panels. If there is functionality not covered by InstallAnywhere's built-in actions and panels, developers can create their own custom components using the Custom Code Application Programming Interface (API).

InstallAnywhere offers an open API that allows developers to write Java code that can run within InstallAnywhere's architecture. Using the API also gives access to additional functionality in InstallAnywhere, such as its unique variables and resource-loading features. Developers can use the API to create custom actions and GUI elements that seamlessly interact with and extend the InstallAnywhere framework.

All custom code that is going to run within the InstallAnywhere framework must be written in Java. The major forms of custom code are actions, panels, consoles, and rules.

- **Custom code actions:** These actions run within InstallAnywhere's action framework alongside the default InstallAnywhere actions.
- **Custom code panels:** These panels run within InstallAnywhere's graphical interface during the installation process. The developer can use the Custom Code API to add panels to the installer that are not provided among InstallAnywhere's default panels.
- **Custom code consoles:** These actions run within InstallAnywhere's console interface during the installation process. Developers can use the Custom Code API to add custom console elements to the installer.
- **Custom code rules:** These rules are evaluated when the actions they are associated with are about to be executed. Custom code rules need to return a Boolean value defining whether the action is to be run.

Zero G Software provides sample custom code actions, panels, consoles, and rules in the Custom Code folder in the root installation directory of InstallAnywhere. These samples can be used as examples of how to implement InstallAnywhere custom code using the API. Additionally, a wide variety of custom code actions and panels are located in the Downloads | Add-Ons | Custom Code area of the Zero G Web site.

Writing Custom Code

Custom Code Actions

Custom code actions allow you to create nongraphical actions that can manipulate data on your target system, affect InstallAnywhere variables, prepopulate various install options, or even execute native code (via JNI or native executions). In fact, custom code actions allow you to perform nearly any action possible with Java.

A Custom Code Action Example

This section describes how to write your own custom code action and leads you through an example (called com.zerog.ia.customcode.samples.SampleAction). This section doesn't explain how to make your code work with InstallAnywhere's advanced designer or the Execute Custom Code action.

NOTE We assume that you know the goals of your action, but have not yet written any code to implement it. After each relevant step, we will show an example of how this can be done.

1. Create your main class file and package it. This is the file that you will specify in the **Class** field in the InstallAnywhere advanced designer (see Chapter 20).

   ```
   package com.zerog.ia.customcode.samples;
   ```

2. To create a custom action, your class must first extend the abstract class com.zerog.ia.api.pub.CustomCodeAction. This class provides the interface through which you will interact with the InstallAnywhere runtime.

   ```
   package com.zerog.ia.customcode.samples;

   import com.zerog.ia.api.pub.*;

   public class SampleAction extends CustomCodeAction
   {
     public void install(InstallerProxy ip) {}
     public void uninstall(UninstallerProxy up) {}
     public String getInstallStatusMessage() {}
     public String getUninstallStatusMessage() {}
   }
   ```

3. Description of public void install (InstallerProxy ip) {}.

The installer calls this method at the point during installation where the custom code action was added. The InstallerProxy instance provides methods to access installer information, set installation status, and control installation flow. SampleAction will display a message to the end-user in a modal dialog.

```
package com.zerog.ia.customcode.samples;

import com.zerog.ia.api.pub.*;
import java.awt.*;
import java.awt.event.*;
public class SampleAction extends CustomCodeAction
implements ActionListener
{
   public void install(InstallerProxy ip){
     // Get Some Variables from the Variable Manager
     String title = ip.substitute ("$SAMPLE_ACTION_TITLE$");
     String msg = ip.substitute ("$SAMPLE_ACTION_MESSAGE$");

     Label l = new Label (msg);

     Button b = new Button ("Close");
     // For internationalization, the button label could be
     // externalized and referenced as follows:
     //
     // Button b = new Button (ip.getValue
     ("SampleAction.Close"));
     b.addActionListener (this);

     // Here we create a dummy Frame to use as the parent
     // for the Dialog - it is never shown.
     Frame myFrame = new Frame();

     Dialog myDialog = new Dialog (myFrame, title, true);
     Dimension bounds = Toolkit.getDefaultToolkit
     ().getScreenSize();

     myDialog.setLayout(new BorderLayout());

     myDialog.add(BorderLayout.NORTH, l);
     myDialog.add(BorderLayout.CENTER, b);
     myDialog.pack();

     // Here we center the Dialog
     Rectangle abounds = myDialog.getBounds();
```

```
          myDialog.setLocation((bounds.width - abounds.width) / 2,
          (bounds.height - abounds.height) / 2);

          myDialog.show();
      }
      public void uninstall(UninstallerProxy up) { }
      public String getInstallStatusMessage() { }
      public String getUninstallStatusMessage() { }
      public void actionPerformed(ActionEvent ae)
      {
        // Dispose the dialog and its hidden parent frame.
        Button source = (Button) ae.getSource();
        Dialog parent = (Dialog) source.getParent();
        Frame fparent = (Frame) parent.getParent();
        parent.dispose();
        fparent.dispose();
      }
   }
```

4. Description of `public void uninstall (UninstallerProxy up) {}`.

   This method is called by the uninstaller at uninstall time before the deletion of any files. The UninstallerProxy instance provides access to any information written at install time. SampleAction will display a small window with a message.

```
public void uninstall(UninstallerProxy up)
{
   String title = "Uninstall";

   Button b = new Button("Close");
   b.addActionListener(this);

   Frame myFrame = new Frame();

   Dialog myDialog = new Dialog (myFrame, title, true);
   Dimension bounds =
   Toolkit.getDefaultToolkit().getScreenSize()

   myDialog.setLayout(new BorderLayout());

   myDialog.add(BorderLayout.NORTH, l);
   myDialog.add(BorderLayout.CENTER, b);
   myDialog.pack();

   // Here we center the Dialog
   Rectangle abounds = myDialog.getBounds();
```

```
      myDialog.setLocation((bounds.width - abounds.width) / 2,
      (bounds.height - abounds.height) / 2);

      myDialog.show();
   }
```

5. Description of `public String getInstallStatusMessage() {}`.

   The installer calls this message to display a status message in the progress bar during installation. The message is displayed while the `install (InstallerProxy ip)` method is called. The method has no effect if the action is a pre-install or post-install action.

   ```
   public String getInstallStatusMessage()
   {
      return "Displaying a small installation message...";
   }
   ```

6. Description of `public String getUninstallStatusMessage() {}`.

   This method is called by the uninstaller to display a status message in the progress bar during uninstall. The message is displayed while the `uninstall (UninstallerProxy up)` method is called.
   ```
   public String getUninstallStatusMessage()
   {
      return "Displaying a long uninstallation message...";
   }
   ```

7. Description of `CustomCodeAction` member variables.

   The `CustomCodeAction` class provides `InstallerProxy` and `UninstallerProxy` as member variables. Use these to access the proxies at any point during execution of the custom code actions, rather than only during installation/uninstallation. Uninstall and install still receive proxies as parameters while called; this is for ease of use as well as for backwards compatibility. You can use either the passed proxy or the member variable proxy and receive the exact same functionality inside these functions. See the Javadoc for `CustomCodeAction` on the Zero G Web site for more information (www.zerog.com/downloads_04.html).

Custom Code Panels

At times you may find that InstallAnywhere's included panels don't meet your needs. InstallAnywhere's API addresses this with the introduction of custom code panels, which are the graphical equivalent of custom code actions. They allow you to present a UI to your end-user in combination with any task that you may need in a graphical installer.

Custom code panels provide you with a framework to which you can add components necessary for your particular task. Each custom code panel extends the core InstallAnywhere **Install** panel and, as such, provides your custom developed panel with the same look and feel and the same available elements as the standard InstallAnywhere panels. The default custom code panel provides the framework for both AWT and Swing elements.

```
public boolean setupUI(CustomCodePanelProxy ip)
{
// clear panel if setupUI is called multiple times
 if(true)
    removeAll();
    // set up layout manager
 setLayout(new FlowLayout());
 Label label1 = new Label("Custom Code Panel Test");
 add(label1);
 return true;
}
```

A Custom Code Panel Example

This section describes how to write your own custom code panel and leads you through an example (named `com.zerog.ia.customcode.samples.SamplePanel`). This section doesn't explain how to make your code work with InstallAnywhere's advanced designer or the Custom Code Panel action.

NOTE We assume that you know the goals of your panel, but have not yet written any code that implements it. After each relevant step, we will show an example of how this can be done.

1. Create your main class file and package it. This is the file that you will specify in the **Class** field in the InstallAnywhere advanced designer.

   ```
   package com.zerog.ia.customcode.samples;
   ```

2. To create a custom action, your class needs to extend the abstract class `com.zerog.ia.api.pub.CustomCodePanel`. This class provides the interface for interacting with the InstallAnywhere installer.

```
package com.zerog.ia.customcode.samples;

import com.zerog.ia.api.pub.*;

public class SamplePanel extends CustomCodePanel
{
   public boolean setupUI(CustomCodePanelProxy
   customCodePanelProxy) {}
   public void panelIsDisplayed() {}
   public boolean okToContinue() {}
   public boolean okToGoPrevious(){}
   public String getTitle() {}
}
```

3. Description of `public boolean setupUI(CustomCodePanelProxy customCodePanelProxy) {}`.

   This method gets called prior to the panel's being displayed. This is useful for initializing the contained components and variables. `SamplePanel` will use another example class, `BrowserLauncher`, to demonstrate how to launch a URL through a custom code panel. To do this, import the class `edu.stanford.ejaldbert.BrowserLauncher` and make sure to include this class file in the custom code panel JAR archive. Use the `setupUI` method to set up the UI and add components to your panel. This step includes adding labels, text fields, buttons, and an ActionListener. You'll want to ensure that you specify a LayoutManager for your panel. Although custom code panels do specify a default FlowLayout, specifying the LayoutManager will make your components appear as you expect within the InstallAnywhere custom code panel framework. This example also creates a few member variables of the `SampleConsole` class.

```
package com.zerog.ia.customcode.samples;
import com.zerog.ia.api.pub.*;
import java.awt.*;
import java.awt.event.*;
import java.io.IOException;
import edu.stanford.cs.ejalbert.*;
```

```java
public class SamplePanel extends CustomCodePanel implements
ActionListener
{
  private boolean inited = false;
  private TextField tf;
  private Button b;

  public boolean setupUI(CustomCodePanelProxy
  customCodePanelProxy)
  {
    // Use a boolean flag here to prevent duplicate GUI
    // elements.
    if (inited == true)
    return true;
    inited = true;

    Label label = new Label ("URL");
    label.setFont(new Font("Dialog", Font.BOLD, 12));

    b = new Button("Go");
    b.addActionListener(this);

    tf = new TextField (40);

    // Get a default URL string from InstallAnywhere and
    // use it if it is not empty.
    String def =
    customCodePanelProxy.substitute("$DEFAULT_URL$");
    System.out.println("Def: " + def);
    if (!def.equals(""))
    {
       tf.setText(def);
    }
    else tf.setText("www.ZeroG.com");

    add(label);
    add(tf);
    add(b);

    return true;
  }
  public void panelIsDisplayed() {}
  public boolean okToContinue() {}
  public boolean okToGoPrevious(){}
  public String getTitle() {}
}
```

4. Description of `public void panelIsDisplayed(UninstallerProxy up) {}`.

   This method is called immediately after the panel is displayed. This is useful for doing some processing while the panel is displayed without having to wait for the `okToContinue` method to be called. Of course, this method will never be called if `setupUI()` returns `false`. `SamplePanel` does nothing during this method and is left empty.

   ```
   public void panelIsDisplayed()
   {
   }
   ```

5. Description of `public boolean okToContinue() {}`.

   This method gets called before the installer continues. If this method returns `true`, then the installer continues to the next action; otherwise the installer prevents the user from continuing. This is useful for verifying end-user input or setting InstallAnywhere variables. In the `SamplePanel` an InstallAnywhere variable is set before the installer continues.

   ```
   public boolean okToContinue()
   {
      // Set an IA variable based upon the textfield's value,
      // then continue.
      customCodePanelProxy.setVariable("$CHOSEN_URL$",
      tf.getText());
      return true;
   }
   ```

6. Description of `public boolean okToGoPrevious() {}`.

   Like `okToContinue()`, this method gets called prior to a return to a previous step in the installer if the end-user clicks the **Previous** button. In the `SamplePanel` this method simply returns `true`.

   ```
   public boolean okToGoPrevious()
   {
      return true;
   }
   ```

7. Description of `public String getTitle() {}`.

   This method returns the string to be displayed as the title of this panel. In `SamplePanel` "Launch URL" is returned as the title.

```
public String getTitle()
{
   return "Launch URL";
}
```

8. Description of `CustomCodePanel` member variables.

    The `CustomCodePanel` class provides `CustomCodePanelProxy` as a member variable. This panel allows developers to access the proxy at any point during execution of the custom code panel, rather than only during `setupUI`. While `setupUI` is called, it still receives `CustomCodePanelProxy` as a parameter (for ease of use as well as backward compatibility). Inside this method, it is important to note that you can use either the passed proxy or the member variable proxy and receive the exact same functionality.

Custom Code Consoles

InstallAnywhere's custom code console provides a similar, customizable framework to that provided by the custom code panel, which allows you to add components of your choosing to a generic InstallAnywhere interface. This console will allow the installer to display text or extract information from the end-user when running in Console mode.

The framework is designed to provide a text-only interface, and as such, the available components are somewhat different.

A simple custom code console might look as follows:

```
================================================================
Test Console
------
Please select one of the following options.
->1- first choice
  2- second choice
  3- third choice
ENTER THE NUMBER FOR YOUR CHOICE, OR PRESS <ENTER> TO ACCEPT THE
DEFAULT:
================================================================
```

A Custom Code Console Action Example

This section describes how to write your own custom code console action, by leading you through an example (`com.zerog.ia.customcode.samples.CustomCodeConsoleAction`). This section doesn't explain how to make your code work with InstallAnywhere's advanced designer.

> **NOTE** We assume that you know the goals of your console action, but have not yet written any code that implements them. After each relevant step, we will show an example of how this can be done.

1. Create your main class file and package it. This is the file that you will specify in the **Class** field in the InstallAnywhere advanced designer.

   ```
   package com.zerog.ia.customcode.samples;
   ```

2. To create a custom console action, your class must first extend the abstract class `com.zerog.ia.api.pub.CustomCodeConsoleAction`. This class provides the interface through which you will interact with the InstallAnywhere runtime.

   ```
   package com.zerog.ia.customcode.samples;
      import com.zerog.ia.api.pub.*;
      public class SampleAction extends CustomCodeConsoleAction
   {
      public boolean setup() {}
      public void executeConsoleAction() throws
      PreviousRequestException{}
      public String getTitle() {}
   }
   ```

3. Description of `public boolean setup() {}`.

   The installer calls this method prior to the console action being displayed. This method is useful for the initialization needed by the action and returns `true` if the console should be displayed. If this method returns `false`, the console is not displayed and the installer continues with the next action. This custom code console action example uses the `setup()` method to populate a vector from an InstallAnywhere variable.

   ```
   package com.zerog.ia.customcode.samples;
      import com.zerog.ia.api.pub.*;
   ```

```
   import java.util.vector;
   import java.util.StringTokenizer;
public class SampleConsole extends CustomCodeConsoleAction
{

   public boolean setup()
   {
      // Use a StringTokenizer to populate the vector
      // 'choices' from the InstallAnywhere variable
      // $SAMPLE_CONSOLE_LIST$

      String list = cccp.substitute("$SAMPLE_CONSOLE_LIST$");
      StringTokenizer st = new StringTokenizer(list, ",");

      while (st.hasMoreTokens())
      {
         choices.addElement(st.nextToken());
      }
      return true;
   }

   public void executeConsoleAction() throws
   PreviousRequestException{}
   public String getTitle(){}
}
```

4. Description of `public void executeConsoleAction() {}`.

   This method is called when the installer is ready to display the console action. Most, if not all, of the console input and output should originate from the call into this action via this method. This example uses the executeConsoleAction method to prompt the end-user to select a choice from a list.

```
public void executeConsoleAction() throws
PreviousRequestException
{
   // Get an instance of ConsoleUtils. We will use
   // ConsoleUtils to help construct the console prompts.
   ConsoleUtils cu =
      (ConsoleUtils)cccp.getService(ConsoleUtils.class);

   // Use the substitute method to get the variable:
   // $SAMPLE_CONSOLE_PROMPT$
   String prompt = cccp.substitute("$SAMPLE_CONSOLE_PROMPT$");

   // Use the built in features of the ConsoleUtils class to
   // ask the user to select from a list
```

```
        int userChoice = cu.createChoiceListAndGetValue(prompt,
            choices);

        // Set the result as an InstallAnywhere variable
        String result = choices.elementAt(userChoice).toString();
        cccp.setVariable(""$SAMPLE_CONSOLE_CHOICE$", result);
    }
```

5. Description of `public String getTitle() {}`.

    This method returns the string to be displayed as the title of this console. This example just returns "Sample Console" as the title.

    ```
    public String getTitle()
    {
        String title = "Sample Console";
        return title;
    }
    ```

6. Description of `CustomCodeAction` member variables.

    The `CustomCodeConsoleAction` class provides `CustomCodePanelProxy` cccp, but instances of the class `ConsoleUtils` must be instantiated specifically.

Custom Code Rules

InstallAnywhere's rules architecture allows you to extend the existing rule set by adding custom code rules. These rules, based on the InstallAnywhere API, provide you with a method of making any action in the InstallAnywhere installer conditional. However, unlike the built-in rules, your code provides the condition. This feature is especially useful in situations where your action is dependant on a variable outside of the InstallAnywhere architecture.

An InstallAnywhere custom code rule is effectively an action that, when executed, returns a simple Boolean value. If the rule returns `true`, the action to which it is attached will install or execute. If the rule returns `false`, the action will be prevented from occurring.

Writing Custom Code

A Custom Code Rule Example

This section describes how to write your own custom code rule and leads you through an example (called `com.zerog.ia.customcode.samples.SampleRule`). This section doesn't explain how to make your code work with InstallAnywhere's advanced designer.

NOTE We assume that you know the goals of your rule, but have not yet written any code to implement it. After each relevant step, we will show an example of how this can be done.

1. Create your main class file and package it. You will specify this file in the **Class** field in the InstallAnywhere advanced designer.

   ```
   package com.zerog.ia.customcode.samples;
   ```

2. To create a custom rule, your class must first extend the abstract class `com.zerog.ia.api.pub.CustomCodeRule`. This class provides the interface through which you will interact with the InstallAnywhere runtime.

   ```
   package com.zerog.ia.customcode.samples;
   import com.zerog.ia.api.pub.*;
   public class SampleRule extends CustomCodeRule
   {
      public abstract boolean evaluateRule()
   }
   ```

3. Description of `public abstract boolean evaluateRule()`.

   This method is called at install-time when the installer is evaluating the rules set on a given installer action. It is very important that this method return quickly so that unnecessary lag is not experienced.

   ```
   package com.acme;
   // You should change this to your own package
   import com.zerog.ia.api.pub.*;
   public class CustomCodeRuleTemplate extends CustomCodeRule
   {
      public boolean evaluateRule()
      {
         //This method resolves all of the InstallAnywhere
         //variables in a string. If the string contains a
         //variable, and resolving that variable then contains
         //another variable, that too will be resolved until all
   ```

```
            //variables have been resolved. If a variable cannot be
            //resolved, it evaluates to an empty string ("").
            String myString = ruleProxy.substitute("$myVariable$");
            //This method returns the value of the named variable.
            //If no variable is
            //defined for that name, returns null.
            String myString = (String)
            ruleProxy.getVariable("myVariable");
            //This method sets the named variable to refer to the
            //value. If the variable was already set, its previous
            //value is returned. Otherwise, returns null.
            Object previousValue =
            ruleProxy.setVariable("myVariable", "theValue");
            //For Internationalization support. Gives access to
            //locale-specific static GUI strings.
            String myString = ruleProxy.getValue("myKey",
            Locale.ENGLISH);
            //For Internationalization support. Gives access to
            //locale-specific static GUI strings. Returns the
            //resource for the user's chosen installation locale.
            String myString = ruleProxy.getValue("myKey")
            return true;
        }
    }
```

4. Description of `CustomCodeRule` member variables.

   The `CustomCodeRule` class provides `CustomCodeRuleProxy` as a member variable. This allows developers to access the proxy at any point during the execution of the custom code rule, rather than only during `evaluateRule`.

Quick Quiz

1. If you added code to the uninstall method in a custom code action, where must you add the action in order for the uninstall method to be called?

   A. Pre-install

   B. Files

   C. Post-install

2. Can custom code be localized?

   A. Yes

   B. No

3. Which type of custom code will run in all supported install modes (GUI, Console, and Silent)?

   A. Custom code action
   B. Custom code panel
   C. Custom code console action

Quick Quiz answers are located in Appendix J.

CHAPTER 20

Developing and Using Custom Code Actions

- **Custom Code and InstallAnywhere Variables**
- **Accessing InstallAnywhere Variables via Custom Code**
- **Executing External Scripts and Executables via Custom Code Action**
- **How to Write Custom Errors in the Installation Log**
- **How to Package and Execute Custom Code with an Installer**
- **Plug-Ins**

Custom Code and InstallAnywhere Variables

For information on variables, please see the section on InstallAnywhere variables (see Chapter 4 and Appendix A). Custom code can both get and set InstallAnywhere variables. This ability can be useful in two cases.

- A project can set InstallAnywhere variables, which can be used as parameters for custom code. For example, if a custom code action is designed to know the directory to which the end-user is installing, use the Set InstallAnywhere Variable action to set `PARAM_1` to `$USER_INSTALL_DIR$`. Then, in the custom code action, call `InstallerProxy.substitute("$PARAM_1$")` to determine its value.
- InstallAnywhere variables may also be used to store return values from custom code actions. These variables can be queried by other actions or rules. To do this, call the method `InstallerProxy.setVariable("PARAM_1",<OBJECT>)` to set the InstallAnywhere variable's value. Remember that these variables are treated as strings and `java.lang.Object.toString()` will be called on them to determine their value in InstallAnywhere. Once `PARAM_1` has been set, it can be accessed in the normal way, using `$PARAM_1$` in a later InstallAnywhere rule or action.

A common problem when accessing the values of InstallAnywhere variables from within custom code is the improper use of the `getVariable()` and `substitute()` methods. The most common problem is the use of `getVariable()` on a Magic Folder object (for instance, `$USER_INSTALL_DIR$`) and subsequent attempt to cast this object to a string. Instead, use `substitute()`, which will resolve the contents of the variable to a string, instead of casting the object.

Accessing InstallAnywhere Variables via Custom Code

Each of the four custom code types has a proxy class that provides methods extending the custom code classes to access information in an InstallAnywhere installer and locate and access resources. Each of these proxy classes provides a method called `getVariable()` and `substitute()`. Both of these methods can be used to access InstallAnywhere variables from within your custom code.

- **substitute**
  `public java.lang.String substitute(java.lang.String var)`

  This method fully resolves a string that may contain embedded InstallAnywhere variables.

  The string returned is guaranteed to resolve all InstallAnywhere variables embedded in the parameter passed to this method. Variables contained (embedded) within the string are resolved fully and recursively. InstallAnywhere variables that are to be resolved are identified by their surrounding dollar signs ($). If no value has been set for a given variable name, that variable is resolved to the empty string.

  For example, calling this method on the string "The files have been $PLACED$ in $USER_INSTALL_DIR$" would return a string with $PLACED$ and $USER_INSTALL_DIR$ resolved to the `String()` values of the objects represented by the InstallAnywhere variables.

  This method is particularly useful for resolving file system paths represented by InstallAnywhere variables for Magic Folders and is the preferred mechanism for retrieving this type of data.

- **getVariable**
  `public java.lang.Object getVariable(java.lang.String var)`

  This method returns the literal object represented by an InstallAnywhere variable.

  InstallAnywhere variables are identified by their surrounding dollar signs ($). If no value has been set for a given variable name, null is returned.

  The `getVariable()` method does not recursively resolve variables. If the intention is to get the string representation of a particular InstallAnywhere variable, the `substitute()` method is generally preferred.

  For example, `getVariable("$USER_INSTALL_DIR$")` would return the MagicFolder object for the current install location, while `substitute("$USER_INSTALL_DIR$")` would return a string representing the absolute path to the current install location.

Executing External Scripts and Executables via Custom Code Action

Here is a simple custom code action that allows you to extract the exit code and output produced when executing a command or target file during install time.

```
package com.zerog.ia.customcode.actions;
import com.zerog.ia.api.pub.*;
import java.net.*;
import java.io.*;
public class EnhancedExecuteTargetFile extends CustomCodeAction
{
    public void install(InstallerProxy ip) throws InstallException
{

try
    {
String fileToExecute = ip.substitute("$FILE_TO_EXECUTE$");
String executeString = "";

if(fileToExecute.endsWith(".sh") || fileToExecute.endsWith(".bin"))
    {
System.err.println("Shell script found - using /bin/sh");
        executeString = "/bin/sh "+fileToExecute;
}
    else
{
        executeString = fileToExecute;
}

System.out.println("About to execute: "+executeString);
final Process p = Runtime.getRuntime().exec(executeString);

final StringWriter errWriter = new StringWriter();
    final StringWriter outWriter = new StringWriter();

Thread thread = new Thread()
    {
public void run()
    {
    InputStream err = p.getErrorStream();
    int c;
    try
    {
     while ((c = err.read()) >= 0)
     {
```

```java
                errWriter.write(c);
              }
            }
            catch (IOException ioe){}
    }
    };
       Thread thread2 = new Thread()
       {
          public void run()
          {
          InputStream err = p.getInputStream();
          int c;
          try
    {
            while ((c = err.read()) >= 0)
              {
      outWriter.write(c);
          }
          }
      catch (IOException ioe){}
          }
    };

    thread.start();
    thread2.start();
    p.waitFor();

    String stdErr = errWriter.toString();
    String stdOut = outWriter.toString();
    String exitCode = new Integer(p.exitValue()).toString();

    System.out.println("StdErr Output: "+stdErr);
    System.out.println("StdOut Output: "+stdOut);
    System.out.println("Exit Code : "+exitCode);

    ip.setVariable("CC_STD_ERR", stdErr);
    ip.setVariable("CC_STD_OUT", stdOut);
    ip.setVariable("CC_EXIT_CODE", exitCode);
}
catch(Exception e)
{
throw new NonfatalInstallException(
   "Execute Command Custom Code Failed while reading Error Stream");
    }
  }
public void uninstall(UninstallerProxy up) throws InstallException
{
}
```

```
public String getInstallStatusMessage()
{
  return "Execute Target File";
}

public String getUninstallStatusMessage()
{
  return "Execute Target File";
 }
}
```

Using InstallAnywhere Custom Code Actions in Uninstall

The custom code action framework provides a key method—`uninstall()`—which allows you to customize the behavior of or add functionality to the InstallAnywhere uninstaller. If your deployment requires any custom actions at uninstall time, you'll need to implement these tasks in a custom code action implementing `uninstall()`. Additionally, this method allows you to specify an uninstall task equivalent to an action that occurs at install time. A single action can utilize install and uninstall methods and can provide **Files**, **Pre-Uninstall**, and **Post-Uninstall** task options.

The uninstall method will only be called if the custom code action is added to the **Files**, **Pre-Uninstall**, or **Post-Uninstall** task. If placed in the **Pre-Install** or **Post-Install** task, the uninstall method in the custom code action will not be called, and all code within the uninstall method will be ignored.

```
public void uninstall(UninstallerProxy up) throws InstallException
{
   System.out.println("This line will be displayed during uninstall");
}
```

The code snippet above simply displays text to standard output. This text will only be displayed if the uninstaller is run in Debug mode.

Debugging Custom Code

In order to debug your custom code, you can simply add `System.out` or `System.err` statements to display information within your code. This output will only be displayed if the installer or uninstaller is run in Debug mode. Please see Chapter 12 for more detailed information on running installers and uninstallers in Debug mode.

Best Practices for Custom Code Development

Use a batch or shell script to combine all of the tasks needed for your custom code development. A single script that compiles your code, packages it, moves files to the correct build location, then builds and executes your InstallAnywhere installer can save time and make your development process much easier.

When you develop and test your custom code, we strongly recommend placing frequent `System.out` and `System.err` statements within your code. This step will allow you to identify possible problems within the code easily.

Advanced Action Methods

- **public interface InstallerResources:**
  public long getAvailableDiskSpace()

  This is a convenient method to get the amount of disk space available on the target system.

- **public java.util.Vector getInstallBundles()**

  This returns a vector of strings that describe the names of all install bundles (features) whose rules currently evaluate to `true`.

  Passing the string name of one of the install bundles (features) contained in the returned vector will cause that install bundle (feature) to be installed.

- **public java.util.Vector getInstallSets()**

  This returns a vector of strings that describe the names of all install sets (features) whose rules currently evaluate to `true`. Passing the string name of one of the install sets (features) contained in the returned vector will cause that install set (feature) to be installed.

- **public java.util.Vector getJavaVMList()**

  This returns a vector of strings that contain the paths to all VMs found on the target system.

  When searching for VMs, the installer will search along the end-user's system path, and in the case of Windows systems, the system registry. This method returns all VMs found on the system.

- **`public long getRequiredDiskSpace()`**

  This is a convenient method to get the amount of disk space required to install the selected product feature on the target system.

- **`public boolean installBundledJRE (boolean installJRE) throws CannotInstallJREException`**

  This instructs the installer to install the bundled Java Runtime Environment (JRE), if it is present, or to not install it.

  If the installer is instructed not to install the bundled JRE, the installer will attempt to choose a system VM for any LaunchAnywhere executables that are to be installed.

- **`public boolean setChosenInstallSet(java.lang.String installSet)`**

  This instructs the installer to install the components included in the specified install set (feature).

  The install set is described by its full name as created in the InstallAnywhere advanced designer or as returned by the call to `getInstallSets()`. Essentially, this call makes the specified install set the new default install set for the installer. Calls to this method will override prior calls made to this method and prior calls made to `setChosenInstallBundles`.

- **`public boolean setChosenInstallBundles(java.lang.String installBundles)`**

  This instructs the installer to install the components included in the specified install bundle(s) (product component).

  The install bundle(s) (features) are described by a comma-separated string containing the full name of all desired install bundles (features) as created in the InstallAnywhere advanced designer or as returned by the call to `getInstallBundles()`. Calls to this method will override prior calls made to this method and prior calls made to `setChosenInstallSet`.

- **`public boolean setChosenInstallSet(java.lang.String installSet)`**

  This instructs the installer to install the features included in the specified install set (feature).

The install set (feature) is described by its full name as created in the InstallAnywhere advanced designer or as returned by the call to getInstallSets(). Essentially, this call makes the specified install set (feature) the new default install set (feature) for the installer. Calls to this method will override prior calls made to this method and prior calls made to setChosenInstallBundles.

- **public boolean setJavaVM(java.lang.String vmPath)**

    This instructs the installer to use the system VM described by the provided absolute path as the VM for all LaunchAnywhere executables installed by this installer.

- **public void setJavaVMList(java.util.Vector newVMList)**

    This method allows the list of VM paths to be set externally to the installer's normal mechanism for gathering and saving paths to system VMs.

    This method will allow the development of actions to validate version information and so forth about a system VM. Setting the VM list prior to the display of the **Choose VM** step will change the VMs listed in the **Choose VM** step, as well as the values returned by getJavaVMList().

How to Write Custom Errors in the Installation Log

Custom actions, panels, and consoles can log errors in the installation using the CustomError classes.

The CustomError object is obtained through the InstallerProxy, CustomCodePanelProxy, and CustomCodeConsoleProxy objects by a request for the CustomError class, as follows:

Given an instance of CustomCodePanelProxy proxy,

```
CustomError error =
(CustomError)proxy.getService(CustomError.class);
error.appendError("the file was not found", CustomError.ERROR);
error.setLogDescription("File Mover: ");
```

```
error.setRemedialText("Blank file was not found. Create a new text
file and place it in the TEMP directory.");
error.log();
```

The code above will log the following text in the installation log.

Summary

```
Installation: Successful with errors.
1      SUCCESS
0      WARNINGS
1      NONFATAL ERROR
0      FATAL ERRORS
Action Notes:
File Mover: Blank file was not found. Create a new text file and
place it in the TEMP directory.
Additional Notes: NOTE - Required Disk Space: 1,046,190; Free Disk
Space: 3,818,479,616
Install Directory: -C:\Program Files\My_Product\
Status: SUCCESSFUL
Additional Notes: NOTE - Directory already existed
File Mover:- Status: ERROR
Additional Notes: ERROR - the file was not found
```

Exercise 20.1 Create a Custom Code Action

1. Set InstallAnywhere variables.
2. Get InstallAnywhere variables.
3. Get Java properties.
4. Use a few methods provided by InstallerResources.
5. Log an error.

Exercise 20.2 Create a Custom Code Panel

1. Get and set InstallAnywhere variables.
2. Display a few components.
3. Use a few methods provided by GUIAccess.

Exercise 20.3 Create a Custom Code Console Action

1. Create a simple custom code console action.
2. Use a few methods provided by GUIAccess.

Exercise 20.4 Create a Custom Code Rule

1. Get and set InstallAnywhere variables.
2. Create a scenario in which the value of an InstallAnywhere variable will set the rule to true or false.

How to Package and Execute Custom Code with an Installer

To create and use custom code in an installer, do the following:

1. Add IAClasses.zip to the classpath.

   The Java compiler will need to reference the classes in this file when compiling the code. IAClasses.zip is located in the root installation directory of InstallAnywhere.

3. Create the action, panel, console, or rule. A good starting point is to use the Java source file templates found in the CustomCode/Templates folder inside the InstallAnywhere installation directory.

4. Compile the source files.

5. Decide which additional files and resources will be needed. For example, images, text files, or other resources may be required.

6. Create an unsigned JAR file that contains the compiled class files and resource files. Signed archives will not function properly with InstallAnywhere's Custom Code API.

> **NOTE** Make sure that the selected archive contains full path information (each file in the archive should be stored with its proper package path). Without this JAR, Java will not be able to find the packaged class files properly.

7. Add an action or rule that executes custom code (such as Execute Custom Code action).

8. Choose the JAR file created in the previous step.

9. Type the fully qualified package and class name, such as `com.acme.MyAction`.

10. Test and debug the action or panel.

    Because InstallAnywhere cannot be run from within an integrated development environment, the best way to debug the custom code is to use the Output Debug Information action or `System.out.println();` statements to print debug output to the console during testing.

NOTE It is critical that the custom code JAR not include the classes and resources from `IAClasses.zip` as this will seriously affect the behavior of the installer and uninstaller.

Plug-Ins

Developers can register custom code as plug-ins with the InstallAnywhere advanced designer. This feature allows properly packaged custom code to be integrated into the design environment, where it will appear in the action palette under the **Plug-ins** tab. Plug-ins are stored within the `<InstallAnywhere>/plugins` folder. Packaging custom code has the following advantages:

- The developer can add them as regular actions without having to specify the JAR and class.
- Custom code usually utilizes InstallAnywhere variables for parameters and return values. If a developer wants to execute custom code multiple times in a project, the global scope of InstallAnywhere variables often forces the developer to be very careful with parameters and return values. Plug-ins have a local scope for parameters.
- Plug-ins are easily portable across development teams.

NOTE Zero G is interested in distributing plug-ins developed by our developers. If you have written a plug-in that you think would be useful to other developers and you would like to share it, please contact our support team at supportteam@zerog.com

Packaging Custom Code as a Plug-In

1. Package the custom code and all of its resources in a JAR (as for regular custom code).
2. Create a properties file called `customCode.properties`. This properties file will specify all of the information InstallAnywhere needs to integrate the plug-in with the advanced designer. Place the properties file in the JAR with no stored path information (at the root level of the JAR).

   The properties file must contain the following properties:

   - `plugin.main.class=<classname>`: This specifies the class that implements the proper member of the InstallAnywhere API for a custom code action, panel, or console (such as a class that implements `com.zerog.ia.api.pub.CustomCodeAction`)
   - `plugin.name=<plug-in name>`: This specifies the name the plug-in will have in the **Plug-ins** tab of the InstallAnywhere advanced designer's action palette.
   - `plugin.type=<action | panel | console>`: This property helps InstallAnywhere determine when the plug-in can be used and which icon to use to represent it in the advanced designer.

   The following properties may also be used:

   - `property.<propertyname>=<propertydefault>`: This property tells the plug-in to populate the action's customizer with a property named the `<propertyname>` and set to the default value of `<propertydefault>`.
   - `plugin.icon.path=<relative path to .png or .jpg file in JAR>`: This property sets a custom 32 × 32 icon for the custom code plug-in in the advanced designer.
   - `plugin.available=<preinstall | install | postinstall | preuinstall | postunintall>`: This property is a comma-separated value list to tell the advanced designer for which tasks to make the plug-in available.

   The following is an example of a properties file for a plug-in:

   ```
   plugin.main.class=com.zerog.ia.customcode.util.fileutils.
       ExtractToFile
   plugin.name=Extract to File
   ```

```
plugin.type=action
plugin.icon.path=myicon.gif
plugin.available=preinstall,install,postinstall
property.ExtractToFile_Source=path/to/file/in.zip
property.ExtractToFile_Destination=$USER_INSTALL_DIR$$/
$myfile.txt
```

Additionally, plug-ins can help InstallAnywhere users with the proper use of the plug-in. Help is displayed in HTML and is launched by the user's pressing a button on the plug-in's customizer. The button only appears if a Help file is provided in the plug-in. To utilize installer Help, do the following:

   a. Create a file called `help.htm`.

   b. Package it in the plug-in JAR (without stored path information).

3. Place the properly packaged unsigned JAR (with the custom code, its resources, and the properties file) in the `<InstallAnywhere>/plugins` directory.

4. Launch InstallAnywhere.

The plug-in will now be visible in the InstallAnywhere action.

CHAPTER 21

Localizing and Internationalizing InstallAnywhere Installers

- **Dynamic and Static Text**
- **Localization and the Internationalized Designer**
- **Specific Localization Concerns**
- **Localizable Elements**

NEARLY EVERY TEXT STRING in an InstallAnywhere project can be localized. Translations of the text of built-in InstallAnywhere screens and dialogs are already provided. The Enterprise Edition supports 29 different locales, and the Standard Edition supports 9. To generate multilanguage installers, click the **Project | Locales** task in the advanced designer, and use the check boxes to select the appropriate languages.

If developers want to modify text strings by locale further, each time an installer is built the string files are output in a folder called `<projectname> locales`, which will be next to the build output folder. The files are named by locale code. For example, the default English (locale code, en) locale file has the name `custom_en`.

These locale files contain the text string grouped by the name of the action to which it belongs. Developers can alter the text string, and upon the next build of the installer, the new localized text will be displayed with the action.

These files contain keys and values for all of the dynamic strings in the project. The keys are generated by the name of the action, with a unique value to represent the unique instance of the action and an additional parameter to signify which dynamic value of the action is being referenced; for example:

```
InstallSet.9733839b90f6.installSetName=Typical
InstallSet.9733839b90f6.description= The most common application
features will be installed. This option is recommended for most
users.
```

The `ProjectLocalizationInfo.txt` file contains the mapping between the actions in the project and their keys in the locale files. Review the `ProjectLocalizationInfo.txt` file for any questions about which action the key references.

Dynamic and Static Text

Text that can be entered into the InstallAnywhere advanced designer is "dynamic text," meaning that the developer can change its value. Text that cannot be edited by the advanced designer is referred to as "static text." Standard items, such as file choosers and text for actions and panels the developer is unlikely to wish to change, have static text. Dynamic text is written to the locale files (located next to the project file). Translations of static text can be found in the <InstallAnywhere>\resource\ i18nresources directory. While developers are unlikely to need to change the static text, InstallAnywhere provides the developer with the option to change the static text.

Almost all dynamic text has default values in the advanced designer. These dynamic values also have default translations. The installer developer must localize every string modified in the advanced designer if he or she wants the translation to match. There are also actions that do not have defaults, such as **Custom Code** and **Get User Input** panels. It is the developer's job to localize these strings as well.

Localization and the Internationalized Designer

Developers can localize not only the installers they create with the InstallAnywhere development environment, but the development environment itself.

The designer writes all changes to dynamic values into the locale file of the same language the advanced designer is running in; so when using the French language variation, dynamic changes are written into the custom_fr file. Using the advanced designer is the correct way to modify this locale file. Changes to the locale files made outside of the advanced designer will be overwritten.

Specific Localization Concerns
Localizing Resources

The developer may find that he or she wants to localize resources (such as license agreements, side panels, billboards, and custom icons) for specific countries. This is possible in InstallAnywhere. Actions such as the **License Agreement** panel and LaunchAnywhere serialize the paths and filenames to their resources and their dynamic strings to the locale files.

The developer can then change these paths and the filenames. For example, to localize the license agreement, do the following:

1. Make sure to include every resource in the **Files** task. Installers will not have access to resources not specified in this task.
2. Find the line in the locale file that contains the text `LicenseAgr.#.FileName`. Specify the filename of the file that contains the localized license agreement (for instance, `License_fr.html`). Do not type the fully qualified absolute pathname to the file—just type the filename itself.
3. Find the line that contains the text `LicenseAgr.#.Path`. Specify the pathname to the file that contains the localized license agreement (on the local file system).

Localizing Custom Installer Labels

Custom labels that match the installer panels are not automatically localized. To match labels, do the following:

1. Build the installer as you normally would.
2. Locate the installer's Locale directory.
3. Open the `custom_en` file in WordPad or another text editor.
4. Search for the `Installer.1.installLabelsAsCommaSeparatedString` variable. This variable should contain the added installer labels.
5. Copy and paste this variable into the other locale files.
6. Finally, provide translations for these labels in their respective files.

Localizing Custom Code

The InstallAnywhere API provides a simple means for localizing custom code actions, panels, and consoles. Here's an example of how to localize a `java.awt.Label` inside a custom code panel. The custom code panel's `setupUI` method should resemble

```
public boolean setupUI(CustomCodePanelProxy ccpp)
{
```

```
Label myLabel = new Label();
myLabel.setText(ccpp.getValue(MyCustomCodePanel.myLabel)));
}
```

The `CustomCodePanelProxy`, `InstallerProxy`, `CustomCodeConsoleProxy`, and `UninstallerProxy` classes provide access to the `getValue` method, which takes a string as a parameter representing the key portion of the key/value pair as defined in InstallAnywhere's international resource files. Developers can create any name for the key that they would like, as long as it doesn't conflict with previously defined keys. Developers can even use a preexisting key to obtain a string that has already been translated in InstallAnywhere's resource files.

To make the new locale keys exist in every installer project, update the static text. To make them exist only in the current project, update the dynamic text. The dynamic text is regenerated every time the developer saves, so update the files every time the project is changed. This is another good reason to have the installer design done before starting the localization process.

Best Practices for Localizing

Complete the installer design before translating the locale files. Changes to the installer design can affect the layout and content of the locale files. Changes to these files may require costly retranslation work.

Stick with the default text whenever possible. All default text is already translated, saving the team time and effort.

Test the installers on systems running in the foreign locale. This will help shake out any errors where the proper strings are not translated in the locale files.

Make sure every resource referenced in the locale files is included in the installer. This is especially true for license agreements, readme's, and other commonly translated documents.

InstallAnywhere's comprehensive locale support is just one of the features that stand out from other deployment solutions. InstallAnywhere Enterprise Edition offers support for 29 different locales, both single-byte

"Western" locales and double-byte locales. Nearly every text string in your InstallAnywhere installer project can be localized, and translations of all of InstallAnywhere's default text are already provided.

Changing Localized Text

It's not necessary to change the localized text in the installer unless one of the following is true:

- You've added or modified installer items that are displayed to the end-user during installation (new components, features, license agreements, important information notes, and so on) that don't have default translations.
- You would like to modify the provided default translation.
- You are using actions that return install panels (such as the **Choose Folder** panel or **Get Password** panel).

Modifying Localized Text

1. Include any localized files (license agreements, graphics for billboards, and so on) in your installer. If these are not included, they won't be included with the installer and won't be available when end-users run the installer. Including these files in your installer means that InstallAnywhere will use them during the install process and install them onto the destination system. If you don't want these files installed, place them in the **Do Not Install** Magic Folder, and they won't be placed onto the destination system.
2. Build your installer. After this first build, a folder named `<projectname> locales` will be created in the same folder as the `.iap_xml` file.
3. A series of files called `custom_en`, `custom_fr`, and so on, will be placed in this Locales folder—one for each language you chose to build for in the **Project | Locales** task in the advanced designer. These are language resource files and contain localized text strings, as well as pointers to filenames containing localized information to embed in your installer.
4. For each language that you want to customize, edit the appropriate language resource file. Use escaped Unicode to encode for these files.

For example, if you want to specify a custom license agreement for French, edit the `custom_fr` file.

> **NOTE** Make sure that your localized license agreements and important note files are added to the installer (via the **Files** task); otherwise, they will not be bundled into the installer.

Changing Default Translations Provided in Language Packs

1. Follow the directions for changing localized text.
2. Modify the language resource files located in the `resource\i18nresources` folder inside of your InstallAnywhere folder. These files contain the defaults for all strings, both the static defaults and the strings that are externalized to the locales (Table 21.1).

Table 21.1 Language Codes

Language	Country Code	Language Group
Catalan	CA	Western
Czech	CS	Eastern
Danish	DA	Western
German	DE	Western
Greek	EL	Eastern
English	EN	Western
Spanish	ES	Western
Basque	EU	Western
Finnish	FI	Western
French	FR	Western
French (Canada)	FR_CA	Western
Hungarian	HU	Eastern
Indonesian	ID	Eastern
Italian	IT	Western
Japanese	JA	Eastern

Table 21.1 Language Codes (Continued)

Language	Country Code	Language Group
Korean	KO	Eastern
Dutch	NL	Western
Norwegian	NO	Western
Polish	PL	Western
Portuguese	PT	Western
Portuguese (Brazil)	PT_BR	Western
Russian	RU	Eastern
Slovak	SK	Western
Slovenian	SL	Western
Swedish	SV	Western
Thai	TH	Eastern
Turkish	TR	Eastern
Chinese (Simplified)	ZH_CN	Eastern
Chinese (Traditional)	ZH_TW	Eastern

Localizable Elements

Installers deployed to non-Latin systems require an international JVM.

Localizing Items in the Installer

See Table 21.2 to determine the correct properties to modify in the language resource files. This table does not include properties from many new actions. For a complete list, please contact Zero G support.

Table 21.2 Localizable Elements

Property	Definition
`Installer.#.ProductName`	Name of the product displayed on the installer title bar
`Installer.#.RulesFailedMessage`	Message displayed if specified rules keep the installer from running

Table 21.2 Localizable Elements *(Continued)*

Property	Definition
`Installer.#.ShortcutDestinationPathMacOS`	Path to where aliases are created during installation on Mac OS (relative to the end-user-selected alias folder chosen during the **Choose Alias Location** step)
`Installer.#.ShortcutDestinationPathWin32`	Path to where shortcuts are created during installation on Windows (relative to the end-user-selected shortcut folder chosen during the **Choose Alias, Link, Shortcut Folder** step)
`Installer.#.ShortcutDestinationPathSolaris`	Path to where links are created during installation on UNIX (relative to the end-user-selected links folder chosen during the **Choose Link Location** step)
`Installer.#.End-userSplashName`	Name of the image file to be displayed as the installer is preparing itself (Note: This is a filename only, not a fully qualified absolute pathname)
`Installer.#.End-userSplashPath`	Pathname to the image file to be displayed as the installer is preparing (Note: This is only a pathname and does not include the filename itself)
`InstallSet.#.Description`	Description of one of the installer's features
`InstallSet.#.InstallSetName`	Name of one of the installer's features
`Intro.#.DisplayText`	Text to display during the installer's **Introduction** step
`Intro.#.Title`	Title to display during the installer's **Introduction** step
`LicenseAgr.#.FileName`	Name of the localized license agreement to be displayed as the installer is preparing itself (Note: This is a filename only, not a fully qualified absolute pathname)
`LicenseAgr.#.Path`	Pathname to the localized license agreement to be displayed as the installer is preparing itself (Note: This is only a pathname and does not include the filename itself)
`LicenseAgr.#.Title`	Title of the **License Agreement** step in the installer
`MakeExecutable.#.DestinationName`	Name of the LaunchAnywhere executable to be created on the destination computer.
`MakeRegEntry.#.Value`	Value to be written into the Win32 registry
`ShortcutLoc.#.MacOSTitle`	Title of the Mac OS **Choose Alias Location** step in the installer
`ShortcutLoc.#.SolarisTitle`	Title of the UNIX **Choose Alias, Link, Shortcut Folder** step in the installer

Table 21.2 Localizable Elements (Continued)

Property	Definition
ShortcutLoc.#.Win32Title	Title of the Win32 **Choose Alias, Link, Shortcut Folder** step in the installer
Billboard.#.ImageName	Name of the billboard image file to be displayed as the installer is preparing itself (Note: This is a filename only, not a fully qualified absolute pathname)
Billboard.#.ImagePath	Pathname to the billboard image to be displayed as the installer is preparing itself (Note: This is only a pathname and does not include the filename itself)
ChooseInstallSet.#.Title	Title of the **Choose Feature** step in the installer
ChooseJavaVM.#.Title	Title of the **Choose Java Virtual Machine** step in the installer
CreateShortcut.#.DestinationName	Name of the shortcut/alias/link to be created on the destination computer
human.readable.language.name	Name of the language represented by the data in this resource file (i.e., English, Español, and so on)
ImportantNote.#.FileName	Name of the text file to be displayed during the **Important Note** step of the installer (Note: This is a filename only, not a fully qualified absolute pathname)
ImportantNote.#.Path	Pathname to the text file to be displayed during the **Important Note** step of the installer (Note: This is only a pathname and does not include the filename itself)
ImportantNote.#.Title	Title of the **Important Note** step in the installer
InstallBundle.#.BundleName	Name of a component
InstallBundle.#.Description	Description text describing a component
InstallComplete.#.DisplayText	Text to display during the **Install Complete** step of the installer
InstallComplete.#.Title	Title of the **Install Complete** step of the installer
InstallDir.#.Title	Title of the **Choose Installation Directory** step of the installer
Installer.#.InstallerName	Name of the installer

APPENDIX A
Standard InstallAnywhere Variables

InstallAnywhere includes a number of default variables that store information essential to the installation process. The variables listed in Table A.1 are standard InstallAnywhere variables.

Table A.1 Standard InstallAnywhere Variables

Variable	Definition	Status
$/$ or $\$	These represent platform-specific file separators, which are most useful to refer to paths in a platform-independent manner. These have the same value as the Java property file separator.	This variable is read-only.
$;$ or $:$	These represent platform-specific path separators.	This variable is read-only.
$CHOSEN_DIALOG_BUTTON$	This variable is set to the return value as set by the end-user's choice in the Show Message Dialog Box action. If the end-user chooses button 1, this variable will be set to 1.	
$CHOSEN_INSTALL_BUNDLE_<#>$	If **Choose Product Features** were enabled, there would be one variable for each feature as given in the variable $CHOSEN_INSTALL_BUNDLE_NUM$. This holds the short name of a feature to be installed. For example, if $CHOSEN_INSTALL_BUNDLE_NUM$ equals 2, then there will be two variables of the form $CHOSEN_INSTALL_BUNDLE_1$ and $CHOSEN_INSTALL_BUNDLE_2$.	This variable is read-only.
$CHOSEN_INSTALL_BUNDLE_LIST$	This variable is a comma-separated list of all install features (short name) chosen for the installation.	This variable is read-only.

Table A.1 Standard InstallAnywhere Variables (Continued)

Variable	Definition	Status
$CHOSEN_INSTALL_BUNDLE_NUM$	If **Choose Product Features** were enabled, this variable would hold the total number of components (as a string) that the end-user had chosen to install.	This variable is read-only.
$CHOSEN_INSTALL_SET$	If **Choose Product Features** were enabled, this variable would hold the short name of the feature chosen by the end-user. If the end-user were to choose to customize the install, this variable would hold the string CUSTOM.	This variable can be set before install time.
$CMD_LINE_ARGUMENTS$	This is a special InstallAnywhere variable that is resolved by the launcher and not by the installer. If this variable is in the LAX property lax.command.line.args, it will resolve to the arguments sent to the LaunchAnywhere executable.	This variable is used by Launch-Anywhere.
$COMMA$	This resolves to a comma (,).	This variable is read-only.
$DEVELOPER_DISK_SPACE_ADDITIONAL$	This variable specifies an arbitrary additional value as a string representing the additional bytes that the Check Disk Space action will add to the computed required disk space for the installation. By default this variable has a value of 0.	Developers may set this variable.
$DOLLAR$	This resolves to $.	This variable is read-only.
$EMPTY_STRING$	This variable represents a null value; it is useful to determine whether or not any variables have been initialized. Variables that have not yet been initialized will have this as their value.	This variable is read-only.
$EXTRACTOR_DIR$	This is the full path to the directory containing the self-extractor executable (from where it was launched).	This variable is read-only.
$EXTRACTOR_EXECUTABLE$	This is the full path to the self-extractor executable (from where it was launched).	This variable is read-only.

Appendix A ■ Standard InstallAnywhere Variables 219

Table A.1 Standard InstallAnywhere Variables (Continued)

Variable	Definition	Status
$FREE_DISK_SPACE_BYTES$	This is the free disk space available on the destination install volume. It is a string that represents the free bytes as determined by the Check Disk Space action. The variable gains its value immediately before the installation of any files or folders listed in the **Install** task.	This variable is read-only.
$IA_CLASSPATH$	This is the classpath as specified in the InstallAnywhere designer environment.	Developers may set this variable in the advanced designer.
$IA_INSTALL_LOG$	Setting this variable will generate an XML-formatted installation log to the $USER_INSTALL_DIR$ location. This document will detail the installation along with warnings and errors.	This variable is read-only.
$INSTALL_LOG_DESTINATION$	As the creation of the install log is the last action of an installation, this variable can be set anytime during pre-install, install, or post-install. The end-user can choose the installation log location.	Developers may set this variable.
$INSTALL_SUCCESS$	This variable alerts the end-user if the installation completed successfully or failed. There are four possible values for this variable: SUCCESS, WARNING, NONFATAL_ERROR, and FATAL_ERROR.	This variable is read-only.
$INSTALLER_LAUNCH_DIR$	This is a full path to the installer's self-extractor.	This variable is read-only.
$INSTALLER_LOCALE$	This is the locale as a string (see `java.util.Locale.toString()`) that the end-user selected at the beginning of the installation.	This variable is read-only.
$INSTALLER_TEMP_DIR$	This is the path to a temp directory for use by an installer. It will be deleted when its use is completed, assuming no items are in use.	This variable is read-only.
$INSTALLER_TITLE$	This is the title of the installer and is displayed in the title bar.	You may set this variable.

Table A.1 Standard InstallAnywhere Variables (Continued)

Variable	Definition	Status
$INSTALLER_UI$	This resolves to the UI mode for the installer.	This variable is read-only, but developers may set it at the start.
$JAVA_DOT_HOME$	This is what the Java property java.home will report.	This variable is read-only.
$JAVA_EXECUTABLE$	This is the path to the chosen Java executable.	This variable is read-only.
$JAVA_HOME$	This is the root of the Java installation.	This variable is read-only.
JDK_HOME	This is the path to the root of a Java Development Kit (JDK) installation. It is only set if the chosen VM is a JDK. If it is not, then this variable will have a blank value.	This variable is read-only.
$lax.nl.env.[ENVIRONMENT VARIABLE NAME]$	[Windows and UNIX only]: Access any system environment variable (for example, access PATH via $lax.nl.env.PATH$) by specifying the variable name as an all uppercase string. These variables are resolved at application runtime, when LaunchAnywhere executes. Developers can also access system environment variables via LaunchAnywhere properties.	This variable is read-only.
$lax.nl.env.exact_case.[Environment_Variable_Name]$	[Windows and UNIX only]: Access any system environment variable (for example, access Path via $lax.nl.env.exact_case.Path$) by specifying the variable name as a string of the exact case as it is defined in the environment. Note that these variables are resolved at application runtime, when LaunchAnywhere executes. Developers can also access system environment variables via LaunchAnywhere properties.	This variable is read-only.

Table A.1 Standard InstallAnywhere Variables (Continued)

Variable	Definition	Status
$NULL$	Currently, this is the same as $EMPTY_STRING$.	This variable is read-only.
$PRODUCT_ID$	This resolves to the value of the product ID in the **Project	Description** task.	This variable is read-only.
$PRODUCT_NAME$	This is the product name.	Developers may set this variable.
$PRODUCT_VERSION_NUMBER$	This resolves to the value of the product version in the **Project	Description** task.	This variable is read-only.
$PROMPT_USER_CHOSEN_OPTION$	This variable is set to the return value as set by the end-user's choice in the Show Message Console Dialog Box action. If the end-user chooses option 1, this variable will be set to 1.	This variable is read-only.
$prop.[JAVA PROPERTY]$	Access any Java property through InstallAnywhere variables. An example is $prop.os.name$, which will return the value of the os.name property.	This variable is read-only.
$REQUIRED_DISK_SPACE_BYTES$	This represents the disk space required by the installer. It is a string representing the required bytes as determined by the Check Disk Space action. The variable gains its value immediately before the installation of any files or folders listed in the **Install** task.	This variable is read-only.
$RESTART_NEEDED$	This tells the installer or uninstaller if the system needs to restart to complete the installation.	This variable is read-only.
$SHORTCUT_NAME$	This variable resolves to "Shortcut" on Win32 systems, "Alias" on Mac OS X and Classic systems, and "Link" on all other systems.	This variable is read-only.
$UNINSTALL_STATUS$	This is the same as $INSTALL_STATUS$, but for the uninstaller.	This variable is read-only.

APPENDIX B
Provided Magic Folders

Table B.1 lists the Magic Folders provided in InstallAnywhere.

Table B.1 InstallAnywhere Magic Folders

Folder Name	InstallAnywhere Variable	Destination
User Installation Directory	$USER_INSTALL_DIR$	This is the installation folder as specified by the end-user. Developers can specify a default value for this variable in the **Project Info** screen in the advanced designer by choosing a location in the Default Install Folder area of the screen.
Programs Folder (Platform Default)	$PROGRAMS_DIR$	This is the default application directory on the destination system (the Program Files folder on Windows, the Applications folder on Mac OS, and the logged-in-end-user's home account on UNIX).
Shortcuts	$USER_SHORTCUTS$	This is the folder specified by the end-user as the shortcuts/links/aliases location. The value of this location can be changed by the end-user if the Choose Alias, Link, Shortcut Folder action is turned on in the installer. Developers can specify a default value for this variable on a per-platform basis by selecting the **Platforms** task in the advanced designer.
System	$SYSTEM$	This variable represents the System folder on the target machine. On Windows 95/98, this resolves to <WINDOWS>\System. On Windows NT/2000, this resolves to <WINDOWS>\System32. On the Mac OS, this resolves to the System Folder. On UNIX, this resolves to /usr/local/bin.
Desktop	$DESKTOP$	This variable represents the desktop on the target machine. This folder only resolves on Windows, Linux, and Mac OS systems.
Temp Directory	$TEMP_DIR$	This variable represents the temp directory on the target machine. When running the pure Java installer on Windows, $TEMP_DIR$ will resolve to the user's home directory.

Table B.1 InstallAnywhere Magic Folders (Continued)

Folder Name	InstallAnywhere Variable	Destination
Startup	$STARTUP$	This is the automatic start-up folder for items that are launched automatically during operating system boot up. This folder only resolves on Windows and Mac OS systems.
Installation Drive Root	$INSTALL_DRIVE_ROOT$	This is the root directory on the volume where the installation is taking place.
Home Directory	$USER_HOME$	This is the home directory of the end-user running the installer. This variable works with all platforms except Mac OS. For users who have already included the variable $UNIX_USER_HOME$, this variable will continue to function with the same definition as $USER_HOME$.
System Drive Root	$SYSTEM_DRIVE_ROOT$	This is the root directory of the system drive.
Java Home	$JAVA_HOME$	This is the home directory of the JVM to be used.
Windows	$WIN_WINDOWS$	This is the Windows directory (Windows 95/98/Me/XP/NT/2000 computers only).
Start Menu	WIN_START_MENU	This is the Windows Start Menu directory (Windows 95/98/Me/XP/NT/2000 computers only).
Quick Launch Bar	$WIN_QUICK_LAUNCH_BAR$	This is the Quick Launch Bar on Windows. On Windows 2000 and XP, the location is relative to the UserProfile Environment variable. On Windows 98 and Me it's relative to the Windows directory.
Do Not Install	$DO_NOT_INSTALL$	This doesn't install the file on the target platform. It is used for files (typically localized license agreements and graphics) that are used during installation, but don't need to remain on the target system.
USER_MAGIC_FOLDER_#	$USER_MAGIC_FOLDER_#$	These variables are user-defined destination install Magic Folders. They install to whichever directories their variable names have been set. To set these variables, use the Set InstallAnywhere Variable action. Note: For UNIX, if the leading "/" is not included in the path before the Magic Folder location, the result is `<directory in which installer double-clicked>/USER_MAGIC_FOLDER_#` because the operating system assumes that any path not preceded by a "/" is below the current directory.

Table B.1 InstallAnywhere Magic Folders (Continued)

Folder Name	InstallAnywhere Variable	Destination
Programs Menu	$WIN_PROGRAMS_MENU$	This is the Windows **Programs** menu (in the **Start** menu) (Windows 95/98/Me/XP/NT/2000 computers only).
All Users Start Menu	$WIN_COMMON_START_MENU$	This is the Windows All Users Start Menu directory (Windows NT/2000 computers only). On Win 9x computers this resolves to the same value as WIN_START_MENU.
All Users Programs Menu	$WIN_COMMON_PROGRAMS_MENU$	This is the Windows **All Users Programs** menu (in the **Start** menu) (Windows NT/2000/XP computers only). On Win 9x computers this resolves to the same value as $WIN_PROGRAMS_MENU$.
All Users Startup	$WIN_COMMON_STARTUP$	This is the Windows All Users Startup folder (in the **Start** menu) (Windows NT/2000/XP computers only). On Win 9x computers this resolves to the same value as $STARTUP$.
All Users Desktop	$WIN_COMMON_DESKTOP$	This is the Windows Common Desktop folder (Windows NT/2000/XP computers only). On Win 9x computers this resolves to the same value as $DESKTOP$.
Fonts	$FONTS$	This is the Fonts directory (on both Windows and Mac OS computers only): $WIN_WINDOWS$\Fonts on Windows; $SYSTEM$:Fonts on Mac OS.
Apple Menu Items	MAC_APPLE_MENU	This is the Apple Menu Items folder (Mac OS computers only).
Control Panels	$MAC_CONTROL_PANELS$	This is the Control Panels folder (Mac OS computers only).
Extensions	$MAC_EXTENSIONS$	This is the Extensions folder (Mac OS computers only).
Preferences	$MAC_PREFERENCES$	This is the Preferences folder (Mac OS computers only): $SYSTEM$:Preferences.
Cleanup at Startup	$MAC_CHEWABLE$	This is the Clean at Startup folder (Mac OS computers only): $SYSTEM_DRIVE_ROOT$:Cleanup At Startup.
User Applications	$MACX_USER_APPLICATIONS$	This is the User Applications directory of the end-user running the installer (Mac OS X only).
The Dock	$MACX_DOCK$	This is the Mac OS X Dock—for shortcuts only. Files cannot be installed to the Dock.

Table B.1 InstallAnywhere Magic Folders (Continued)

Folder Name	InstallAnywhere Variable	Destination
/usr/local/bin	$UNIX_USR_LOCAL_BIN$	This is the /usr/local/bin directory (UNIX computers only).
/opt	$UNIX_OPT$	This is the /opt directory (UNIX computers only).
/usr/bin	$UNIX_USR_BIN$	This is the /usr/bin directory (UNIX computers only).

NOTE Developer-defined Magic Folders are not available in Standard Edition.

APPENDIX C
Actions

Tables C.1 to C.3 list the install, general, and panel actions available in InstallAnywhere.

Table C.1 Install Actions

Action	Editions	Description
Copy File	E	Copy a file from one location to another location on the end-user's system.
Copy Folder	E	Copy a folder from one location to another location on the end-user's system.
Create Alias, Link, Shortcut	E S	Create an alias (Mac OS X), symbolic link (UNIX and Linux), or shortcut (Windows).
Create Folder	E S	Create a new folder on the end-user's system. If the folder already exists, this will not delete the existing folder.
Create LaunchAnywhere for Java Apps	E S	Create a launcher to start the installed Java application.
Create Uninstaller	E S	Create the uninstaller and several additional files needed by the uninstaller. Zero G recommends that the uninstaller be installed into its own folder.
Delete File	E	Delete a file from the end-user's system.
Delete Folder	E	Delete a folder from the end-user's system.
Expand Archive	E S	Expand a ZIP file (.zip, .jar, .war, .ear) or decode a Mac binary file (.bin) on the end-user's system.
Install Archive	E S	Install a ZIP file (.zip, .jar) from the installer onto the end-user's system. This action appears automatically when a ZIP file is added.
Install File	E S	Install a file from the installer onto the end-user's system. This action appears automatically when files are added.
Install from Manifest	E	Install all of the files and folders specified in the manifest file on the end-user's system.

Table C.1 Install Actions (Continued)

Action	Editions	Description
Install HP-UX Depot	E	Install and uninstall HP-UX depot files through the Install HP-UX Depot action. The developer needs to specify the package name within the depot file, which can contain multiple packages. In order to install multiple packages in the same depot, add one action for every package you want to install. This will not increase the size of the installer.
Install Linux RPM	E	Install and uninstall Linux RPMs through the Install Linux RPM action. These RPMs can either be bundled with the installer or preexisting on the system. If the RPM is relocatable, and the **Relocatable** check box is set in the action customizer, the RPM will be installed to its location in the file tree. Additionally, the RPM can be set to ignore dependencies (similar to the `--nodeps` option for the command-line RPM tool) and to force the installation (`--force`).
Install Merge Module	E	Install a merge module as if the merge module were run as a separate silent installer.
Install PowerUpdate Client	E S	Create a PowerUpdate Check for Updates client for the installed application. This requires a downloaded client ZIP from a PowerUpdate server.
Install Solaris Package	E	Install and uninstall Solaris package files through the Install Solaris Package action. These packages can either be bundled with the installer or preexisting on the system. The developer must enter the name of the package. Additionally, InstallAnywhere supports bundling admin and response files for the packages with the installer. For more information on these files, consult the man pages for `pkgadd(1)`, `pkgask(1)`, and `admin(4)`.
Install SpeedFolder	E S	Dynamically pick up files at build-time from a folder. All files will be installed as one single, fast operation. (Tip: Use SpeedFolders for large installations with many files or builds that occur automatically.)
Move File	E	Move or rename a file from one location to another location on the end-user's system.
Move Folder	E	Move or rename a folder from one location to another location on the end-user's system.
Register Windows Service	E	Start, stop, or pause a Windows service on the end-user's system.
Set System Environment Variable	E	Set Environment variables on the end-user's system. This is compatible with Windows and UNIX only. UNIX Bash, sh, ksh, zsh, csh, tcsh shells are supported.
Set Windows Registry—Multiple Entries	E	Set multiple Windows registry keys, data, and values on the end-user's system.

Table C.1 Install Actions (Continued)

Action	Editions	Description
Set Windows Registry—Single Entry	E S	Set an individual Windows registry key, data, and value on the end-user's system.

Table C.2 General Actions

Action	Editions	Description
Add Comment	E S	This action is designed to allow developers to add a simple comment to the installer.
Add Jump Label	E	Use this action to branch off the installation conditionally. By applying InstallAnywhere rules, developers may jump end-users to a specific part of the installation, depending on the specifics of their system or install. Use this action in conjunction with the Jump to Target action. This action is available during the install sequence, but not within the files.
Execute ANT Script	E	This action allows developers to execute scripts designed for the Apache Jakarta Project's Ant application. If this action is selected, ANT will be bundled with the application. Only developers familiar with ANT should use this action. For more information, go to http://ant.apache.org.
Execute Command	E	This action allows developers to execute a command as they would at any command-line interpreter. This action is useful for executing applications that are already installed on the system. This command line is entered just as the system's command line would be.
Execute Custom Code	E S	This action allows developers to extend InstallAnywhere's functionality. InstallAnywhere's API is purely Java-based and allows developers to do nearly anything that is possible in Java. The Execute Custom Code action represents the noninteractive interface for this API.
Execute Script/Batch File	E	This action allows developers to enter the text to a script or batch file, which will then be executed from within the installation.
Execute Target File	E S	This action launches any executable or opens a document that is included in the installer. If the target is a document that has the appropriate application associations set up, then the document will be opened in the correct application. This action is available only during and after the installation of files.
Find Component in Registry	E	This action discovers whether a component exists on a system through the cross-platform registry; it also finds existing component versions, their locations, and if there are multiple instances of a particular component on the destination system.

Table C.2 General Actions (Continued)

Action	Editions	Description
Get Windows Registry Entry	E	InstallAnywhere allows developers to access information stored in the Windows registry through this action. It also allows developers to retrieve or check for the existence of a key or value and store that information in InstallAnywhere variables to be used in the installation.
Jump to Target	E	Related to the Add Jump Label discussed above, this action allows developers to jump to a specific point in an installation. When controlled by InstallAnywhere rules, this action gives developers a conditional method of moving nonlinearly through an install. This action is available during the **Files** and **Sequence** tasks.
Launch Default Browser	E S	This action allows developers to launch the user's default Web browser with specified arguments. It can open a URL or a file on the system. This action is available during the **Sequence** task.
Modify Text File—In Archive	E	This action allow developers to alter text files found in Zip-format archives.
Modify Text File—Multiple Files	E	This action allow developers to alter multiple text files. It can also be used to properly change line endings for a large number of files.
Modify Text File—Single File	E	This action allow developers to the contents of a single file.
Output Debug Information	E S	The InstallAnywhere installer includes comprehensive debugging. By running the installer in Debug mode, developers can diagnose many issues. This action allows developers to output specific information either to the console or to a file. Developers can output the entire contents of the InstallAnywhere variable manager, the install tree, Java Properties, and other information related to the installation.
Output Text to Console	E S	This action outputs specified text to the debug console, which is useful for measuring the progress of a noninteractive installer in Silent or Console mode or the progress of a noninteractive portion of the installation.
Perform XSL Transform	E	This action allows developers to specify an Extensible Stylesheet Language transform, or XSLT, and target. Predefined XSLTs can be found in the `<InstallAnywhere>\resource\extras\presets` directory.
Perform XSL Transform—In Archive	E	This action works the same as the Perform XSL Transform action, but does so for files in an archive. This action is useful for configuring Web applications in WAR, EAR, and JAR files.
Restart Windows	E S	This action will restart a Windows system. The system will reboot as soon as this action is reached, so use it carefully and only in conjunction with rules.

Table C.2 General Actions (Continued)

Action	Editions	Description
Set InstallAnywhere Variable—Multiple Variables	E S	The root of any InstallAnywhere installation, these actions allow developers to specify values for, or to create, InstallAnywhere variables. These actions are used throughout the installation and can be used to control nearly any aspect of the installation.
Set InstallAnywhere Variable—Single Variable	E S	Set InstallAnywhere Variable—Multiple Variables
Show Message Dialog	E	This action creates a modal dialog that requests end-user input. The message dialog box will appear over the currently displayed panel and can be used to force the end-user to return to the previous panel, exit the installer, or input information. When controlled by rules, this action can be used as a data verification tool.
Start, Stop, Pause Windows Service	E	If the application is interacting with a Windows service, the installer may need to manage that service. This action, when the installer is run with sufficient privileges, allows the installer to stop, start, or pause registered Windows services.

Table C.3 Panel Actions

Action	Editions	Description
Choose Alias, Link, Shortcut	E S	Added as part of the default project, this panel allows the end-user to choose an installation location for shortcuts (Windows), aliases (Mac), and links (UNIX).
Choose Features to Uninstall	E S	This panel allows the end-user to select the features to uninstall.
Choose File	E	This panel allows installers to request that the user select a file based on certain criteria and set its result as an InstallAnywhere variable. The variable can then be used later in the install.
Choose Folder	E	This panel allows developers to request that the user select a folder based on certain criteria and set its result as an InstallAnywhere variable that can be used later in the install.
Choose Install Folder	E S	Part of the default project, this panel allows the user to choose the primary installation folder. It is not necessary that this panel be included, as without it, the installer will select the default specified in the **Project	Platforms** task.
Choose Install Set	E S	This panel allows developers to request that the end-user choose an install set or features to install.

Table C.3 Panel Actions (Continued)

Action	Editions	Description
Choose Java VM	E S	This panel allows developers to have the end-user select the JVM to be used for any installed LaunchAnywhere launchers. Developers can specify the type of VM that the end-user should select, and the panel will search the system for an appropriate VM.
Choose Uninstall Type	E S	This panel allows the end-user to select whether to install all or part of the application.
Custom Code Panel	E	InstallAnywhere's Custom Code API allows developers to create custom panels where necessary.
Disk Space Check	E S	This panel performs a disk space check on the installation destination system based on the end-user's chosen install location and the end-user's chosen features. If there is not enough disk space to perform the install, then the installer will prompt the end-user to free the required disk space or choose another install location. This panel is automatically added before files are installed. The action does not appear in the list.
Display Message	E S	This panel allows developers simply to display a text message to the end-user during the installation. This can be useful for conveying information about installation choices that the end-user has made. This panel is also particularly useful in debugging installer issues having to do with InstallAnywhere variables.
Find File/Folder	E	This panel implements a search process that, depending on specifications made by the developer, will search portions of the file system for a specific named file, or a file matching a certain pattern. The end-user can also choose a matching file.
Get Password	E	This panel allows developers to request a password from the end-user. Developers can choose to validate the password against a list of specified passwords (enabling the Index feature that allows different passwords effectively to unlock different features) or they can simply store the entered password in a variable (as when requesting a password to be used in a configuration routine).
Get Serial Number	E	Implementing InstallAnywhere's built-in serial number verification and creation routines, this panel allows developers to add serial number functionality to the installer. Developers can choose to generate any number of serial numbers for any number of products. Serial numbers can represent unique products or sets of products. As a result, this action allows developers to create rules that can manage all aspects of the installation based on rights granted by the serial number the end-user has entered.

Table C.3 Panel Actions (Continued)

Action	Editions	Description
Get User Input—Advanced	E	The older, smarter, and more capable brother of the **Get User Input** panel, this panel allows developers to get input from the user by using multiple input types and setting multiple variables. This action can use radio buttons, check boxes, text fields, and menus—all on the same panel.
Get User input—Simple	E	This panel allows developers to request input from the end-user.
Important Note	E S	This panel allows developers to display a text or HTML file without the radio buttons found on the **License Agreement** panel. It is particularly useful for displaying readme or errata-type documents.
Install Complete	E S	This panel displays information about the installation's status to the end-user. It also optionally displays if a restart is needed on a Windows system. It is available only after files have been installed.
Introduction	E S	Part of the default project, this panel offers an introduction to the installation.
License Agreement	E S	This panel allows developers to display a license agreement to the end-user. The end-user must choose to accept the agreement to continue. Developers can set the default state of the radio buttons (accept or decline) and choose a file to use for a license agreement. The **License Agreement** panel can also use HTML files, which gives developers a degree of control over text formatting and allows them to link to external documents.
Pre-Install Summary	E S	This panel summarizes information collected and evaluated prior to the installation of files. It allows the developer to customize what information is presented. It is included in the default InstallAnywhere project.
Scrolling Message	E	This panel allows developers to enter long text in a message panel that includes scroll bars. This is particularly useful for instructions.
Uninstall Complete	E S	This panel displays information that the uninstaller has completed.
Uninstaller Introduction	E S	This panel offers an introduction to the uninstaller.

Console Actions

Console actions (commonly called consoles) are the means for requesting installer end-user input when using a command-line interface (see Table C.4). When the end-user selects a console installation, console actions will be used instead of panel actions.

Table C.4 Console Actions

Action	Editions	Description
Choose Features to Uninstall	E	This console allows the end-user to select the features to uninstall.
Choose Install Folder	E	This console chooses the primary installation location.
Choose Install Sets	E	This console allows developers to request that the end-user choose an install set or features to install.
Choose Java VM	E	This console allows developers to have the end-user select the JVM to be used for any installed LaunchAnywhere launchers. Developers can specify the type of VM that the end-user should select, and the panel will search the system for an appropriate VM.
Choose Link Folder	E	This console allows the user to determine where to install UNIX links.
Choose Uninstall Type	E	This console allows the end-user to select whether to install all or part of the application.
Custom Code	E	InstallAnywhere's Custom Code API allows developers to create custom consoles where necessary.
Display Message	E	This console allows developers simply to display a text message to the end-user during the installation.
Get Password	E	This console allows developers to request a password from the end-user.
Get Serial Number	E	This console allows end-users to generate a list of serial numbers as well as request them from the end-user.
Get User Input	E	This console allows developers to request input from the end-user.
Install Complete	E	This console displays information about the installation's status to the end-user. It is available only after files have been installed.
Install Failed	E	This console should be displayed when a console installer has generated an error.
License Agreement	E	This console allows developers to display a license agreement to the end-user.
Pre-Install Summary	E	This console summarizes information collected and evaluated prior to the installation of files.
Ready to Install	E	This console alerts the end-user that the installer is about to install files.
Show Message Console 'Dialog'	E	This console displays a message dialog to the end-user.
Uninstall Complete	E	This console displays information that the uninstaller has completed.
Uninstaller Introduction	E	This console offers an introduction to the uninstaller.

Common Properties

Table C.5 contains common properties found in action customizers in InstallAnywhere.

Table C.5 Common Properties

Property	Description
Comment	Sets the name of the action in the visual tree
Do not uninstall	Tells an action to not attempt to undo the results of the action at uninstall time
If file already exists on end-user's system	Overrides the default behavior for how to resolve conflicts between installed files and preexisting files
In classpath	Puts the item on the classpath for all LaunchAnywhere executables installed
Installed file/existing file	Determines whether the file is being installed or already exists on the end-user's system
Override default UNIX /Mac OS X permissions	Sets the file permissions to a specific value for this action
Path	Shows the path where the action will be installed
Show indeterminate dialog	Brings up an indeterminate progress bar to show progress to the end-user while an external process is executing
Source	Shows the path where the item currently exists on the developer's system (displays the source path if source paths are being used)
Store process' exit code in	Sets the value of the InstallAnywhere variable to the process' exit code
Store process' stderr in	Sets the value of the InstallAnywhere variable to the process' standard error
Store process' stdout in	Sets the value of the InstallAnywhere variable to the process' standard out
Suspend installation until process completes	Pauses the installer until the launched process completes

Panel Action Settings

Panel actions (commonly called panels) are the means for requesting user input through a graphical interface.

Graphic installers may show the installation steps through a set of labels, or words that represent the step. Installers may also display specific images for the steps. When **Images** is selected in the **Installer UI | Look and Feel | Installer Panel Additions | Type of Additions to Installer Panels** task, the customizer for the panel in the **Pre-Install** and **Post-Install** tasks will enable the use of the **Image Settings** tab. If **List of Installer Steps** is selected, the **Label Settings** tab will be enabled.

> **NOTE** These settings are unavailable to panel actions in the uninstaller. Panel actions in the uninstaller use the default values set in the **Installer UI | Look and Feel** task.

Image Settings

Use panel image settings to choose a specific image to display on the chosen panel. Developers may choose to use the default panel image, display an image specific to that panel, or display no image at all.

Label Settings

The **Label Settings** tab in the customizer enables developers to preview labels and icon images. Labels are highlighted and marked as the installation progresses. The installer build process will autopopulate the list based on the panel titles.

> **NOTE** Using the **Installer UI | Look and Feel** task's **Installer Panel Additions** tab and the **Labels Settings** tab found on each individual panel's customizer, developers can assign multiple panels to the same label. Thus, if there are numerous steps or if the installer has several panels for the same step, the interface can be adjusted as needed.

To control label order or to edit the content of the label, in the **Installer UI | Look and Feel** task's **Installer Panel Additions** tab use the arrows and other control buttons found to the left of the list of panels.

Help

Selecting **Enable installer help** in the **Installer UI | Help** subtask provides a Help feature for the installer program. Developers may set a single Help message, which they can define in this window. To customize Help for each installer screen, select **Use different help** for each text panel. Add the customized Help in the **Help** tab of the action customizer at the bottom of the **Pre-Install** and **Post-Install** tasks.

Selecting **HTML** allows greater formatting control of the message, but not of the title bar. To change formatting, use HTML formatting tags, such as

`<B>MyHelp</B> <I>Information</I>`

which displays as **MyHelp** *Information*.

Additional Action Information

LaunchAnywhere

A LaunchAnywhere executable, or LAX, is a file used to launch a Java application on any LaunchAnywhere-compatible platform (all Windows, UNIX platforms, and Mac OS X). LaunchAnywhere enables end-users to double-click on an icon (Windows or Mac OS X) or type a single command (UNIX) to start a Java application. The LAX is also in charge of configuring the Java application environment by setting the classpath; redirecting standard out and standard error; passing in system properties, environment variables, and command-line parameters; and many other options.

The launcher looks at a configuration file, `<MyLauncherName>.lax`, to determine how the launcher runs. This `lax` file is created during the installation and is placed in the same location as the launcher.

Please see the list of LAX properties located in Appendix I.

Manifest Files

Manifest files are text files that specify a list of files and directories. The manifest file has a certain format (listed below). The format specifies the file's source, its destination (which is relative to the location of the action in the visual tree of the **Files** task), and optionally, which UNIX file permission it should have and if it should be placed on the classpath. At build time, this file is analyzed, and its contents are placed into the installer.

Manifest File Format

For files:

```
F,[SOURCEPATH]relative_path_to_source_file,./
  relative_path_to_destination_file
F,absolute_path_to_source_file,./relative_path_to_destination_file
```

To put files on the classpath:

F,absolute_path_to_source_file,./
  relative_path_to_destination_file,cp

To set a file's permissions on UNIX:

F,[SOURCEPATH]relative_path_to_source_file,./
  relative_path_to_destination_file,755

For directories:

D,[SOURCEPATH]relative_path_to_source_dir[/],./
  relative_path_to_destination_dir[/]
D,absolute_path_to_source_dir[/],./
  relative_path_to_destination_dir[/]

Examples:

F,IA_HOME/path/to/source/file.txt,./destination/path/
  thisfile.txt
F,/absolute/path/to/source/file.txt,./destination/path/
  thisfile.txt,cp,655
D,IA_HOME/path/to/dir,./destination/path/dir
D,/absolute/path/to/dir,./destination/path/dir

APPENDIX D
Build Tools

A build properties file template named `Build.properties` can be found in your InstallAnywhere application folder inside `resource/build`. Table D.1 lists some build tool options.

Table D.1 Build Tool Options (Part 1)

Option	Description

-v	Print InstallAnywhere product version
	`C:\Program Files\InstallAnywhere 6 Enterprise>build.exe -v`
	`InstallAnywhere 6 Enterprise`

-p	Use specified build properties file
+	Add platform to build
-	Remove platform from build

The arguments listed in Table D.2 modify the add (+) and remove (–) platforms arguments.

Table D.2 Build Tool Options (Part 2)

Option	Description
a,A	AIX without VM option
av,AV	AIX with VM option
h,H	HP-UX without VM option
hv,HV	HP-UX with VM option
j,J,o,O	Pure Java option
l,L	Linux without VM option
lv,LV	Linux with VM option

Table D.2 Build Tool Options (Part 2) (Continued)

Option	Description
s,S	Solaris without VM option
sv,SV	Solaris with VM option
u,U	Generic UNIX without VM option
n,N	Named UNIX without VM option
nv,NV	Named UNIX with VM option
w,W	Windows without VM option
wv,WV	Windows with VM option
x,X	Mac OS X without VM option
web	Build Web installers
cd	Build CD-ROM installers
opt	Optimize by platform
merge	Build merge modules

APPENDIX E
Exit Codes

The command-line build tool returns one of the exit codes listed in Tables E.1 to E.7 based upon the results of the build.

Table E.1 Resource-Related Exit Codes

Code	Status
cancelled1	Missing resources; build abort cancelled by preferences

Table E.2 Project File–Related Exit Codes

Code	Status
101	Project load error
102	Project copy load error
103	Project file not found
104	Project file is read-only
199	Project file unknown error

Table E.3 Command Line Options–Related Exit Codes

Code	Status
200	Illegal build flag
201	Insufficient build flag

Table E.4 VM Pack–Related Exit Codes

Code	Status
300	VM Pack replaced
301	VM Pack not found
302	VM Pack illegal format
399	VM Pack unknown error

Table E.5 File Write Errors

Code	Status
400	File write not found
401	File write busy
402	File write protected
403	File write error
499	File write unknown error

Table E.6 File Read Errors

Code	Status
500	File read not found
501	File read busy
502	File read protected
503	File read error
599	File read unknown error

Table E.7 Other Errors

Code	Status
-1	Other error/unknown error
0	No errors; build completed successfully without errors or warnings
666	Insufficient rights in directory
799	Unknown internal error

APPENDIX F

Parameters

After defining the task, specify any parameter necessary for the build settings:

```
<buildinstaller
  IAlocation="C:\Program Files\InstallAnywhere 6 Enterprise"
  IAProjectFile="C:\Projects\myproject.iap_xml"
  additionalparameter=value
/>
```

Replace the IAlocation with the absolute path to your own InstallAnywhere application folder. If InstallAnywhere cannot be found, ANT will search for it in one of the default locations or look in the registry to find where InstallAnywhere was installed.

Specify the path and filename of the project to build in the IAProjectFile parameter.

All other properties are optional. The parameters closely match the properties found in the build properties file. The Table F.1 shows the available parameters.

Table F.1 Platform Target Parameters

Attribute	Description	Required
IAProjectFile	Specifies the location of the InstallAnywhere project that you want to build	Yes
IALocation	Specifies the location where InstallAnywhere is installed	No*
propertiesfile	Specifies the location of a build properties file you can use (if used, all other attributes are ignored)	No
failonerror	Stops the build process if the command exits with a return code other than 0 (defaults to false)	No

* If IALocation is not specified, the task will search for a copy of InstallAnywhere to run against. If InstallAnywhere is not installed in one of the default locations, then the task will check the InstallAnywhere product registry for a valid location.

NOTE Remember, in order for the InstallAnywhere **ANT** task to work, you will need to add iaant.jar to $ANT_HOME/lib.

Tables F.2 to F.4 list the various platform, build, and installer options available.

Table F.2 Platform Options

Option	Value
BuildLinuxWithVM	true/false
BuildLinuxWithoutVM	true/false
LinuxVMPackLocation	Path
BuildHPUXWithVM	true/false
BuildHPUXWithoutVM	true/false
HPUXVMPackLocation	Path
BuildAIXWithVM	true/false
BuildAIXWithoutVM	true/false
AIXVMPackLocation	Path
BuildSolarisWithVM	true/false
BuildSolarisWithoutVM	true/false
SolarisVMPackLocation	Path
BuildNamedUNIXWithVM	true/false
BuildNamedUNIXWithoutVM	true/false
NamedUNIXVMPackLocation	Path
NamedUNIXTitle	Path
BuildWindowsWithVM	true/false
BuildWindowsWithoutVM	true/false
WindowsVMPackLocation	Path
BuildMacOSX	true/false
BuildPureJava	true/false

Table F.3 Build Options

Option	Value
BuildCDROMInstaller	true/false
BuildWebInstaller	true/false
BuildMergeModule	true/false
BuildReadOnlyMergeModule	true/false
BuildOutputLocation	Path
OptimizeCDROMInstaller	true/false
OptimizeWebInstaller	true/false
OptimizeMergeModule	true/false
AutoPopulateLabels	true/false
AutoCleanComponents	true/false

Table F.4 Installer Options

Option	Value
InstallerStdErrRedirect	Path
InstallerStdoutRedirect	Path
InstallerValidVMList	String
InstallerInitialHeapSize	Integer
InstallerMaxHeapSize	Integer
UNIXDefaultUI	Silent/Console/GUI

Examples

```
<taskdef name="buildinstaller"
classname="com.zerog.ia.integration.ant.InstallAnywhereAntTask"/>
<buildinstaller

    IAlocation="C:\Program Files\InstallAnywhere 6 Enterprise"

    IAProjectFile="C:\Projects\myproject.iap_xml"

    BuildLinuxWithVM="true"
    BuildMacOSX="true"
    BuildWebInstallers="true"
    OptimizeWebInstallers="true"
    InstallerStdErrRedirect="C:\console.txt"
    />
```

APPENDIX G
Language Codes

Table G.1 lists the language codes used in InstallAnywhere.

Table G.1 Language Codes

Language	Country Code	Language Group
Catalan	CA	Western
Czech	CS	Eastern
Danish	DA	Western
German	DE	Western
Greek	EL	Eastern
English	EN	Western
Spanish	ES	Western
Basque	EU	Western
Finnish	FI	Western
French	FR	Western
French (Canada)	FR_CA	Western
Hungarian	HU	Eastern
Indonesian	ID	Eastern
Italian	IT	Western
Japanese	JA	Eastern
Korean	KO	Eastern
Dutch	NL	Western
Norwegian	NO	Western
Polish	PL	Western
Portuguese	PT	Western

Table G.1 Language Codes (Continued)

Language	Country Code	Language Group
Portuguese (Brazil)	PT_BR	Western
Russian	RU	Eastern
Slovak	SK	Western
Slovenian	SL	Western
Swedish	SV	Western
Thai	TH	Eastern
Turkish	TR	Eastern
Chinese (Simplified)	ZH_CN	Eastern
Chinese (Traditional)	ZH_TW	Eastern

APPENDIX H
Localizable Elements

Installers deployed to non-Latin systems require an international JVM.

Localizing Items in the Installer

See Table H.1 to determine the correct properties to modify in the language resource files. This table does not include properties from many new actions. For a complete list, please contact Zero G support.

Table H.1 Localizable Elements

Property	Definition
Installer.#.ProductName	Name of product displayed on installer title bar
Installer.#.RulesFailedMessage	Message displayed if specified rules keep the installer from running
Installer.#.ShortcutDestinationPathMacOS	Path to where aliases are created during installation on Mac OS (relative to the end-user-selected alias folder chosen during the **Choose Alias Location** step)
Installer.#.ShortcutDestinationPathWin32	Path to where shortcuts are created during installation on Windows (relative to the end-user-selected shortcut folder chosen during the **Choose Alias, Link, Shortcut Folder** step)
Installer.#.ShortcutDestinationPathSolaris	Path to where links are created during installation on UNIX (relative to the end-user-selected links folder chosen during the **Choose Link Location** step)
Installer.#.End-userSplashName	Name of the image file to be displayed as the installer is preparing itself (Note: This is a filename only, not a fully qualified absolute pathname)
Installer.#.End-userSplashPath	Pathname to the image file to be displayed as the installer is preparing (Note: This is only a pathname and does not include the filename itself)
InstallSet.#.Description	Description of one of the installer's features

Table H.1 Localizable Elements (Continued)

Property	Definition
`InstallSet.#.InstallSetName`	Name of one of the installer's features
`Intro.#.DisplayText`	Text to display during the installer's **Introduction** step.
`Intro.#.Title`	Title to display during the installer's **Introduction** step
`LicenseAgr.#.FileName`	Name of the localized license agreement to be displayed as the installer is preparing itself (Note: This is a filename only, not a fully qualified absolute pathname).
`LicenseAgr.#.Path`	Pathname to the localized license agreement to be displayed as the installer is preparing itself (Note: This is only a pathname and does not include the filename itself)
`LicenseAgr.#.Title`	Title of the License Agreement step in the installer
`MakeExecutable.#.DestinationName`	Name of the LaunchAnywhere executable to be created on the destination computer
`MakeRegEntry.#.Value`	Value to be written into the Win32 registry
`ShortcutLoc.#.MacOSTitle`	Title of the Mac OS **Choose Alias Location** step in the installer
`ShortcutLoc.#.SolarisTitle`	Title of the UNIX **Choose Alias, Link, Shortcut Folder** step in the installer
`ShortcutLoc.#.Win32Title`	Title of the Win32 **Choose Alias, Link, Shortcut Folder** step in the installer
`Billboard.#.ImageName`	Name of the billboard image file to be displayed as the installer is preparing itself (Note: This is a filename only, not a fully qualified absolute pathname)
`Billboard.#.ImagePath`	Pathname to the billboard image to be displayed as the installer is preparing itself (Note: This is only a pathname and does not include the filename itself)
`ChooseInstallSet.#.Title`	Title of the **Choose Feature** step in the installer
`ChooseJavaVM.#.Title`	Title of the **Choose Java Virtual Machine** step in the installer
`CreateShortcut.#.DestinationName`	Name of the shortcut/alias/link to be created on the destination computer
`human.readable.language.name`	Name of the language represented by the data in this resource file (i.e., English, Espanol, and so on)
`ImportantNote.#.FileName`	Name of the text file to be displayed during the Important Note step of the installer (Note: This is a filename only, not a fully qualified absolute pathname)

Table H.1 Localizable Elements (Continued)

Property	Definition
ImportantNote.#.Path -	Pathname to the text file to be displayed during the **Important Note** step of the installer (Note: This is only a pathname and does not include the filename itself)
ImportantNote.#.Title	Title of the **Important Note** step in the installer
InstallBundle.#.BundleName	Name of a component
InstallBundle.#.Description	Description text describing a component
InstallComplete.#.DisplayText	Text to display during the **Install Complete** step of the installer
InstallComplete.#.Title	Title of the **Install Complete** step in the installer
InstallDir.#.Title	Title of the **Choose Installation Directory** step of the installer
Installer.#.InstallerName	Name of the installer

APPENDIX I
LaunchAnywhere Executable Properties

The properties that LaunchAnywhere can modify are defined in Table I.1.

Table I.1 LaunchAnywhere Executable Properties

Property	Definition
lax.application.name	This is the name of the application that the launcher executes.
lax.class.path	This is the classpath for the application. By default, it is set to $IA_CLASSPATH$ (the classpath specified in the InstallAnywhere designer environment). When specifying the classpath, either forward or backward slashes ("/" or "\") may be used as directory separators, and either colons or semicolons may be used for path separators—InstallAnywhere will substitute the proper characters based on the installation platform. Mac end-users should use slashes for directory separators and not colons as InstallAnywhere will treat colons as path separators.
lax.command.line.args	This is a list of arguments passed to the application's main method. These are specified in exactly the same way they would be on the command line. For example, if the application is invoked as java myApp arg1 arg2, set this property to _arg1 arg2_. Be sure to place quotes around any arguments that have spaces. When it is necessary to pass in an argument that is only known at install time (for instance, the installation directory), use an InstallAnywhere variable.
lax.java.compiler	[Runtime only—cannot be set via "Edit Properties..."]: This is the JIT (just-in-time) compiler being used for execution of this application.
lax.main.method	This is the name of the application's starting method that the LaunchAnywhere executable should invoke.
lax.mainclass	This is the class that gets launched by the LaunchAnywhere executable. This class must contain a method with a name defined by the lax.main.method property.
lax.nl.current.vm	This is the pathname of the VM executable currently being used by this application.

Table I.1   LaunchAnywhere Executable Properties (Continued)

Property	Definition
lax.nl.env.<lowercase>	[Windows and UNIX only]: You can access any System Environment variable (for example, access path via $lax.nl.env.path$) by specifying the property name as an all-lowercase string. These properties are resolved at application runtime, when LaunchAnywhere executes. You can also get access to System Environment variables via InstallAnywhere variables.
lax.nl.env.<UPPERCASE>	[Windows and UNIX only]: You can access any System Environment variable (for example, access PATH via $lax.nl.env.PATH$) by specifying the property name as an all-uppercase string. These properties are resolved at application runtime, when LaunchAnywhere executes. You can also get access to System Environment variables via LaunchAnywhere variables.
lax.nl.env.exact_case	[Windows and UNIX only]: You can access any System Environment variable (for example, access Path via $lax.nl.env.exact_case.Path$) by specifying the property name as a string of the exact case as it is defined in the environment. Note that these properties are resolved at application runtime, when LaunchAnywhere executes. You can also get access to System Environment variables via LaunchAnywhere variables.
lax.nl.env.path	[Runtime only—cannot be set via "Edit Properties…"]: This is the system path for the computer this application is running on.
lax.nl.java.compiler	This property defines the name of the JIT compiler that your application should use. If you set this option to no value (i.e., blank), the default JIT will be used. You can also name a specific JIT by defining it in this property. This property should be set to off if no JIT is to be used.
lax.nl.java.launcher.main.class	This is the class that contains the main method called by LaunchAnywhere.
lax.nl.java.launcher.main.method	This is the name of the main method called by LaunchAnywhere.
lax.nl.java.option.additional	The value of this property will be written to the command line verbatim. JVM properties or settings not directly supported by current LAX configuration properties can be included as part of the command line used to invoke Java.
lax.nl.java.option.check.source	This is set to on or off to tell the VM to verify byte codes.
lax.nl.java.option.debugging	This turns on debugging in the VM so that an application can be debugged.
lax.nl.java.option.garbage.collection.background.thread	This determines whether to have a low-priority background thread that does garbage collection. It is set to on or off.

Table I.1 LaunchAnywhere Executable Properties (Continued)

Property	Definition
lax.nl.java.option.garbage.collection.extent	This is set to one of the following values: min: Garbage collect everything except classes. full: Garbage collect everything.
lax.nl.java.option.java.heap.size.initial	This defines the initial heap size for the installer that will be invoked. This number is always specified in bytes, not kilobytes or megabytes, and is analogous to the VM parameter –ms or Xms. The default is 16,777,216 (16MB).
lax.nl.java.option.java.heap.size.max	This defines the maximum heap size in bytes for the installer that will be invoked. This number is always specified in bytes, not kilobytes or megabytes, and is analogous to the VM parameter -mx or Xmx. The default is 50,331,648 (48MB).
lax.nl.java.option.verbose	This is set to any of the following values: gc: Output garbage collection messages. normal: Output all normal verbose messages. all: Output all normal and garbage collection messages. none: Do not output any verbose messages.
lax.nl.java.option.verify.mode	This sets when Java will verify classes for security and errors. Values can be remote, all, or none.
lax.nl.message.vm.not.loaded	This is the message to show the end-user in a dialog box if no VM can be found.
lax.nl.valid.vm.list	This is the list of VMs that this LaunchAnywhere executable will allow the Java application to be run against. The value for this property can be any space-delimited combination of the following: ALL (any VM) JDK (any Java JDK) JRE (any Java JRE) J1 (any Java 1 VM) J2 (any Java 2 VM) JRE_J1 (any Java 1 JRE) JDK_J1 (any Java 1 JDK) JRE_J2 (any Java 2 JRE) JDK_J2 (any Java 2 JDK) MSJ (the Microsoft VM [jview]) The value of this property will also override the value listed in lax.nl.current.vm if the VM listed in that property is not of a valid type. The order of the valid VM list specifies the precedence in which VMs found on the system should be chosen if a valid VM is not listed in lax.nl.current.vm.

Table I.1 LaunchAnywhere Executable Properties (Continued)

Property	Definition
lax.nl.win32.microsoftvm.min.version	This is the minimum version of the Microsoft VM that this LaunchAnywhere executable will find.
lax.resource.dir	This is the platform name in exact case.
lax.root.install.dir	This is the root directory of the entire installation (same as $USER_INSTALL_DIR$).
lax.stderr.redirect	This is the location of your application's stderr output. Set it to null to suppress, console to write to a console window, or any filename to output to a file. Note: If you are specifying a pathname to a Windows file, make sure to use escaped backslashes (i.e., c:\\myfolder\\output.txt).
lax.stdout.redirect	This is the location of your application's stdout output. Set it to null to suppress, console to write to a console window, or any filename to output to a file. Note: If you are specifying a pathname to a Windows file, make sure to use escaped backslashes (i.e., c:\\myfolder\\output.txt).
lax.user.dir	This is the end-user directory for your application (represented by "."). You can also specify any arbitrary absolute or relative path. A relative path is relative to the launcher.
lax.version	This is LaunchAnywhere's version number.
LISTPROPS	This property lists all system properties available to the Java application (it can take any value.) Stdout and stderr must be redirected to see the results of this output.

APPENDIX J
Quick Quiz Answers

Chapter 6: An Introduction to the Advanced Designer
From page 58

Answers: 1. B | 2. A, B | 3. A

Chapter 8: Basic Installer Customization
From page 81

Answers: 1. C | 2. B | 3. B

Chapter 9: Installer Organization
From page 94

Answers: 1. B | 2. C

Chapter 10: Introduction to Advanced Actions and Panel Actions
From page 100

Answers: 1. C | 2. C | 3. A

Chapter 15: Source and Resource Management in InstallAnywhere
From page 148

Answers: 1. D | 2. B

Chapter 16: Advanced Interface Options
From page 152

Answers: 1. A | 2. B

Chapter 17: Advanced Organizational Concepts
From page 163

Answers: 1. A | 2. A | 3. D | 4. D

Chapter 19: Custom Code
From page 190

Answers: 1. B | 2. A | 3. A

Index

$ (and variables), 195, 218
    in pathname, 143, 146
    use rules, 81, 161
$:$, 217
$;$, 217
$\$, 217
$/$, 117–119, 217
-1 error, 169
\ backslash, 119, 253, 256
/ forward slash, 119, 253
/ (UNIX), 121
+ option, 167
/opt, 122
– option, 167

A

option (AIX without VM), 167
absolute path, 33, 112, 116, 144, 195, 201
Abstract Window Toolkit (AWT), 66, 69, 181
ActionListener, 182
actions, 30–31
    advanced, 96–98
    console, 30, 108–109
    custom code, 177–180, 196–202
    general, 30, 97, 103–105
    install, 101–103
    jump, 151–152
    list of, 101–113
    panel, 30, 105–108
    plug-in, 31, 204–206
    properties, 109–110
    reordering, 96
    rules, 31

Add Billboard, 72
Add Comment, 103
Add Files to Project, 21–22
Add Jump Label, 103
Add Launcher, 47–48
adding advertised variables, 161
adding components, 93
adding features, 94
adding merge modules, 161
adding platform to build, 167
adding source paths, 143, 146
Additions to GUI Installer Panels, 29, 67
admin, 102
Adobe Systems, 2
advanced action methods, 199–201
advanced actions, 96–98
Advanced Designer, 26
    actions, 96
    button, 44
    dynamic and static text, 208–209
    exercise, 45–53
    locale files, 209
    Magic Folders, 118
    plug-ins, 204
    starting, 20
    tasks, 44
Advanced Get User Input, 107, 151
advertised variables, 157, 160–161
AIX, 167, 172
alias, 10, 48, 101, 106, 215, 221
All Users Desktop folder, 122
All Users Programs menu, 121
All Users Start menu, 121
All Users Startup folder, 122

259

Allowable UI Modes, 66
animated graphics, 11
answers to quizzes, 257–258
ANT, 103, 170–173
Apache Foundation Jakarta Project, 103, 170
Apple Menu Items, 122
approximate merge module size, 160
assigning files to components, 93
authentication and merge modules, 159
authoring environments, 2–3, 26
authoring modes, 20
Auto Populate, 71
autoclean components, 173
automated build environments
    ANT build integration, 170–173
    build tools, 166–168
    command-line build facility, 166
    exit codes, 168–170
autopopulate labels, 173
av option (AIX with VM), 167
awk, 147
AWT (Abstract Window Toolkit), 66, 69, 181

B

background images, 29, 67, 69, 70
backslash (\), 119, 253, 256
batch file, 104, 199
billboards, 11, 16, 29–30
    animated GIFs, 68
    image pathname, 216
    size of, 30, 72
.bin, 101
blank icons, 49
boolean rules, 31, 50, 73
`boolean setupUI()`, 182
Borland, 2
branding, 12
browser, 17, 52, 104
`BrowserLauncher`, 182
`build executable`, 166
Build Installer, 23

Build Log, 64
build options, 62–64, 159–160, 173
build platforms, selecting, 170
build properties file template, 167
build settings, parameters, 171–172
build tool options, 167–168
building a basic installer, 21–24
building a console-enabled installer, 133
building a silent-mode installer, 136
building with Advanced Designer, 45–53
build-time merge modules, 158–159
bundle list, 217
Bundle Merge Module at Build Time, 156, 158
bundle name, 216
burning CD-ROM installers, 63–64
buttons, 182, 217
byte codes, 254

C

case sensitivity, 79–80, 128, 220, 254, 256
cd option, 168
CD-ROM installers, 26, 62–64, 168
CD-ROM option, 173
Change Disk Name or Space, 63
Check Disk Space, 218, 221
check end-user chosen language, 74
check file modification timestamp, 74
check file/folder attributes, 74
Check for Updates, 102
check if file/folder exists, 74
check platform, 74–75
Choose Alias, Link, Shortcut, 46, 48, 106, 120, 133, 215–216
Choose an Action, 96
Choose Features to Uninstall, 106, 108
Choose File, 106
Choose Folder, 106
Choose Install Folder, 62, 106, 108
Choose Install Set, 106
Choose Install Sets, 85, 89–93, 108
Choose Installation Directory, 216

Choose Java Virtual Machine (JVM), 35, 106, 108, 116, 216
Choose Link Folder, 108
Choose Main Class, 22
Choose Product Features, 218
Choose Uninstall Type, 106, 108
$CHOSEN_DIALOG_BUTTON$, 217
$CHOSEN_INSTALL_BUNDLE_#$, 217
$CHOSEN_INSTALL_BUNDLE_LIST$, 217
$CHOSEN_INSTALL_BUNDLE_NUM$, 218
$CHOSEN_INSTALL_SET$, 218
class field, 177, 181
classes, 22, 203–204
classpath, 22, 110, 219, 253
Clean Components, 93
Clean-up at Startup, 122
client-side installer experience, 6–11
$CMD_LINE_ARGUMENTS$, 218
colon, 119, 253
comma, 200, 205, 217, 218
$COMMA$, 218
command-line
    arguments, 253
    build facility, 166
    builds, 145
    console installer, 133
    exit codes, 168
    installation, 30
    interface (console), 27
    requests, 30
Comment, 99, 103, 109
common properties, 109–110
compare InstallAnywhere variables, 74
components, 86
    adding, 93
    assigning files, 93
    modifying automatically, 89
    organization, 88–89
    removing, 93
concept review, 124–130
conditional logic, 73–81
console actions, 30, 108–109
console installers, 132–135
console mode, 27, 67, 132
console output, 126–127
console.app, 128–129
console-mode installers, 12, 132–135
consoles, 108–109, 185–188
Control Panels folder, 122
Copy File, 101
Copy Folder, 101
copy load error, 168
country codes, 213–214
CP icon, 22
Create Alias, Link, Shortcut, 35, 101, 116
Create Folder, 101
Create LaunchAnywhere for Java Apps, 101
Create New Project option, 21
Create Uninstaller, 101
creating serial numbers, 107
custom code
    actions, 177–180, 194–204
    consoles, 185–188
    debugging, 198
    localization, 210–211
    panels, 106, 108, 181–185
    plug-ins, 204–206
    rules, 188–190
Custom Code Application Programming Interface, 176
custom icons, 22, 48–49
custom installer labels, 210
custom rule, 74
Custom User Input, 155
CustomCodeAction, 180
CustomCodeConsoleProxy, 201
CustomCodePanel, 181–185
CustomCodePanelProxy, 201
customCode.properties, 205
CustomError, 201–202
customization
    conditional logic, 73–81
    look and feel, 66–73
customizer, 48, 50–51, 75
    merge module, 162

D

Debug mode, 104, 198
debugging, 254
    custom code, 198
    during development, 126
    and Display Message, 76
    LAX, 128
    Mac OS X installer, 128
    output, 43, 57, 104, 105, 129–130, 204
    post-development, 126–130
    UNIX/Linux installer, 127–128
    Win 32 installer, 126–127
default
    actions, 49
    browser, 104
    icons, 48, 71
    initial heap size, 255
    installer location, 24
    overwrite, 55
    panels, 45–46
    permissions, 110
    project name, 21
    source paths, 146
    text, 211
    timestamp, 55
    translations, 213–214
    variables, 217–221
Delete File, 101
Delete Folder, 101
design-time merge modules, 158–161
desktop folder, 120
developer experience, 20–24
$DEVELOPER_DISK_SPACE_ADDITIONAL$, 218
development strategies, 40–41
disk space, 10, 199, 200, 218–219, 221
Disk Space Check, 106
disk-burning application, 63–64
$DISK_SPACE_REQUIRED$, 160
Display Message, 76–77, 106, 109, 130
Distribution subtask, 63
do not install, 109, 121

Dock (Mac OS), 122
$DOLLAR$, 218
double-byte locales, 211–212
drag-and-drop, 47
DVD installers, 62–64
dynamic text, 208–209, 211

E

.ear, 101
Eastern languages, 213–214
Edit Advertised Variables, 157, 161
editions, InstallAnywhere, 4
8-bit color requirement, 2, 3
embedded variables, 195
embedded virtual machines (VMs), 23
empty string, 221
$EMPTY_STRING$, 218
en (locale code), 208
end-user experience, 6
end-user input, 78–81
Enterprise Edition, 4
environment variable, 220
errata documents, 77
errors, 36, 97, 171
    codes, 168–169
    CustomError, 201–202
    debug output, 130
    install failed, 109
    standard error, 110
    testing in foreign locales, 211
    variables, 117
escaped backslashes, 256
evaluate custom rule, 74
exact case, 220
executables, 112, 128, 196–198, 218, 253–256
Execute Action panel, 51
Execute ANT Script, 103
Execute Command, 103
Execute Custom Code, 103
Execute Script/Batch File, 104

Execute Target File, 104
executeConsoleAction, 187
$EXECUTE_FILE_TARGET$, 51
exit codes, 110, 168–170, 196–197
exitcode, 100
Expand Archive, 100, 101
Extensible Stylesheet Language Transform (XSLT), 105, 147
Extensions folder, 122
external scripts, 196–198
$EXTRACTOR_DIR$, 218
$EXTRACTOR_EXECUTABLE$, 218

F

-f, 135
failonerror, 171
feature-level uninstall, 138
features, 85
    adding, 94
    independence of, 89
    organization, 87
file attributes, 74
file installation tree, 47, 50
file is read-only error, 168
file modification timestamp, 74
File Modification Timestamp Behavior, 54–55
file not found error, 168
file read errors, 169
file separators, 119, 217
file unknown error, 168
file write errors, 169
Find Component in Registry, 53, 93, 104, 154
Find File/Folder, 107
FlowLayout, 181–182
folder attributes, 74
folders, copying, 101
Fonts, 122
forward slash /, 119, 253
free disk space, 106, 199–200, 219
$FREE_DISK_SPACE_BYTES$, 219

G

garbage collection, 254–255
general actions, 30, 97, 103–105
get InstallStatusMessage(), 180
Get Password, 98–99, 107, 109
Get Serial Number, 107, 109
get UninstallStatusMessage(), 180
Get User Input, 14–15, 79–80, 109
Get User Input—Advanced, 107, 151
Get User Input—Simple, 107
Get Windows Registry Entry, 104
geterrorstream(), 196
getInstallBundles(), 200
getInstallSets(), 200–201
getJavaVMList(), 201
getTitle(), 188
getVariable(), 194–195
GIFs, 22, 49, 68
GMT (Greenwich Mean Time), 55
graphics mode, 69
GUI, 27–30
GUI panel additions, 67

H

h option (HP-UX without VM), 167
handler, 51
heap size, 58, 255
Help, 68, 111
    components, 88–89
    HTML, 73, 111
Hewlett Packard, 2
home directory, 120
HP-UX, 102, 167, 172
HTML, 6, 29
    distribution, 63
    formatting tags, 111
    Help files, 68, 73
    Important Note, 77, 107
    License Agreement, 76, 107
human.readable.language.name, 216
hv option (HP-UX with VM), 167

I

-i, 133, 135
i2, 2
IAClasses.zip, 203
$IA_CLASSPATH$, 219, 253
ia_debug, 128
IA_HOME, 142
$IA_INSTALL_LOG$, 219
IALocation, 171–172
$IA_PROJECT$, 142
IAProjectFile, 171
.iap_xml, 166
IBM, 2
ICNS file, 49
ICO files, 22
icons, 22, 48–49, 150, 205
If file already exists on end-user's system, 109
illegal build flag, 168
images, 70, 111, 150
Important Note, 77, 107, 216
importing a merge module, 156, 161–162
In classpath, 110
infinite loop, 35
initial heap size, 255
install
    actions, 101–113
    bundles, 199
    errors, 11
    sets, 84–85, 87, 90
    timestamp, 55
Install Archive, 101
Install Complete, 17, 58, 107, 109, 216
Install Failed (error), 109
Install File, 102
Install from Manifest, 102
Install HP-UX Depot, 102
Install Linux RPM, 102
Install Merge Module, 102
Install Only If, 77–78, 80, 81
Install PowerUpdate Client, 102
Install Solaris Package, 102
Install SpeedFolder, 102
Installation Drive Root, 120
installation log, 54, 219
installation log errors, 201–202
installation planning, 40–41
Installation status, 219
Installed file/existing file, 110
installer
    arguments, 58
    environment, 3–4
    modes, 27
    options, 173
    title, 219
    types, 26–27
    versions and IDs, 53–54
Installer Applet, 6–11
$INSTALLER_LAUNCH_DIR$, 219
$INSTALLER_LOCALES$, 219
InstallerName, 216
InstallerProxy, 177, 180, 194, 201
$INSTALLER_TEMP_DIR$, 219
$INSTALLER_TITLE$, 219
$INSTALLER_UI$, 220
$INSTALL_LOG_DESTINATION$, 54, 219
$INSTALL_SUCCESS$, 219
install-time merge modules, 159
insufficient build flag, 168
insufficient rights in directory error, 169
Intel, 2, 3
interlaced GIF files, 49
international support, 4
Introduction panel, 13, 107
Introduction text, 215
introspecting added files, 48
in-use files, 54
Iona, 2

J

J1, 255
J2, 255
.jar, 101
JAR files, 48, 203–204

Java, 58
- application launcher, 31–32
- custom code, 176
- enabled platforms, 23
- executable, 220
- property, 221
- source file templates, 203

Java Abstract Window Toolkit (AWT), 66, 69, 181
Java Home folder, 121
Java Runtime Environment (JRE), 200, 255
Java Virtual Machine (JVM)
- supported, 3–4, 35, 106, 108, 116, 201, 216
- and timestamps, 55

$JAVA_DOT_HOME$, 220
$JAVA_EXECUTABLE$, 220
java.home, 220
$JAVA_HOME$, 35, 116, 121, 220
JDK, 220, 255
JDK_HOME, 220
JDK_J1, 255
JDK_J2, 255
JIT (just-in-time) compiler, 253, 254
j,o option (Pure Java), 167
JRE, 200, 255
JRE_J1, 255
JRE_J2, 255
jump actions, 151–152
jump labels, 103, 151
Jump to Target, 104
jx.log, 128

K

key concepts, 25–36
key files, 88, 93–94, 154

L

l option (Linux without VM), 167
Label Settings, 111
labels, 182
- localization, 210
- order and icons, 150

languages, 3–4, 28–29, 63, 74
- codes, 213–214
- name of, for resource file, 216

Launch Default Browser, 104
LaunchAnywhere, 31–32
LaunchAnywhere executables (LAX), 112, 128, 218, 237, 253–256
$LAUNCH_APPLICATION$, 79–81
lax. properties, 253–256
LAX_DEBUG, 129
$lax.nl.env.[]$, 220, 254
$lax.nl.env.exact_case.[]$, 220, 254
LayoutManager, 181–182
License Agreement, 76, 215
- console, 109
- HTML, 76, 107
- localized, 213
- merge modules, 62, 155

links, 10, 15, 48, 101, 106, 221
links (UNIX), 215
Linux, 3, 56, 167, 172
List of Installer Steps, 71
LISTPROPS (properties list), 256
load error, 168
locale, 29
- code, 208
- files, 29, 74, 209, 211
- as string, 219

locales, 208
Locales subtask, 57
localizable elements, 214–216
localization, 28–29, 207
- custom code, 210–211
- custom installer labels, 210
- localizable elements, 214–216
- modifying text, 212–213
- resources, 209–210

localized license agreements, 213, 215

Locate Merge Module at Install Time, 159
look and feel, 150
    of installer, 29, 66–73
        maintaining with templates, 154
Lucent, 2
lv option (Linux with VM), 167

M

M (on icons), 162
Mac Apple menu items, 122
Mac OS, 3, 122, 135, 215
Mac OS X, 168, 172
    installer debugging, 128
    options, 56
    permissions, 110
    VMs, 58
$MAC_CHEWABLES$, 122
Magic Folder object, and `getVariable()`, 194
Magic Folders, 33–35, 116–119, 122
main class, 253
main method, 253, 254
manifest files, 36–37, 112–113
match regular expression, 74, 81
merge, 168
merge option, 156
merge modules, 27, 62–64, 154–157
    adding, 161
    authenticating, 159
    build-time, 158–159
    creating, 159–160
    customizer, 162
    design-time, 158–159
    importing, 161–162
    install-time, 159
    option, 173
    read-only, 156, 160
    size, 160
    size optimized, 157
merging pre-install task, 162
missing resources, 145
modes, 66–67

Modify Text File, 104
modifying components, 89
Move File, 102
Move Folder, 102
MSJ, 255
multilanguage installers, 208
multiplatform installation, xviii–xix, 2–4
multiple labels, 152

N

n option (named UNIX without VM), 167
naming files dynamically, 91
native code, 177
nonoptimized merge modules, 158
Nortel, 2
null, 221
$NULL$, 221
nv option (named UNIX with VM), 167

O

OfficeSuite, 21
okToContinue, 184
Open Select Target, 62
opening projects without resource-checking, 144
operating systems, 3, 56, 62
opt (optimize by platform option), 168
optimize, 168
optimize CD-ROM installer, 173
optimize merge module, 173
optimize Web installer, 173
optional installer arguments, 58
organization, 90–93
    components, 88–89
    features, 87
    install sets, 87
Organization task, 86–88
out-of-memory conditions, 58
Output Debug Information, 104, 130, 204
output location option, 173

output text to console, 105
Override default UNIX/Mac OS X permissions, 110
overwrite behavior, 54–56
overwrite options, 56

P

-p option, 167
panel(s), 110
    actions, 30, 96–98, 105–111
    additions, 150–152
    custom code, 181–185, 202
    images, 150
    labels, 150
    in pre-install, 98–99
parameters, for build settings, 171–172
password, 107
Path, 110
path information, 203
path separators, 217
pathname, 253
Perform XSL Transform, 105
pixel size
    billboards, 30, 72
    progress pane, 71
pkgadd, 102
pkgask, 102
platform options, 172
platform target parameters, 171–172
platforms, 2, 56, 74
plug-ins, 31, 97, 204–206
Post-Install, 79–80
post-install/uninstall actions, 96–97
Post-Uninstall, 44, 198
PowerUpdate, 32
PowerUpdate Client, installing, 102
predefined source paths, 142, 146
Preferences Control panel, 144
Preferences folder, 122
pre-install, 45–46, 57, 77, 98–99

Pre-Install summary, 108–109
pre-install task, and merging, 162
preserve timestamp, 55
Pre-Uninstall, 198
pre-uninstall, 97–99
Print InstallAnywhere Variables, 130
Print Java Properties, 130
product ID, 139, 221
product name, 221
product registry, 53
product version, 167, 221
`$PRODUCT_ID$`, 221
`$PRODUCT_NAME$`, 221
`$PRODUCT_VERSION_NUMBER$`, 221
Programs Folder, 120
Programs Menu, 121
`$PROGRAMS_DIR$`, 34, 120
progress bar, 11
progress pane, size of, 71
project file–related exit codes, 168
project files, 36
project loading, 145
Project Loading preference, 144
Project Locales, 29
Project Wizard, 20–24, 26
`ProjectLocalizationInfo.txt`, 208
`$PROMPT_USER_CHOSEN_OPTION$`, 221
properties, 109–110
    file, 135, 205
    localization, 214–216
`propertiesfile`, 171
`$prop.[JAVA PROPERTY]$`, 221
`public void install`, 178
`public void uninstall`, 179
Pure Java, 167, 172
Pure Java installer debugging, 128

Q

Quick Launch Bar, 121
quiz answers, 257–258

R

R (rule indicator), 78, 96
radio buttons, 79
RAM requirements, 2, 3
read errors, 169
readme, 77
read-only merge modules, 156, 160, 173
read-only variables, 217–221
Ready to Install console, 109
recursion error, 117
RedHat Package Management (RPM), 56, 102
Register Windows Service, 102
regular expressions (regexp), 74
relative path, 112, 135, 256
Relocatable, 102
remove platform from build, 167
removing components, 93
renaming files, 91
reordering actions, 96
Replace InUse Files after Restart, 54
$REQUIRED_DISK_SPACE_BYTES$, 221
requirements
    authoring environment, 2–3
    installer environment, 3–4
    resolution, 2, 3
resolving variables, 189–190
resource manager, 144–147
resource-related exit codes, 168
resources, checking, 144
response files, 135–136
restart, 221
Restart Windows, 105
$RESTART_NEEDED$, 221
reusability, of projects, 154–155
root directory, 120
root of installation, 117
RPM, 102
rules, 50, 74–78
    custom code, 188–190
    logic, 31

S

s option (Solaris without VM), 167
SampleAction, 177
SampleConsole class, 182–183
SCM (source control management), 145
script file, 104
Scrolling Message panel, 108
sed, 147
self-extractor, 218, 219
semicolon, 253
Send stderr, 57
Send stdout to, 57
separators, 217, 253
serial number creation and verification, 107
server-side installer experience, 12–17
Set InstallAnywhere Variable, 105
Set System Environment Variable, 103
Set Windows Registry, 103
setChosenInstallBundles(), 200–201
setChosenInstallSet, 200
setup(), 186
setupUI(), 182, 184
sharing plug-ins, 204
shell configuration file, 143
shell script, 199
shells, 103
$SHORTCUT_NAME$, 221
shortcuts, 10, 15, 48, 101, 106, 215, 221
    executability of, 51
Shortcuts folder, 120
Show indeterminate dialog, 110
Show Message Console Dialog, 109, 221
Show Message Dialog, 105, 217
silent installers, 135–136
silent mode, 67
silent-mode installers, 12, 27
single-byte locales, 211–212
single-click install, 6
size
    billboards, 30
    installer disks, 63

merge modules, 160
    splash screen, 29
size optimized merge modules, 157–158
slashes, 119, 253, 256
software stack installation, xviii
Solaris, 102, 167, 172
Source, 110
source control management (SCM), 145
Source Path Management, 145–147
source paths, 142–144
    adding, 143, 146
    creating, 147
    default, 146
    predefined, 146
SpeedFolders, 35–36, 99, 100
    installing, 102
splash screens, 67, 69, 215
    pathname, 215
    preferred size, 29
SSH, 132
Standard Edition, 4
    Magic Folders, 122
standard variables, list of, 217–221
Start, Stop, Pause Windows Service, 105
Start Installer, 7
Start Menu, 121
start-up folder, 120
static text, 208–209, 211
`stderr`, 57, 100, 110, 112, 129, 197, 256
`stdout`, 57, 100, 197, 256
Store process' exit code in, 110
Store process' `stderr` in, 110
Store process' `stdout` in, 110
`StringTokenizer`, 187
subinstallers, 156
`substitute()`, 194–195
suite installer, xviii, 154, 158, 159
Sun, 2
Suppress First Window, 51, 59
Suspend installation until process completes, 110
`sv` option (Solaris with VM), 167

Swing, 181
Swing mode, 7, 29, 67–71, 181
System Drive Root, 121
`$System Drive Root$`, 118
System Environment variable, 254
system folder, 120
`System.err`, 198–199
`System.out`, 198–199
`System.out.println()`, 204

T

target file, 104
task actions, 99
TELNET, 27, 132
temp directory, 120, 219
templates, 26–27, 62–64, 154–161, 203
testing, 23, 52
    in foreign locales, 211
text editors, 36
text fields, 182
time zones, 55
timestamps, 54–56, 74
    JVMs, 55
translating locale files, 211
translations, static text, 209
Try Web Install, 52–53
TTY, 67

U

u option (Generic UNIX without VM), 167
UI mode, 220
Unicode, 212
uninitialized variables, 218
`uninstall`, 180
uninstall, 97
    custom code actions, 198
    equivalent, 100
    feature-level, 138
    status, 221

Uninstall Complete, 108, 109
uninstaller, 31, 110, 138–139
Uninstaller Introduction, 108, 109
UninstallerProxy, 179, 180
$UNINSTALL_STATUS$, 221
Universal Unique Identifier (UUID), 93, 154
UNIX
    / in installation location, 121
    build, 62
    debug, 129
    generic and named, 167, 172
    links, 108
    permissions, 110
    silent installers, 135
    X-windows, 133
UNIX VMs, 58
UNIX/Linux installer debugging, 127–128
unknown internal error, 169
updating folder locations, 143
uppercase strings, 220, 254
User Applications, 122
user home folder, 142
User Installation Directory, 120
user interface, 28–30
User Magic Folder, 117, 121
$USER_HOME$, 120, 142
$USER_INPUT_RESULTS$, 80
$USER_INSTALL_DIR$, 34–35, 90, 99–100, 116–117, 120, 194, 256
$USER_SHORTCUTS$, 35, 116, 120
/usr/bin, 122
/usr/local/bin, 122
UUID (Universal Unique Identifier), 93, 154

V

-v option, 167
$VARIABLE$, 77
variables, 32–33, 74, 77
    $, 161
    advertised, 157
    custom code, 194–198
    embedded, 195
    Magic Folders, 34–35, 116–119
    read-only, 217–221
    resolving, 189–190
    source paths, 142–143
    standard, 217–221
    uninitialized, 218
vector of strings, 199
verbose messages, 255
verify mode, 255
version, minimum, 256
version number, 221, 256
versioning, 28
versions and IDs, of installers, 53–54
virtual machines, 57–58
VM, 116, 201
.vm files, 62–63
VM heap size, 58
VM list, 199, 255
VM not loaded message, 255
VM pack–related exit codes, 169
VM packs, 62–63

W

w option (Windows without VM), 168
.war, 101
Web Installer Applet, 6–11
Web installer option, 173
Web installers, 26, 62–64, 126–130, 168
web option, 168
Western languages, 213–214
Win32 installer debugging, 126–127
Win32 registry value, 215
Windows, 168, 172, 215
    directory, 121
    options, 56
    silent installers, 135
Windows All Users Programs menu, 121
Windows All Users Start Menu, 121
Windows All Users Startup, 122

Windows Common Desktop, 122
Windows Programs Menu, 121
Windows Quick Launch Bar, 121
Windows Start menu, 121
Windows VMs, 58
Wizard (IA Project Wizard), 20–24
write errors, 169
writing custom code, 176
    actions, 177–180
    consoles, 185–188
    panels, 181–185
    rules, 188–190
wv option (Windows with VM), 168

X

x option (Mac OS without VM), 168
XML files, 36, 147
XML-formatted installation log, 219
XSL transformations, 36, 105, 147
X-windows, 133

Z

0 (no errors), 169, 171
Zero G Web site URL, xiv
.zip, 101
ZIP files, 48, 101

informIT

www.informit.com

YOUR GUIDE TO IT REFERENCE

Articles

Keep your edge with thousands of free articles, in-depth features, interviews, and IT reference recommendations — all written by experts you know and trust.

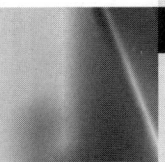

Online Books

Answers in an instant from **InformIT Online Book's** 600+ fully searchable on line books. For a limited time, you can get your first 14 days **free**.

Safari
TECH BOOKS ONLINE

Catalog

Review online sample chapters, author biographies and customer rankings and choose exactly the right book from a selection of over 5,000 titles.

Wouldn't it be great

if the world's leading technical publishers joined forces to deliver their best tech books in a common digital reference platform?

They have. Introducing
InformIT Online Books
powered by Safari.

Specific answers to specific questions.
InformIT Online Books' powerful search engine gives you relevance-ranked results in a matter of seconds.

Immediate results.
With InformIT Online Books, you can select the book you want and view the chapter or section you need immediately.

Cut, paste and annotate.
Paste code to save time and eliminate typographical errors. Make notes on the material you find useful and choose whether or not to share them with your work group.

Customized for your enterprise.
Customize a library for you, your department or your entire organization. You only pay for what you need.

Get your first 14 days FREE!
For a limited time, InformIT Online Books is offering its members a 10 book subscription risk-free for 14 days. Visit **http://www.informit.com/onlinebooks** for details.

Register Your Book

at www.awprofessional.com/register

You may be eligible to receive:

- Advance notice of forthcoming editions of the book
- Related book recommendations
- Chapter excerpts and supplements of forthcoming titles
- Information about special contests and promotions throughout the year
- Notices and reminders about author appearances, tradeshows, and online chats with special guests

Contact us

If you are interested in writing a book or reviewing manuscripts prior to publication, please write to us at:

Editorial Department
Addison-Wesley Professional
75 Arlington Street, Suite 300
Boston, MA 02116 USA
Email: AWPro@aw.com

Visit us on the Web: http://www.awprofessional.com